THE COLLECTED WORKS OF
G. K. CHESTERTON

X

PART III

THE COLLECTED WORKS OF
G. K. CHESTERTON

X

COLLECTED POETRY

PART III

Compiled and edited
with an Introduction
and Notes by
Denis J. Conlon

IGNATIUS PRESS   SAN FRANCISCO

CONTENTS

GENERAL EDITORS' INTRODUCTION

Throughout his life, G. K. Chesterton penned nearly a thousand poems that described his reaction to people and events.

Although Chesterton's intended audience consisted of his beloved common men, even the critics enjoyed and admired his verse. In the July 1927 issue of the *Observer*, Sir John Collings Squire said this about Chesterton the poet:

> His greatest distinction lies in the hold he has upon the fundamentals of human life, considered both in its social and its metaphysical aspects. In an age of new questions he has reiterated old answers; in an age of skepticism he has laughed at the laughers with a hilarity less hollow than theirs; in an age which tends in excuse baseness, even when it does not explain it away he has flown the banners of honour, fidelity, and generosity; in an age of mass-regimentation he has stood for the sanctities of the individual's soul. And above all—a fact in whose presence all his levities, quibbles, occasional injustices, easy assumptions, and prejudices pale into insignificance—living in a period when the value of life itself has been widely questioned (and, by that very fact, impoverished) he has maintained that "it is something to have been," showing the world the spectacle of one man enjoying the thousand miracles of the day, though the sword of Damocles hang over his head as it hangs over the heads of us all. There lies his "optimism" not in any shallow Panglossian delusions, either about the present or about the future. In point of fact this self-proclaimed optimist habitually maintains that society has gone most of the way to the dogs, and will probably complete the course. "Earth will grow worse ere men redeem it, And wars more evil ere all wars cease."

This volume contains the third part of the great man's collected poems. We are pleased and honored that two of the leading Chestertonians, Mr. Aidan Mackey and Dr. Denis J. Conlon, have collaborated in the assembling of these volumes to which they have contributed many previously uncollected poems.

Mr. Aidan Mackey is the founder of the Chesterton Study Centre, has served as Chairman of the Chesterton Society, and is author of *G. K. Chesterton: A Prophet for the 21st Century* among many other publications. He has devoted over half a century to promoting the memory and works of G. K. Chesterton.

Dr. Conlon, emeritus professor of English Literature and Culture at the University of Antwerp, numbers *G. K. Chesterton: The Critical Judgements* and *G. K. Chesterton: A Half Century of Views* among his publications. He also served as editor of Volumes VI, X Part II, XI, and XIV of *The Collected Works of G. K. Chesterton* and was chairman of the G. K. Chesterton Society from 1995 to 2007.

In Volume X, Part 1, Mr. Aidan Mackey published almost 500 poems, over half of which he had discovered while searching the attic of Top Meadow after the death in 1988 of Dorothy Collins, Chesterton's literary executrix. In Volume X, Part II, Dr. Denis J. Conlon presented the fruits of his researches in the British Library and elsewhere, covering the years up to 1900. This Volume X, Part III, is the final installment of his research: turn-of-the-century poems discovered after the publication of Part II and the poetry of the subsequent years up to 1936 not included in the previous books.

George J. Marlin
Richard P. Rabatin
General Editors

Dale Ahlquist
Patricia Azar
Joe Mysak
Associate Editors

INTRODUCTION

By Denis J. Conlon

Speaking on January 11, 1934, to the Distributist League at Gatti's Restaurant in London Gilbert Chesterton summed up what he called his moral, mental and spiritual condition in an impromptu triolet:

> My writing is bad,
> And my speaking is worse;
> They were all that I had,
> My writing is bad;
> It is frightfully sad,
> And I don't care a curse.
> My writing is bad,
> And my speaking is worse.

Chesterton, recognised as one of the greatest speakers of the century, was once again indulging his habit of digging the grave of his literary reputation. Ironically, he did so in an off-the-cuff verse form that many poets have found almost impossible to tackle at leisure, but it is a late example of his denigrating his own work quite typical of his attitude right from the beginning of his career when in 1898 he wrote, "I do not feel as if things like the Fish poem are really worth publishing. I know they are better than many books that are published, but Heaven knows that is not saying much.... With regard to this occasional verse I feel a humbug. To publish a book of my nonsense verses seems to me exactly like summoning the whole of the people of Kensington to see me smoke cigarettes...." His self-effacement coupled with a tendency to lose poems and a penchant for publishing them in obscure, now long forgotten magazines ensured that much of his work was mislaid; other poems were presented to friends and only reemerged years later after his death, and his wife kept the poems he addressed to her strictly to herself. He was, of course, a powerhouse pouring forth poetry, and his prodigious memory, not to be confused with his forgetfulness, could at the drop of a hat recreate, or more correctly rewrite, the missing verses. New versions proliferated as they were conjured up as occasion demanded, one example among many being "The Nativity", which appeared in differing forms over many years.

Chesterton never seems to have collected his own poems. *The Wild Knight* (1900) was put together, financed and promoted by Edward Chesterton, his father, while *Poems 1915* and *Wine, Water and Song* were, due to GKC's long illness in 1914–1915, sent to the press by his wife. Either she or the publisher, influenced by the libel case against his brother resulting from the Marconi affair, changed lines to avoid any further prosecutions. In *The Song of Quoodle* "Old Gluck" (Sir Isidore Gluckstein) was censored and replaced by "The Jew", thus making a valid comment on the exclusion of the public from parkland seem like an anti-Semitic diatribe. Later collections were assembled with similar lack of sensitivity by secretaries, until at last for the third 1933 edition of *Collected Poems* (issued by a new publisher) Chesterton himself did glance over the collection, made a few minor changes but decided to leave things as they were, with the poems still printed chronologically back to front. He probably felt as he had in 1905 in his note to the second edition of *The Wild Knight*: "I leave these verses as they stand, although they contain innumerable examples of what I now see to be errors of opinion.... there are verses I cannot take so seriously as to alter them. The man who wrote them was honest; and he had the same basic views as myself. Besides, nobody need read the book: I certainly beg to be excused." All the collections were, however, notable for their omissions: it would be remarkable if a fond parental choice of verses were to include everything the poet had produced or evaluate its worth dispassionately, and more remarkable indeed if a wifely hand could fall upon verses written before her marriage, particularly those apparently written for an earlier love. In Chesterton's case the situation was compounded by the poet's own inability or unwillingness to turn up his lost work. The outcome was the disappearance for up to a century of the greater part of GKC's poetic output, in particular most of that written before 1900 when he was twenty-six years old and his muse was at its freshest. In Chesterton's case inspiration never did dry up, but it is probably fair to say that after his illness in 1914 and especially after he took up the burden of editing *The New Witness* (later *G. K.'s Weekly*) he was not able to pour forth his verses with the previous abandon. Nonetheless, "there is good news yet to hear and fine things to be seen" in his later work.

It is difficult to assess the status of any writer when work is missing, and two-thirds of his poems were missing from Chesterton's *Collected Poems*. Of course, many of his contemporaries were aware of some of the omissions, but their opinions were based only on the material known to them. We know that John Betjeman commented favourably during radio and TV shows on poems such as "The Secret People", which he saw as "a potted History of England", and that in 1953 Alfred Noyes was to say, "In his real self Chesterton was essentially a poet. His *Lepanto* and *The Ballad of the White Horse* will live, but fine as they are, there are still finer things in some of his shorter poems."[1] Those opinions from perhaps the last two poets to make a successful living from their poetry is supported by opinions from others such as Charles Williams: "One of the first poets of our time",[2] and André Maurois:

> There are visitors to the Zoo who gaze at the hippopotamus or the elephant and think these great creatures would be more nearly perfect if they were different. But the hippo and the elephant are facts ... Without his paradoxes, without his jokes, without his rhetorical switchbacks, Chesterton might perhaps be a cleverer philosopher. But he would not be Chesterton. It has often been supposed that he is not serious, because he is funny; actually he is funny because he is serious. Confident in his truth, he can afford to joke.... During an age of morbid rationalism, Chesterton reminded men that reason is indeed a wonderful tool, but a tool that needs material to work on, and produces nothing if it does not take the existing world as its

[1] Alfred Noyes, "The Centrality of Chesterton", *The Quarterly Review* (January 1953): 45–50.
[2] Charles Williams, *Poetry at Present* (Oxford: Oxford University Press, 1930), pp. 97–113.

object.... To Chesterton as to Browning, the universe stands constant, solid—wondrous, under all the theories built up by intelligence, each as different from the others as were the reports of the blind men on the elephant. In that universe, with Chesterton's help we can grow deep spreading roots, and the shifting winds of the mind cannot drag us out of the soil for those brief and glorious flights that can only end in a quick fall. [3]

In 1961, a generation later, Anthony Burgess, once again basing his opinion only on *Collected Poems*, was to say:

He is not a great poet, but he was incapable of turning a mean rhyme, and he was too fond of language ever to admit the bathetic or pedestrian. If his poems are unsubtle, that is in keeping with the "public" quality of all his writing—a concern with broad strokes and bold colour, a love of the oratorical. Poems like "The Rolling English Road" and "The Donkey" remain superb recitation pieces, and Chesterton would be pleased to know that public bar audiences are better prepared to hear them than are Hampstead drawing-rooms. He had an easy mastery of traditional verse forms including difficult ones like the ballade, and he learned much from such practitioners as Villon how to make his rhymes and images bite. Chesterton never had a moonlight or twilit phase in his poetic development: there was always boldness, wit, even anger. And he could write light verse which remains funny without being facetious. [4]

Possibly the "moonlight or twilit phase" is now available in these present volumes, but P. J. Kavanagh thought in any case that "Chesterton's poems are usually thoughts expressed in verse, or emotion expressed thoughtfully." [5] Another poet who looked favourably on GKC's verse was W. H. Auden, who stated his position in 1970: "I

[3] André Maurois (Emile Herzog), *Poet and Prophet* (London: Cassell, 1933), pp. 141–74.

[4] Anthony Burgess, Introduction to G. K. Chesterton, *Autobiography* (London: Hutchinson, 1969), pp. 3–7.

[5] P. J. Kavanaugh, *The Bodley Head Chesterton* (London: Bodley Head, 1985), pp. x–xxvii; American edition: *A Chesterton Anthology* (San Francisco: Ignatius Press, 1985).

have always liked Chesterton's poems"[6] and then four years later expanded his view:

Consciously or unconsciously, every poet takes one or more of his predecessors as models. Usually, his instinct leads him to make the right choice, but not always. In Chesterton's case, for example, I think that Swinburne was a disastrous influence.... It is due to Swinburne that, all too often in his verses, alliteration becomes an obsessive tic.

Both in his prose and his verse, [Chesterton] sees, as few writers have, the world about him as full of sacramental signs or symbols. I would not call him a mystic like Blake, who could say: "Some see a heavenly host singing Holy, Holy, Holy." Chesterton never disregards the actual visible appearance of things. Then, unlike Wordsworth, his imagination is stirred to wonder, not only by natural objects, but by human artifacts as well. Probably most young children possess this imaginative gift, but most of us lose it when we grow up as a consequence, Chesterton would say, of the Fall.

In verses such as ["The Song of Quoodle"], there is little, if any, trace of Swinburnian influence. Behind them one detects the whole tradition of English comic verse, of Samuel Butler, Prior, Praed, Edward Lear, Lewis Carroll and, above all, W. S. Gilbert. It was from such writers, I believe, that Chesterton, both in his verse and his prose, learned the art of making terse aphoristic statements which, once read or heard, remain unforgettably in one's mind. I cannot think of a single comic poem by Chesterton that is not a triumphant success. *Greybeards at Play*—until it was sent to me by John Sullivan, Chesterton's bibliographer, I had never heard of its existence: I have no hesitation in saying that it contains some of the best pure nonsense verse in English, and the author's illustrations are equally good. By natural gift, Chesterton was, I think, essentially a comic poet."[7]

The poetic muse descended early on the young Chesterton, who before the age of ten was writing competent pastiches, after which he found his own voice, rapidly developing precocious solemnity alongside light-hearted and eclectic tones. His output from the late

[6] W. H. Auden, *Chesterton's Non-Fictional Prose* (London: Faber and Faber, 1970), pp. 11–18.

[7] W. H. Auden, "The Gift of Wonder", in *G. K. Chesterton—A Centenary Appraisal*, ed. John Sullivan (London: Paul Elek, 1974), pp. 73–80.

1880s throughout the 1890s was phenomenal, as he experienced first love and began to run the gamut of a variety of religious positions. During this time, he spent two years at University College London training to be a book illustrator, before going to work as a publisher's reader for a firm specializing in Spiritualist tracts. Every spare moment seems to have been devoted to poems in an amazing variety of styles, almost all of it destined to be put away and forgotten for over a century, with the exception of those few contained in *The Wild Knight and Other Poems*.

Once Chesterton had in 1900 given up working as a publisher's reader and become a journalist, he soon gained an ever-growing reputation as a literary critic and social commentator, with his poetry turning more in the direction of the political and social lampoon and ballade. Nonetheless, he was able to retain a lightness of touch which ensured that even the bitterest satirical attack was always acclaimed as a comic masterpiece. On a more solemn note he found time to undertake great recitation pieces such as *The People of England (The Secret People)*, *Lepanto* and his tribute to King Alfred, *The Ballad of the White Horse*.

The great outpouring continued until in the 1920s he took on more and more editorial duties on *G. K.'s Weekly*, alongside his weekly article for the *Illustrated London News*, and undertook lecture tours. His light-hearted banter became more and more confined to the private poems he exchanged over the years with groups of young people with whom he always seemed to have a ready rapport, a rapport which does not, however, appear to have extended to the parties to which GKC was invited *(The Jazz* and *All Through the Night)*. Eventually in the 1930s his work load did restrict him, and his poems appeared far less regularly. This meant that there were far fewer poems to be lost, but many still escaped the net. It is almost certain that there are some which have escaped this latest sweep, but that is in the nature of the Chestertonian game. Gilbert Chesterton was almost certainly the most prolific poet of his age, one whose verse so entered the public consciousness that they became part of the bric-à-brac of the mind. Soon after the death of GKC Herbert Palmer found his verse full of preachings, politics and arresting hymns of hate.... Chesterton, in spite of his frequent blare and bombast, has been extraordinarily successful in infusing true poetry into his thundering orchestra. God speaking through him, he knows no restraint, but comes at you, marches up the street and round the corner, a rage of music and colour that seeks to hold up the traffic.... But poetry that is merely like that does not necessarily contain the enduring line, the wonderful stanza, and it is astonishing that in the verse of Chesterton there is so much that is really fine.... There is plenty of magic in Chesterton's verse, not exactly the delicate elfish magic of Yeats or Walter de la Mare, a rather flick-in-the-eye magic if you like, but none the less evident. Sometimes, indeed, he achieves it when flying right into the jaws of bombast he steers miraculously clear, or when formulating a paradox he gets beyond the truth of paradox to the creation of the rose that shines upon the lips of truth. Then there is the Chesterton who is memorable because he says something very droll, even though it be penetratingly satirical.... But Chesterton was a sort of God's fool, the Almighty's chosen jester, who fearlessly took liberties, secure in most instances beneath his cap and bells.[8]

This third volume of Chesterton's poetry completes the task of giving an oversight of an avalanche of poems, just a few of which would have made the reputation of lesser poets.

[8]G. K. Chesterton and His School", *Post-Victorian Poetry* (London: Dent, 1938).

BIOGRAPHICAL NOTE

Gilbert Keith Chesterton was born on May 29, 1874, at 32 Sheffield Terrace, Campden Hill, London, in the shadow of the water-tower that was to figure so prominently in *The Napoleon of Notting Hill*. He was the second child of the family, but he was to lose his elder sister, Beatrice, when he was three years old, a loss offset by the birth of his brother, Cecil, in 1879.

GKC's father, a Unitarian, belonged to the well-known family of estate-agents but chose to take little active part in the business, and after his death in 1922 there seem to have been no business connections between the two parts of the family. In 1881, the Chestertons moved to 11 Warwick Gardens, near the Earl's Court Exhibition Centre, where until 1906 the overpowering feature was the Great Wheel which "filled heaven with the wheel of stars". The topography of the two areas was to influence GKC's work throughout his career. Over the years, a biographical folklore grew up that suggested that he did not speak or read until extremely late in life, a folklore contradicted by his dictating stories at the age of three and writing poems from the age of eight.

From Warwick Gardens, Chesterton attended first Colet Court (Bewsher's), the preparatory for St. Paul's School and then later the main school itself. He would seem to have been a shy, reticent schoolboy, but he was not the numbskull depicted in the folklore, as, besides winning the school poetry prize, he carried off the French prize, founded the Junior Debating Club and from 1891 published poems in magazines such as *The Debater*, *The Pauline* and *The Union Magazine* and then in 1892 his first publicly published poem in *The Speaker*. A tall, slim youth, he seems to have acquired some skill at fencing, croquet, tennis, golf and ice-skating. Instead of following his friends to Oxford, GKC spent a few months at Calderon's College of Art in St. John's Wood before registering in 1893 at University College, London, where he trained to be a book-illustrator by reading courses in French, English and Latin (A. E. Housman was his tutor), accompanied by a drawing class at the Slade School of Art (Augustus John was a fellow student). In his second year he dropped Latin and Art in favor of history and political economy. The years until 1895, when he took a job as a reader, first with Redways the spiritualist publishers and then with Fisher Unwin, saw him starting to write with immense application as novels, poems, dramas and articles flowed from his pen. Little if any appears to have been published at the time, but he had an immense reservoir of work, especially poems, on which he was able to draw for the rest of his life.

His work as a cartoonist and later as a reviewer and essayist enabled him to achieve enough financial security by 1901 to marry Frances Blogg and settle first in Edwardes Square and later in Battersea at Overstrand Mansions. He became a regular columnist on the *Daily News* and the *Illustrated London News* as well as making a name for himself as poet, critic, novelist and short story writer. In 1908 the death of his wife's brother by suicide had a profound effect on her health, and so in 1909 the Chestertons moved to Beaconsfield, then a peaceful country retreat, to the west of London. For a short while the cascade of books and articles and public debates slowed, but then once again he got into his stride until some years later in 1914–1915 his own grave illness brought a halt. A year after his recovery he temporarily took over the editorial chair of his brother's paper, *The New Witness*, when Cecil volunteered for the front, a task which became permanent in 1918 upon his brother's death. *The New Witness* was revived as *G. K.'s Weekly* in 1925, when it became standard bearer for the Distributist Movement, a political and economic programme much influenced by Leo XIII's encyclical *Rerum Novarum*.

In 1922 Chesterton, who in the 1890s had run the gamut from Unitarianism through Puritanism, Spiritualism and agnosticism before discovering his own Orthodoxy in the Christian Social Union and the Anglo-Catholic wing of the Church of England, overcame his long-standing doubts over papal infallibility and was received into the Roman Catholic Church at the age of forty-eight by his friend Fr. J. O'Connor, the model for Father Brown. His books *St. Francis of Assisi*, *The Everlasting Man* and *St. Thomas Aquinas* followed that conversion, but they contain little that he would not have written at any stage in his career. That career now took new turns as he undertook lecture tours in the United States, Poland and Spain, visited Palestine and Italy, and then began to broadcast regularly for the BBC. He was nominated for the Nobel Prize for Literature in 1935, but in the end no prize was awarded for that year. At the time of his death on June 14, 1936, he was beyond doubt one of the best known and best loved figures in literature and journalism.

NOTE TO THE PRESENT VOLUME

The poems are presented in chronological order of their composition, showing Chesterton's development as a poet. The volume begins with turn-of-the-century poems too late for inclusion in Volume II. Poems known to have been written between 1900 and 1936, other than those included in Part I, have been included here. The year 1900 is important because it marks the divide between the private and the public poet.

It should be noted that Chesterton flung his genius so far and wide that there can be no guarantee that poems won't continue to be found in the most unexpected places for a long time to come; in fact it is almost a certainty. For that reason we refrain from maintaining that this collection is in any way complete, although every effort has been made to ensure that we have included as much as could be found.

DJC

ACKNOWLEDGMENTS

I wish once more to thank Dr. Richard Christophers of the British Library Department of Manuscripts for his continued help and guidance which have proved invaluable in the compilation of this collection. Likewise Geír Hasnes was lavish with his advice and in particular allowed me free access to his as yet unpublished Bibliography of Chesterton's works.

I am particularly indebted to the Nicholl family, above all to Gilbert Chesterton's friend Mrs Joan Huffer (née Nicholl) for her help and hospitality, and to Frances Huffer, her daughter, who shepherded me through the streets of Paris and across the fields of France to her mother's home and back again. I must record an equal debt for their help and hospitality to Philip and Caroline Morgan-Smith, Barbara Nicholl's son-in-law and daughter who opened up for me their treasure trove of poems. Peter Cockerill, Dorothy Nicholl's son, was instrumental in putting me in touch with his aunt and cousins.

Yet again I acknowledge the help of Cdr. David Braybrooke, LVO, RN, of the late Stephen Medcalf, and of Dale Ahlquist. As ever Nigel Rees has been more than willing to lend his aid. Paul Chown very kindly went out of his way to send me a copy of "Our Angel, Michael" as a token of his enjoyment of Parts I and II.

The staff of the Swalecliffe Branch of the Kent County Library Service, in particular Fiona Bainbridge, have provided me with a service far beyond the call of duty. I must also thank Ignatius Press and its long-suffering copy-editors, especially Carolyn Lemon and Vivian Dudro, for their patience.

Finally, as ever and as I complete the task he began so long ago in Part I of this project, I needs must express my appreciation of Aidan Mackey's unstinting support and co-operation over many years.

Any imperfections, infelicities or omissions are to be laid at my door rather than theirs.

DJC

LIST OF ILLUSTRATIONS

Gilbert Chesterton posed as an artist, 1890

I

POEMS OF THE 1890s

[LOVE IS ENOUGH II]

Love is enough for the loving, love without self's alloy,
Its mighty breast enfolding the flame of a secret joy.
Love is enough for the loving as pure of envy and strife,
It is poured as a fiery torrent from the brimming urns of Life.
Love is no money-changer, to weigh the return as gold,
Love is not weak nor selfish, nor faileth, nor groweth old,
Love is as strong as death, his wings to the stars unfurled,
His feet in the deepest places of the chambered underworld.

Though the frowns and smiles of the loved be as fights that are lost
    and won,
Though the cry on the lips of thousands be light to the praise of
    one,
Though the light of our life that kindleth be set in another's eyes,
Love doth not die in the darkness or wander away in the sighs.
Love is a crown to the loving, a mystical shrine untrod,
A secret lent to the spirit by the breath of the living God.
He stands in the innermost temple, and often in hours unsought
We hear the might of his stirring through the roar of of the lovers of
    thought.
He rings with a lingering glory the dusky shapes we see
That move in a twilight chamber in the haunts of memory.

Love is no jester and courtier, no trifler in folly and guile,
To sing at a rosèd casement and watch for a wanton's smile.
Love is an earnest spirit, so patient and lonely and strong,
And the woe of his lips is silent, and the time of his torture is long,
His hope is high and distant, his path is steep and hard,
He giveth his all and watcheth, till God shall relieve his guard.
Keep we the might of his presence, a flash of the light of the Lord,
A breath of the mighty nature that shaketh its good abroad
That so we may be as the angels and rise to the loftiest lot
Of him who is highest of all things that he giveth and asketh not,

Cf. "[Love is Enough]", *Collected Poetry*, Part II, p. 41.

3

Who giveth a self and a will and a place in the ordered plan
Gives also the love of a God for the half-hearted worship of man,
As the awful eyes that are watching and the silent lips that bless
Are turned on the ways of his thousands in a great unconsciousness.

Love is enough for the loving, and let it suffice unto me,
As the golden eve is sinking on darkening wood and lea,
As the sun streams out in glory and floods the course of the spheres,
As the earth rolls out its treasure in patience through the years,
As the humblest rose breaks out from the earth in a simple trust,
So shall the gifts of the loving be the crown of a living dust,
No spot on the earth of God can take what it never gave,
None, but bounds of Hell, and the rotting space of the Grave.

(1890)

BENEATH A MICROSCOPE

The trees were dwarfed, the clouds were riven,
His feet were mountains lost in heaven;
He rose through strange new skies alone,
The Earth dropped from him like a stone,
And his own limbs beneath him far
Seemed tapering down to touch a star.

He found his head, shaggy and grim,
Staring among the cherubim.
The seven celestial floors he rent
Then found one crystal dome that bent
Over his head as clear as hope,
And cowered beneath a microscope.

(ca. 1890)

Cf. "A Fairy Tale", Collected Poetry, Part I, p. 210 and "The Elephant", Part II, p. 288.

[BRAND THE MIGHTY]

Two strong men came to the knee of the King
And they kissed the hand with the signet ring,
And they craved a word, ere the day went by
When Brand the Mighty was marked to die.

Said one, Prince Herne of the Sea-heights tall,
As he spake to the King alone in his hall,
"The day must dawn, and the day must fly
When Brand the Mighty is marked to die,
For Brand was haughty and proud and bold,
And he scorned my name in the days of old.
And I have served you with tongue and with sword,
With the hosts of a chief and the lands of a lord.
Let him die today ere the West is red.
That my honour live in the blood of the dead."
The King flushed red and the King flushed bright:
"Well said, Lord Prince, thou speakest aright.
To horse with this scroll and like whirlwind away,
For Brand the Mighty shall die today."

Said one, Red Orme of the Sea-girt Wall,
As he spoke to the King in the lonely hall:
"The day may dawn and the day may fly
When Brand the Mighty is marked to die,
For Brand is tender and true at core,
And he did me grace in the days of yore,
And as he turned me from rapine and sin
To a rude King's man without title or kin,
And as I have served you with pike and with gun,
By the hours I have served and the deeds I have done,
Let Brand be pardoned by royal grace
That the man I love may stand for a space."
The King waxed pale and the King waxed white:
"Well said, brave Orme, thou counsellest right.
To horse with this pardon, let fly and away,
Lest Brand the Mighty should die today."

Red Orme, flung in saddle, the town left behind,
O'er uplands and meadows he flew like the wind,
And before him forever with panting breath
Prince Herne dashing on with the message of death.
Each swept through the hamlets ...
In a thunder of hoofs and a drift[ing of] dust.

. . . .

On dash of spurs, he had passed him well,
When his charger staggered, lurched and fell.
Alone on the meadows, 'neath sun and star,
And the herald of death rode on afar.
No word said Orme, but he rose from [his] knee.
On the steed and the land and the Prince looked he,
And when Herne crested the hill with a shout,
He drew from his holster a pistol out,
And there came a crack o'er the lonely lea,
And a wreath of smoke that floated free,
And the groan of a fall o'er the meadows still,
And Orme rode slowly up to the hill.
He rode past hedge and he rode past grain,
And past Prince Herne, shot dead through the brain.

On a city market a scaffold stood.
And the people thronged for the work of blood,
For the sun of the day was in the sky
When Brand the Mighty was marked to die.
And the block was black and the axe was in hand
When a haggard rider reeled to a stand
In the place: and his words with a madness ring,
"A pardon, a pardon: I come from the King."
The pardon was read and the rabble cheered,
But the headsman frowned and the judges sneered:
"At the eleventh hour: this word of the crown.
Well: hasten and pull the scaffold down."
The rider knitted his brows: cried "Stay!"
"No haste to carry the axe away.

In the meadows green scarce far a span
I wot there lieth a murdered man.
A man I smote with the craft of Cain.
Come, headsman: shoulder the axe again."

This is the fate Red Orme came by
When Brand the Mighty was marked to die.

(ca. 1890)

THE NUN

Slow through the Gothic arches dim the paved walk she trod,
The dark-robed virgin of the Cross, the lonely bride of God;
'Neath clustering columns' shadows vast, 'neath fiery windows' gleam,
Through glimmering aisle and cloisters cool she moved as in a dream.
Nor saw the pines in ordered gloom, the rose in living red
Mocking the chilling columns round the rosèd stains o'erhead,
But with a slow and noiseless step, with eyes upon the floor,
She passed and faded from my sight, a dream of times of yore.
But still those grave pathetic eyes upon my fancy staid (sic),
Those solemn eyes, the silent lips, the pale and cloistered maid,
The eyes that might not dim or flesh with woman's joy or strife,
The lips that might not speak the word that thrills the world to life,
The maid for whom through pictured panes alone God's sunlight
    gleams,
Who feeds a sexless tortured soul and mad ecstatic dreams,
Whose cheek must never flush to words spoke in a lonely dell,
But pale to saintly glories and to tempting shades of Hell.
Oh, can her gloomy sacrifice by God be felt as good,
Who sears out her blinded soul the flower of womanhood?
Does He that left the Eden flower to honour care and strife
Dwell most within this world of death or yonder world of life?
Does not from yonder lark that sings far in the fiery skies
Than cloistered hymns and litanies [far] finer anthems rise?
Is not a sweeter breath of heaven from yonder hawthorn blown
Than on the dreamy incense rolls from altar steps of stone?

Does not the mother by the fire amid her children fair
Show nearer unto faith and God than your pale dreamer there?
What craft has bent the maiden down to fate so dark and grim,
Has pent a woman's spirit free in yonder cloisters dim?
What reckless suicidal grief has urged yon guileless maid
To plunge her soul and body deep in yonder ghostly shade?

'Twas from a mad, unmanly rout, a reckless world she fled, ...

(incomplete 1891)

SUNSET

The drooping day was spreading his golden wings in the West,
And the sun like a glorious star flamed bright on his dying breast,
Barred with its golden mists and crowned with its turrets of fire.
I saw in the western seas the city of day expire.

Oh had I the wings of a dove far over the woods to flee
And wing my way in the dusk o'er the foam of the evening sea,
To pass through the fiery gates to the sunset lands away
And flutter in fairy gardens and the evening courts of day.

But how? No sunset-fields, no living glories are there.
The clouds are grey and heavy and space is hollow and bare.
The soft mist low on the fen and the red cloud bright in the West
Are of one chill fabric of vapour by varying sunlight drest,
Dull walls of a sombre mist that the blurred horizon mar,
Aglow with the lightening rays of a lonely and distant star!

Do I not know around me old bonds still holy and dear,
Which viewed by analysis dull are earthly and common and near.
The motherhood bent o'er the cradle that glows in the firelight of
    men,
That broods in the eagle's eyrie and cowers in the wild cat's den,
The bells with their holiest peal in the love-bond of husband and wife
That grows from its dreamy dawn to its crown in the toiling of Life.

(ca. 1891)

DUST TO DUST

"Dust to dust" the old-world story curst us for our father's deed,
"Dust to dust" the new agnostic cries in his material creed.
Grew a whisper through the ages, with that gloomy doom at strife,
Breaking out in myth and madness, "Dust to dust", but life to Life,
Dust to dust, to earth and lichen, leaf and blossom, moss and sod,
Life to life, through living aeons centering in the living God.
"God is God of all the living" cried the heart that was divine.
Would to God that for an instant it were so in yours or mine.
Feel a shadow stand beside, still in all we seek or shun,
Walk beneath the living Father as we walk beneath the sun.
This were more than all atonement, miracle, redemption, grace,
If we felt the love and sorrow as they pass across his face,
Felt the fiery goad to honour of the trust without an end,
Felt the maddening shame of sin before the watching of a friend.
If thou canst not, man of Europe, feel the place within thy needs
Of the vast and vivid Life which is the soul of all the Creeds,
Tell not me of rites and credos, churches and regenerate birth,
Child of dust and evolution, live thy breath up on the earth!

                                                    (ca. 1892)

[INFERNO]

Then I turned into a palace, where in spangled bowers secluded
Jewelled dames in languid splendour dazed wild manhood's burning
    gaze,
Mingling in their glittering dances, in their whispering joys uniting,
Revelling in their golden pleasure in the tapers' golden blaze.

"Look" the voice replied, and straight way, by its side my eyes
    encountered
By those proud and beauteous ladies, by those gay and haughty men,
Dimly seen a swarthy savage, by his beaded harlot crouching,
Whose close-looped barbarian jewels lit the darkness of his den.

Then I pointed to the distance where with tempest roar and darkness
Whirled the myriad wheels of [commerce], smoked the myriad
    towers of trade,
Where the rolling smoke o'er all things, thickening o'er the crowded
    city
Hid the furnace glare gigantic, where the nation's works are made.

(ca. 1892)

DEATH

Who art thou, awful presence tall
    Draped dim in ghostly grey,
Who tearest my children from my arms,
    Yet turnest thy head away?

Oh are thy features fair or foul,
    Thy presence stern or wild?
Oh let me see the face of him
    Who bears away my child.

Nay, to the living I am veiled,
    Thy doom I may not give,
My face is hid, for never man
    May look on it and live.

Then to the silent and unknown
    Thy mortal tribute pay
Who while he makes his stern demand
    Must turn his head away.

But when thy boat has battled long
    In life's tempestuous sea,
From out the stillness and the gloom
    My voice may call for thee.

Then shall the shroud of the unknown
    Fall slowly from my brow,
And thou shalt gaze upon me then,
    As these are gazing now.

(ca. 1892)

[MARY]

Mary, lonely is my heart,
   Lonely it must ever be,
While the gay and gorgeous throng
   There is little chance for me.

Nay, I will not speak the word
   That would pain and sorrow breed,
Must be blind while others gaze,
   Must be dumb while others plead.

Neither will I ask that Fate
   Deck with that outward grace
Which may give a meaner soul
   Prize of Atalantic race.

Blasphemy it were to wish
   Thee the gilded tyrant's thralls,
Loved I will be for my soul
   Or will not be loved at all.

               (ca. 1892)

POLYGAMY

(On a lady writing in favour thereof)

Is it a woman who speaks,
A daughter of Eden's Queen,
Whose fair form in the blaze of the forest
On the bright orbed tree is seen?

Is it a woman who speaks
'Neath the Mother's spirit eyes,
As she stands by her world-old mate
In the blue star-world of the skies?

Shame it were that a man,
Save some Prince of the gorgeous East,
Should dare in a Saxon land
To be shown this blasphemy's priest.

Shame be it that a man
Should insult his sisters so,
But how, if a woman counts
This slavery dark and low?

How if a woman's brow
With less than the harlot's shame
Be lifted before the world
And this doctrine of infamy name?

That here is sex in a harem for a man
To pet and pleasure and play,
As low as his pack of hounds,
And why not as many as they?

Not that the one exist for the one
As it was when Eden began,
But the man exists for the lust,
And the woman exists for the man.

Not that one exist for the one
As it was when love was begun,
But the one needs use in the many,
And the many exist for the one.

Whither now are we going,
Of what may this thought be the seed
What will strong manhood become,
If this be the woman's creed?

                              (ca. 1892)

THE HOUSE OF LIFE

Twilight and firelight,
The dreaming embers glow
Pa[rti]tioned was I
And divided even so
The World of the things we dream
And the House of the things we know.

Dark house of life,
At moments even in thee
Through rifts of the dark old dwelling
There cometh to mine and me
The rise of the unknown star,
The roar of an unknown sea.

Swift, solemn moments,
Mystical whisper and doubt,
When our facts and the old house strong
And the [rooms] we move about
Seem shadows cast through the casement
From something that standeth without.

(ca. 1892)

[THE LIVE-LONG DAY]

Where suns and stars like lamps that burn, encircle the space untrod
They stand, Life's innermost circle, the mystical sons of God,
And they furl their wings of sunrise and unto the question hark
That God asketh of every living thing at the dying of day into dark:
"Where hast thou been the day long, at labours of sin and of worth,
And what hast thou done for the deathless hope, the crowning fate
    of the earth?"
And sadly answered the angels, as worn with a thankless lot,
"We toil on the Earth for ever, and Man beholdeth it not.
He hath fashioned a fancied angel in the type of his mortal clay
And he sees not the angel armies that fend him night and day."
Then to a star-lit angel the lord of the Angels spake,
"Where hast thou been the live-long day, what labours to mark or
    to make?"
"From the dark mist floods of space, from the rivers of night and day
We lift our crowns into brightness, we move on a mighty way,
We watch from the walls of midnight that rise from the endless seas,
We guide the bark of the mortal man through ocean mysteries."

(incomplete, ca. 1892)

THE HYMN OF THE UNKNOWN GOD

"As I passed by I beheld a temple to the Unknown God."
Acts [16:1–4.]

Not only old Hellenic pomps with shout and flare of torches
Have throned that ruler in the ways and wreathed him in the porches,
Not only old philosophies that groped through starry mazes
Have seen that silent shadow cast gigantic o'er the spaces,
Have heard from chasms vague and void, through all the brain's
commotions
On the waste shoreline of the soul the roar of endless oceans.

Wherever human hearts can stir and human creeds can falter,
Glooms out behind the sculptured gods the darkness of his altar,
Wherever men have hearts of men, then hearts will rise, confessing
His speechless formulas of prayer in groping and in guessing.
The faiths of men are fair and high and brave the men that bore
them,
They spurned the proud and dared the fray and flared to ashes for
them,
The breath out of a vaster world behind the types and stories,
But who is he that hath not felt a flash of inner glories
Beneath the seas of day and night that flood the spheres with
changing
The moving of a deeper force through unknown Kingdoms
ranging,
That yawning of a sudden doubt the silent deeps revealing,
That shadow of an unknown form athwart the threshhold stealing.
Therein are tolerance and hope, and liberty and kindness,
And all the larger thoughts of men and all the dreams of blindness.

O God Unknown, unknowable, O riddle everlasting,
O'er all, a blessing and a curse, thy haunting shadow casting.

Cf. "The Unknown God", *Collected Poetry*, Part II, p. 126.

The churches die and land's new faiths with gods and legends throng
   them,
But still, throughout a thousand faiths, thy place is still among them,
The deathless mystery of things thou art and fallest never.
Still earth is earth, and man is man, and thou a god for ever.

(ca. 1892)

THE ICONOCLAST [II]

They called me cold and a scorner and proud in the sight of my
   eyes,
They have seen me a spreader of shadow, a breather of mysteries.
Lord of my soul—thou seest, thou hearest the voice that cries.

I am spurned by the wise and the mighty, I am shunned by the
   myriad crowd,
They flee with curses from me and cry on my pride aloud.
God, I am at thy feet, thou knowest if I be proud.

I have no cause to be proud, nor to covet standing alone,
I think but as one among thousands, nor need seek for a union.
I do but carry a ménage—as each man carries his own.

I am not haughty or cruel, ye have no cause to flee,
Only mournful a little, and worn with the things I see.
I only carry my message—would God I could let it be.

The world is grown peaceful of doctrine and merciful in its words,
It's healing the wounds of dogma and sheathing the nation's swords,
And the song of joy and of pity is high on the minstrel's chords.

The world is grown peaceful of doctrine, forgiving again and again,
It clamours about the sinner and crowns him and heals his pain,
But the Pharisee weepeth without and cries for the mercy in vain.

(ca. 1892)

Cf. "The Iconoclast", *Collected Poetry*, Part II, p. 101.

OMAR

Because the fierce earth stiffens to a moon,
Because all life festers and falls in dust,
Because our hordes are crumblings of a crust,
Therefore, we stare like daisies at the noon.
Laughing aloft, like sons of kings at play,
Lords of the live earth's treasures for a day,
Because of this, because these things are so,
Because the hours rush by us with one cry,
We grasp the cup that soon shall shattered be,
We toss the crown that soon shall fade below,
We flame and scatter like the Autumn leaves:
The raw earth made us and the earth receives.

Because the earth flowers round the feet of God,
Because his hands unseal the golden day,
Because he knows and giveth ere we pray,
Therefore, stars, land and great seas nod.
Therefore I smite my breast and strive and sweat,
Panting to pay an undemanded debt.
Because of this, because God's barns stand wide
Giving our pleasure, asking not a gain.
Therefore I burn to share his crown of pain,
To bear his signs in feet and hands and side.
Let others have his comfort, I his care.
Therefore I fast and cry aloud ... spare.

                                        (ca. 1892)

A BABE WAS BORN

A babe was born in Bethlehem
    —A thousand such are born:
But with its starlike halo broke
    The dark world's golden morn.
O selfish rulers of the home,
    Mothers and sires we see,

The child may come again on earth
　　—Say, know ye which is he?

A craftsman toiled in Nazareth
　　—A thousand such have toiled:
But from his strokes the world church rose,
　　Earth's giant sins assoiled.
Ho, graspers, owners, taskmasters,
　　The scourge yet in your hands,
He that has worked may work again
　　—Say, know ye where he stands?

A captive died on Calvary
　　—A thousand such have died:
But his lost cry redeemed the world,
　　The voice of one that cried.
You, judges, princes, governors,
　　Whose myriads bow the knee,
The sword is yours, the blood is yours
　　—Say, know ye which was he?

　　　　　　　　　　　　　(ca. 1893)

MIRACLES

A humble man moved o'er the down
Beneath a hill-hid eastern town.
He viewed all mildly, like a King,
And, like a child, touched everything.
The sheep around, the bird above,
Were gathered to his lonely love.
He passed the cloud, the sparrow's wing,
And left them all a song to sing.

He touched the wild flowers, and they flame,
Red banners of his royal name,
Tall fiery symbols of the heart
That, careless, in God's gifts take part,
Signs of the tranquil blaze that shone
About the gentler Solomon.

He moved, and touched them with a spell,
And left them all a tale to tell.

He brake the bread, he filled the wine
That gleamed into a blood-red sign.
The coarsest grain to blessings turned,
The dimmest wine in glory burned
To knit in glistening bonds and rare
His own together everywhere,
Even as the board bound true as He
The unlettered twelve of Galilee.
He touched the common food of man
And left it with a gracious plan.

                                        (ca. 1893)

[MORE THAN A GOD]

Better than leagues of elfin land,
One dandelion by loose gales fanned,
Better than gardens of dreams and gloam
The spare moss gilding the roofs of home.
Fair are the myths with dragon and star,
But these are better than fair—they are.

Better than shapes of the proudest pen,
One nameless man of the mobs of men,
Better than golden centuries' gleam,
One roaring cycle of steel and steam,
Times divine doth the dreamer give,
But these are more than divine—they live.

Better than shapes of a coming grace,
Hands and feet and a living face,
Better this than the great unsent,
Though the hand be pierced and the feet be rent.
Radiant gods ye may seek beside,
But he was more than a God—he died.

                                        (ca. 1893)

THE WORLD'S TRAGEDY

I come, I come, o sons of men, my triumph roars at last,
Yet with the weight of this my staff I scarce can tread so fast.
'Twas worth the patient wandering years, the fight with want and sin,
To see, with pomp and crowded streets, my kingdom ushered in.
My mantle trails along the stones, man's best imperial crown
Sits hard about my brows—so hard, methinks, the blood runs down.

I come, I come, o sons of men, Jerusalem I come,
My mighty men the halt and lame, my counsellors the dumb.
Raised on the highest steeps of time, with power to bless and ban,
I come, I come, o sons of men, the crownèd son of man.
O brothers, sisters, little ones, whose homes were poor as mine,
My heart went to you through the mists of all the dreams divine.

I dropped the crust, I seized the staff, I trod the homeless wold,
No king of all my foes could fling the hateful taunt of gold.
I sought the meanest lives that felt the Father's rain and sun,
I bent above the harlot's shame, and she and I were one,
Pride after pride I stripped away, that all earth's mightiest cull,
Lower and lower down I bent, and still my heart was full.
O brothers, sisters, broken ones the world's hard judges slay,
O captives at the gibbet's foot, I join you too today.

O brothers, sisters, toiling ones hereafter that shall rise,
To break the glebe in other lands, to sweat 'neath other skies,
Too well I know, for all my choice, too well, too well I see
That age's dust and sage's doubt may turn your hearts from me,
That you, in glare of newer times, again may join the cry
With rulers and with men of wealth, the shout of "Crucify!",
That yet again the noise may come, the lazy sophist's scorn,
That ye too may deride me dead, whom I have loved unborn.

(ca. 1893)

NINA [VIVIAN]

The green-ribbed apple tree loads fruit on leaves
                              Is justified.
The deeps of corn are shifted into sheaves
                              Blessed, set aside.
A straight wall runneth round it. Each receives
                              Great peace and pride.
Sister, all other needs have moved,
                              In faint lights shed,
Adventure and the daydream of life loved,
                              And won and wed,
But thou art sacred, happy, crowned, removed,
                              Divine and dead.
Dead: with thy lover from the Heaven of Love,
                              A sunset place.
On all life's battle, blow and shout and shove,
                              Thou lookest grace.
Is it not ours to look and see above
                              Our star: thy face?
Sister, we played together: we can trace
                              Our childhood's day.
Sister, we laughed together: for that grace
                              Grant what I pray:
To serve thee, smite for thee and find thy face
                              Set other-way.
                                        (ca. 1893)

IDA [VIVIAN]

Earth be fair to thy feet, my sister,
Gold grass under and clouds on high.
May the days be full and the years, my sister,
Sweet, for the sake of a year gone by.

The artist Comely Vivian and his family were neighbors of the Chestertons. His three daughters—Nina, Ida and Violet—were a big part of GKC's life in the 1890s. See "Nina" in *Collected Poetry*, Part II, p. 317.

Year of their fate, their year, my sister,
Something for us too, ends in it now:
We have been friends, we twain, my sister,
Never was merrier friend than thou.

Not for us was the best, my sister,
Sacred raving and crowning wild.
Sunny and sane we stood, my sister,
Looked on the wonderful thing and smiled.

Not as ours are the strong bonds, sister,
Not as ours are the links that last,
We take hands at the cross-roads, sister,
Not the worse for the past thing past.

That which you could not give, my sister,
That which I did not give, nor could:
Crown thee and bless thee, I pray, my sister,
For the sake of a twelvemonth's sisterhood.

(ca. 1893)

[VIOLET VIVIAN]

Thine are the twelve great triumphs, Love our Lord,
Thine the red banner and the burning sword.
Hell's walls down wrecked: yet more accord:

More than the infernal Temples wrecked. Yea more.
Thou hast unlatched the cottage [door]
Yea: Thou hast entered home: and all is o'er.

Friend, to have made thee friend, without release,
Win thee and swear, this wonder shall not cease.
We conquered sin: but now we conquer peace.

Star thy still eyes with wish and wonderment,
Invade thine even order with event,
Light in their deep contentment discontent.

To claim by thee a seat established
Even in the circle of the broken bread,
May not for this a man hold up his head?

We who are war-worn, we who take and give,
We can o'erlook love, live and let live
But can thy terrible grey eyes forgive?

There clean and awful, keepeth watch and ward
The star of truth that sundereth like a sword.
Ah, can this spirit love me, Love, our Lord?

In those clear eyes: as wells of crystal clear
Love is alive: Yea, I have seen love here,
And I am shaken of a sacred fear.

Write this thing of me: till the star-dome rend
He gave me love, who gives and doth not lend;
As one that wins a bride, I won a friend.

(ca. 1893)

WORLD-LOVER

The little leaves of green and gold,
     Wherein my feet go lovingly,
And past the thatches brown and old,
     The sea-grey meadows by the sea;
How should the thistledown that flies
     Give back my laugh or head my rhyme,
Or all the daisies' elfin eyes
     Have looked on me at any time?
Only a man, unknown, unseen,
     Who deems the green leaves truly green.

A shorter, slightly variant version of the first three stanzas appeared in *Collected Poetry*, Part I, p. 217 under the title "[Green Leaves]".

How should all men who toil and rove
  Have heard my feet amid the din,
Or vision how my lonely love
  At every casement looketh in?
And no man knows how grows in power
  My care for earth's divine old dust
For who shall kiss the sun for flower
  That warms the just and the unjust?
So I: a life unknown, unseen,
  That deems the green leaves truly green.

Fair-blooded faces, maiden brows,
  Blue eyes adrift as dreaming sea,
But not for me the sea-star shows
  Nor any fair face flames for me:
But could a man enwrap his arms
  About the whole earth fierily:
Through seas and seasons, snows and calms,
  Then, of a great truth, I were he:
Even I, a man, unknown, unseen,
  Who deems the green leaves truly green.

But in the deafening day of God
  Then will I stand and speak a word,
"Lo: I have neither pen nor rod,
  Nor any mighty work, good Lord.
Lo: this thing only is my pride,
  For this one thing have I upstood:
I wandered long, I wandered wide,
  And found Thy good earth passing good.
This much at least, a soul unseen
  Who deemed the green leaves truly green."
            (from *The Club*, undated but
                catalogued in St. Paul's
              School Library as 1893)

THE BRIDAL OF THE LAWGIVER

Of great limbs gone to chaos,
    Of a great face turned to night,
From the grey old earth's first twilight,
    The song of a man of might,
The man of the shattered tables,
The man of the changing rod,
The man that gave to the nations
The ten great words of God.

(A city of monstrous temples
    With giant stairs between,
Where gleamed the eyes as jewels
    Of titan gods unclean,
The glittering shapes and colours
The ghastly hues, and gay
Colossal and fantastic
The Pharaoh's city lay.

And round the feet and altars
    Of those tremendous gods
With murmuring and shrieking,
    With bridles and with rods,
The floods of naked races,
The ebbing human seas
That served for days undying
The undying Ptolemies.)

. . . .

The Midian pools and rivers
    In silver wander wide,
But they gleamed as red a sunset
    When Mesu took his bride.

See Exodus 2:1–22. Mesu is Moses, who fled from Egypt and settled in the land of Midian, where he married one of the seven daughters of Jethro.

The Midian slopes are shaggy
With struggling sheep at play,
But day was dark with vultures
On Mesu's wedding-day.

Like lilies by the waters
   Did Jethro's daughters stand
With green and golden garments,
   A dark and braided band.
Like lilies in the tempest,
They swayed and caught and clung,
As hoarse with yells and laughter
Men crashed the reeds among.

"Are you the starry maidens
   Come down on earth to play?"
"Are you the brood of Memnon[1]
   That you should bar our way?"
"Our flocks are rich and countless
And wearied of hot hours:
Hence: bondmaids of a bondman.
Get hence: the pool is ours."

Clear as a lute at evening
   Did Jethro's fairest speak,
"Rob, if you need the robbing,
   For slaves can rob the weak:
But round these brooks and shallows
Our father's flocks did go:
When you and all your kindred
Caught garbage from the crow."

Then Ptah the son of Nimrod[2]
   Snatched staff in ire and heat:

[1] In Greek mythology, Memnon was a king of Ethiopia who conquered Egypt and parts of Mesopotamia; he also fought at Troy.

[2] Ptah is the name of the Egyptian prime creator. In Genesis, Nimrod, the grandson of Noah, builds a large kingdom beginning at Babel.

But one that sat beside the well
   Sprang swiftly to his feet
A shadow towered over them
Two cubits and a span,
And Mesu stood amongst them,
A strange and mighty man.

"Whence I have come I know not,
   Whither I go God knows,
Ask whence the snow cometh,
   Say where the waste wind blows,
But thee and thine that know thee
My own right hand shall know:
Ere from this place the maidens
Three cubits' length shall go."

Then spake the son of Nimrod,
   "Spawn of the shore-mud, go:
Shall he that strikes the eagle
   Bend at the flies his bow?
Back, dastard, back, insulter,
Soul of a bulrush, back!"
And the great throat of Mesu
Bayed back against the pack:

"Not against wolf or jackal,
   Son of a houseless cow,
Not against elk or eagle
   Your bow is bended now.
Thick with a thousand weapons
Stand as a great tower stands,
And I will come against thee
With hate and my two hands,
With justice and my body,
And so the tale begins."
With that there sang about his head
Full thrice three javelins.

Mesu, the son of Isak,[3]
  Stood like a naked tree
—And slow and stern and fearless
  Against the foe came he:
Three javelins hissed beside his ear,
Four shivered in the sand:
—And right into their midst he came
And smote them hand to hand.

Not soft as lotus gardens,
  Not gay as dance is gay,
Their lot who thronged to battle
  When Mesu stood at bay,
Stern as the gates of Sheol,[4]
Stark as the burying-stone,
Their lot who stood together
When Mesu stood alone.

'Neath hands of weapons naked,
  'Neath arms as arms of clown,
Down went the braided chieftain,
  The curlèd prince went down.
With yells and oaths and laughter
They come, and still they come,
Till ten lips howled for slaughter
When four were smitten dumb.

. . . .

                    (incomplete, ca. 1894)

---

[3] The father of Moses is not named in Exodus, but Isaac, the son of Abraham, is one of the Hebrew patriarchs.

[4] Sheol is the Hebrew word for the unseen land of the dead.

ESOTERIC BUDDHISM

Thou pale Saint-Prince of the Orient
    Star-crowned with the mystic light,
With the smile of the still Nirvana
    In thine eyes as dark as night.

With thy smile so calm and exalted
    On the groaners who gnash and weep
Bidding them dream in thy guidance
    To the heavens of a dreamless sleep.

Fair art thou Prince of the East,
    Thine armies are starry and bright,
Thy glorified spirits as bright and as calm
    As the splanging hosts of the night.

Fair art thou Prince of the East,
    And a day dream fair it may be
To dream that thy hierachied powers
    Are the lords of the ages to be.

Fair art thou Prince of the East,
    Thou may hold the spoilt children of joy,
Thy bitter renunciation
    In their soft scented hands as a toy.

They may prate of thy calm exalted
    So gentle and strong,
While they roll in the halls of splendour
    And are friends with the mammon of wrong.

Wherever the ragged toiler
    Lies cowering in horrible gloom,
The plague-struck in scores
    Lie heaped in one rotting room.

Wherever the groaning masses
    Are gasping in anguish wild,
Mayhap they may turn from the Rajah's son
    To dream of the carpenter's child.

And men may turn in their sorrow
   'Neath tyrant or oligarch's ban
To him who carried the glory of God
   In the unranked glory of Man.

The pampered children of Dives
   May revel in gorgeous dream
Of the blaze of the jewelled Palace
   And the worshipping nabob's gleam.

But the toiling children of hunger
   May find a gospel more dear
Was adored in the shepherd's wonder
   And preached in the fisherman's ear.

Fair art thou Prince of the East
   In thy Kingdom gemmed and pearled
But ours still is that worn Galilaean
   Whose Kingdom was not of the world.

                     (ca. 1895)

[ALONE, ALONE]

Alone, alone on the sunny world
With the blue sky over my head,
With never a hope or wish in my heart
To kindle the soul that was dead.

Alone, alone in deepening dusk,
Darkened by ghostly forms
With a horror chill at my lonely heart,
No strength or comfort warm.

Alone, alone, in the starlight world
Girt by the cool, deep air,
With the heart beating high in the silence around
In a solemn glory of prayer

                     (ca. 1895)

THE BABE UNBORN [II]

If all the skies were full of clouds
And all the hills of grass,
And all the towns of chimney pots,
How well the time would pass.

If only summer leaves were green
And summer skies were blue,
And roads ran up across the hill,
I know what I should do.

If there were coloured books to read,
And four-legged beasts to ride,
And real doors to knock at,
And real men inside,

I think that if they gave me leave
Within that world to stand,
I would be good for all the day
I spent in fairyland.

They should not hear a word from me
Of folly or of scorn,
If only I could find the door,
If only I were born.

(1895)

LEGEND OF THE PESSIMIST [II]

God sat by the foam of the golden sea
That which is called eternity:

And stars and worlds were ever more
Cast as shells up on the shore.

Cf. "The Babe Unborn" and "By the Babe Unborn", *Collected Poetry*, Part I,
pp. 194, 197.
Cf. "Legend of the Pessimist", *Collected Poetry*, Part I, pp. 59–60.

The Lord God's riddle the Lord God said
  "The daisy-crown has a ring of red."

Past chaos-giants adrift and dim,
  The soul of the pessimist answered him:

"Heaven are jaws devouring slow,
  —This is the thing my tongue shall show."

Strong stars flickered and dark skies bowed
  As the Lord God laughed in his place aloud.

"How wilt thou show this, mighty one?"
  "—Give me five gifts and it is done."

"Rib me round with a living frame
  —A little gift to begin the game.

Arch my brow like the sky's own dome
  —Merrily on our work doth come—

Set in it eyes like suns that see
  —How shall I else make nought of thee?

Carve my lips, like a trumpet's curled,
  Fashioned to flout thee and thy world.

Breath like thunderclap; kiss like strife,
  Wake within me the star of life."

Titan travail of world-wide wings.
  Wrought is the wonder of wondrous things.

Sunshine thickens and grasses thrive,
  Over and under a man alive.

His eyes as suns do, burn and beat
  Down at the daisy at his feet.

Only a word his lips have said,
  "The daisy-crown has a ring of red."

Read God's riddle, he that knows,
  Down in the fields where the daisy grows.

                              (ca. 1895)

LOVE LYRICS BY AN EDUCATIONALIST

The evening star is fair in heaven,
   The rose leaves linger fair before you,
And ten years hence or so I feel
   That I shall certainly adore you.
The holy educational eye
   Observes with penetration priestly
That life with you will ten years hence
   Be less ingeniously beastly.

Yes: Only shortly to be beloved,
   Repulsive as you are at present,
You shall be grander than a lord,
   As grand as an Adelphi peasant.
Of eighteenth century graces you
   Shall be a careful grave concoctor
And try them on your family—
   Until they scream and fetch the doctor.

You shall wear jewellery in tons,
   Your coats shall every day be new,
Your hair be black; your nose be hooked
   —What cannot education do?

The student, ruthless reaper
   Of truths from every clime
May note these facts: in some way
   Soon after a certain time
Not far from a place (these details
   Grow tedious I'm afraid)
There at that hour precisely
   Something was made.

Let sceptics vainly sneering
   Explain this sign sublime
That this should be made of all things
   There, at that very time.
What all this was, I know not,
   But since, as you will find,

It has nothing to do with the song I sing,
   We needn't mind.

About the thing itself now
   I will confess a doubt,
I wish I knew how they worked the hooks
   And how the ends pulled out,
And what they did with the old blue back
   And the salt and the copper wire,
But as it has nothing to do with us,
   We won't enquire.

About that thing I spoke of,
   It must be plain confessed
That for Shape—and Tone—and Flavour
   It ranked one of the best.
It filled up half the bedroom
   And worked with a kind of spur,
But in the tale I tell, I admit,
   It doesn't occur.

               (ca. 1896)

LE JONGLEUR DE DIEU [II]

But God beside one sea walketh,
   With breakers, wall on wall,
In trackless heights they gather,
   Into deafening ruins fall.
Drifts through the sunken temples,
     Shoulders the shattered ships,
     The sea that God hears breaking,
     The laughter on my lips.

Mine is the praise God heareth,
   Mine is the joy, and his,

Cf. "Le Jongleur de Dieu", *Collected Poetry*, Part II, pp. 254–56.

That has felt his feet in the darkness
  On the brink of a truth's abyss.
I have seen what all men seek for,
    But the woods are choked with mirth,
    But the flower at my feet is cunning
    With the hope at the heart of the earth.

In clefts as livid as chaos,
  Loose as creation's verge,
Kept I in youth the vigil,
  Plied I in youth the scourge,
Till the real, bare and blinding,
    Came like apocalypse,
    And like flame from the lips of a prophet
    It laid a laugh on my lips.

                      (ca. 1896)

IRONY

I climbed the pedestal of Fate,
  I clutched the cold colossal feet,
Crying to be the ribbon green
  Where her dim hair grows deep and sweet.

I trampled on the ruined thrones,
  The crowns of all the aims and art,
Begging to be the violet
  That heaves above the heart of hearts.

I have not been the ribbon green,
  The flowers that on her bosom nod,
I did not see the dreadful smile
  Upon the secret face of God.

"You shall not be the ribbon green",
  The lips of living thunder spake,
"But you shall be the hempen rope
  That binds her body to the stake."

You shall not be purple blooms
  That make her fragrant as the glen,
But you shall be the yellow flame
  That slays her for the sport of men.

Then said I slow, "When rods of thorn
  Broke on the living Christ, Lord God,
Did not men gather and adore
  A relic in the broken rod?"

"And mean and fallen though I be—
  One thing is more to me than I,
Each motion of that noble face
  That smote me like a battle cry."

I know what thing is worth the world.
  Lord of the World, know this thing well
—One eye's flash worthy of herself
  Than my whole body cast in hell."

"O Potter, bending o'er the pots,
  For honour and dishonour made,
The terrors gather round her head
  But thou and I were not afraid.

                              (ca. 1897)

GOLD LEAVES

  Lo! I am come to autumn
    When all the leaves are gold;
  Grey hairs and golden leaves cry out,
    The year and I are old.

  In youth I sought the prince of men,
    Captain in cosmic wars,
  Our Titan, even the weeds would show
    Defiant, to the stars.

  But now a great thing in the street
    Seems any human nod,

Where shift in strange democracy
    The million masks of God.

In youth I sought the golden flower
    Hidden in wood or wold,
But I am come to autumn
    When all the leaves are gold.
                                        (ca. 1897)

THE WORLD'S LOVER

My eyes are full of lonely mirth:
    Reeling with want and worn with scars,
For pride of every stone on earth,
    I shake my spear at all the stars.

A live bat bears my crest above,
    Lean foxes nose where I have trod,
And on my naked face the love
    Which is the loneliness of God.

Outlawed: since that great day gone by—
    When before prince and pope and queen
I stood and spoke a blasphemy—
    'Behold the summer leaves are green.'

They cursed me: what was that to me
    Who in that summer darkness furled,
With but an owl and snail to see,
    Had blessed and conquered all the world?

They bound me to the scourging-stake,
    They laid their whips of thorn on me;
I wept to see the green rods break
    Though blood be beautiful to see.

Beneath the gallows' foot abhorred
    The crowds cry 'Crucify!' and 'Kill!'
Higher the priests sing, 'Praise the Lord,
    The warlock dies'; and higher still

Shall heaven and earth hear one cry sent
  Even from the hideous gibbet height,
'Praise to the Lord Omnipotent,
  The vultures have a feast tonight.'

(ca. 1897)

[THE LONELY CHILD]

There was a child that sat alone
  Playing with ball and toy,
Turning a painted windmill wheel
  In loneliness and joy,
But the mill was the wheel of all the stars
  And the balls were the sun and the moon.

He set a starry doll's house up
  With painted door and rafter,
Opened and shut the little doors
  With everlasting laughter.
He made it gay with a little doll
  Wooden and violet
But the dolls were all the sons of men,
  The prophets and the Kings.

(ca. 1897)

THE PILGRIM FATHERS

A Nation sat upon a sea-girt throne
  In the grey morning of the world alone
And swore with hidden face and lifted hand
  An oath that none may wholly understand.

But as the lands and ages rose and reeled
  Letter by letter is the speech revealed,
The broken fragments of that primal vow
  Scattered about the world, we read them now.

"Are not the gleaning of the grapes of God
　　More than the vintage of the Gentiles trod?
The Kings of old lie swathed in gilded pall,
　　But my cast raiment shall be more than all.
The nations go with banners and great state,
　　Sending their mightiest men to war with fate,
But mine shall spring from dropped and ruined things:
　　My refuse nations and my convicts Kings."

Between the swarthy skies and livid seas
　　A ship fled, hung between eternities,
From Kingly craft and priestly power it fled.
　　"Get forth and die," the lying Agag said—
And from between a hopeless sea and sky
　　Came the answer, "This blood does not die."

(ca. 1897)

THE STRANGE SERVANT

I have a sword, I have a staff,
A ruined tower: a meadow,
A crazy servant, hoar and blind
That like my shadow walks behind,
　　Forgotten like my shadow.

His head is like a hoary star
With eyes of laughter lonely,
When I go fishing for my wish
He runs and fills the sea with fish,
　　Before my passage only.

When I go forth with axe in hand
He goes before my going.
He builds the woods before my face,
He passes o'er a naked place
　　And leaves the forest growing.

He brings the wood, he brings the meat
Or in strange empty hours
In floating daydreams swift and sparse
He turns the wheel of all the stars
   Or fills a field with flowers.

Only far before he goes before
That he before my coming
Ere stars or oceans were unfurled
Laid the foundations of the world.
   (Hark, the bees are humming.)
            (ca. 1897)

LINES TO WATERLOO STATION [II]

Come hither, Fisher Unwin,[1]
   And leave your work awhile,
Uplooking in my face a span
   With bright adoring smile.
All happy leaping publishers
   Round Paternoster Row,
Gay Simpkin, dreamy Marshall
   And simple Sampson Low,
Come round, forgetting all your fears,
   Your hats and dinners too,
While I remark with studied calm,
   "Hurrah for Waterloo!"

Nay start not, fearful Putnam,
   I sing no warrior's fall
(Macmillan, smile again, and dry
   The tears of Kegan Paul)

Cf. "Lines to Waterloo Station", *Collected Poetry*, Part I, p. 446.

[1] The name of Chesterton's employer followed by all the other publishers within reach of GKC's office in London.

But seldom on the spot I sing
    Is heard the peal of guns,
Men do not charge for batteries,
    They only charge for buns.
No chief expires, no trumpet
    I blow, except my own,
But harmless season tickets
    Expire without a groan.

I've been in all the waiting-rooms,
    I never chanced to see
An army: but observant
    I never claimed to be—
If someone through my body drove
    A bayonet like a spit,
I listened to Miss Frances Blogg[2]
    And did not notice it.

Yet still thy Gladstone bags shall woo
    Thy labels' bashful kiss,
Geologists shall reconcile
    Thy cake with Genesis,
For out of thee the Sacred Seven[3]
    Went forth to better spheres
And left the Bard upon the shore
    With chocolate and tears.

When dark and low the moon hath sunk,
    The booking-office shut,
When wolves howl in the waiting-rooms
    (Be still, O David Nutt),
When over the First Class Carriages
    Have moss and ivy grown
Under the sad and naked stars
    A figure walks alone:

---

[2] GKC's fiancée, later in 1901 his wife.
[3] Frances Blogg and her friends who had departed for a holiday in France.

His hair is white, and in his eyes
  A blessing fierce with hate,
And in his fingers high in air
  He clutches One-and-Eight[4]
He seeks not how to separate
  His neck-tie from his hair;
He walks upon the railway-line,
  His soul is buried there.

                              (1898)

DEDICATED

She was my sister[1] one night more: she stood
My own new sister for one day of seven.
I hardly knew her then: I thought her good,
A very little space too good for heaven.

Till the night came: when laughing undeterred,
We scored with spirit writings scroll and slate,
And darkly, line by line, I spelt one word,
And every fibre swore a war on fate.

Mocking it doomed her the cloister shelves
Where love and war and tears and laughter cease,
Crypts where the sexless slanderers of themselves
Eat darkly the forbidden fruit of peace.

                              (1899)

[4] One shilling and eight pence (one-twelfth of a pound in pre-decimalised currency).

[1] GKC's sister-in-law Gertrude Blogg, who died in a traffic accident in 1899. It would appear that her death had been foretold in some game with a planchette or ouija board. See "A Nunnery", *Collected Poetry*, Part II, p. 185.

[CHOSEN II]

You are the man that is marked with a star
   Set for aye on the old earth's lyre,
You have been loved of the well-beloved,
   Even desired of the world's desire.

I heard a song that the fairies sang,
   The flowers are red and the fields are green
But pale in the midst of green and red
   Is the man who knew the heart of the Queen.

He is marked from the scrolls of time
   Never to snigger or sulk or tire.
You have been loved of the well-beloved,
   Even desired of the world's desire.

They were many about her path,
   They were many, but you were one,
Here, if you will, is a song that ends,
   Here, if you will, is a song begun.

Time to come has its plots in store—
   Time that is past can ne'er turn liar,
You have been loved of the well-beloved,
   Even desired of the world's desire.

Life in your eyes was pale and proud
   Bleak winds battered you where you stood
Lonely—"O man", the prophet said,
   "Hath He not shown you that which is good?"

Count no crown too mighty for thee,
   Turn not back from a whole hell's fire,
You have been loved of the well-beloved,
   Even desired of the world's desire.

                (ca. 1899)

Cf. "Chosen", *Collected Poetry*, Part I, pp. 343–44.

Gilbert Chesterton and Frances Blogg during their engagement, 1898.

II

POEMS ADDRESSED TO
RHODA BASTABLE
1898–1909

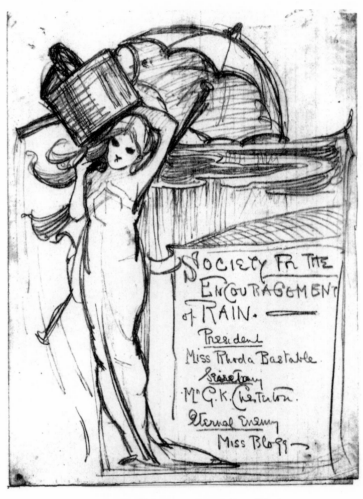

Society for the Encouragement of Rain.
President: Miss Rhoda Bastable;
Secretary: Mr. G. K. Chesterton;
Eternal Enemy: Miss Blogg

11 Warwick Gardens,
W.

Dear Miss Bastaple
The nonsense I venture to
send you by this post, though quite
rough and written on odds and ends
is slightly more durable in form
than the pencil sketches I did
on Sunday. Consequently I beg
you to accept it as a memorial
of the Encouragement of Rain
Society. Believe me
Yours very sincerely
Gilbert Chesterton

11 Warwick Gardens, [London] W. Dear Miss Bastaple [sic] The nonsense I venture to send you by this post, though quite rough and written on odds and ends is slightly more durable in form than the pencil sketches I did on Sunday. Consequently I beg you to accept it as a memorial of the Encouragement of Rain Society. Believe me Yours very sincerely Gilbert Chesterton

Rhoda Bastable, secretary of Chesterton's debating club, was the cousin of Frances Blogg, who became GKC's fiancée in the summer of 1898. Other poems to Rhoda Bastable include the following in *Collected Poetry*, Part I: "A Happy Xmas", p. 279, "Inscription for Rhoda Bastable", p. 205, "Song to an Old Tune" and "A Standing Invitation", p. 316, "To Rhoda", p. 335 and "To Rhoda, Otherwise called Rohda", p. 336.

THE POET AND NATURE

I love to see the little stars
All dancing to one tune.
I think quite highly of the Sun
And kindly of the Moon.

The Mountains all in order set
Sit drinking up my tea.
The Great Niagara Waterfall
Is never shy with me.

I am the Tiger's confidant
And never mention names.
The Lion drops the formal "Sir"
And lets me call him James.

Cf. "From the Publications of the Encouragement of Rain Society", *Collected Poetry*, Part II, pp. 249–50 and "The Oneness of the Philosopher with Nature", Part II, pp. 355–65.

Into my ear the blushing Whale
Stammers the truth: I know
Why the Rhinocerus [sic] is sad
– Ah, Child! 'Twas long ago—

I am akin to all the Earth
Linked in the vast Design.
The aged Pig will often wear
That strange sweet smile of mine.

My niece the Barnacle has got
My piercing eyes of black.
The Elephant has got my nose;
        I do not want it back.

And I, who loved the Octopus
Since we were boys together,
Who have no secrets from the shark,
Shall I then fear the weather?

I love to bask in sunny fields
But when that hope is vain
I go and bask in Baker Street
All in the pouring rain.

The Snow, where fly, by some strange law,
Hard snowballs without noise
O'er streets untenanted, except
By good unconscious boys?

The Wind, that gives our reeling aunts
The deep pure joy secure
Of training the satiric powers
Of the deserving poor.

O Rain and Hail and Thunderbolts
Snow, Fire and General Fuss
Come to my arms—Come all at
    once;
O photograph me thus.

                    (1898)

THE FISH OUT OF WATER

Observe these pirates, bold and gay
   That sail a gory sea;
Notice their bright expression:
   The handsome one is Me.

We plundered ships and harbours,
   We spoiled the Spanish Main,
But Nemesis watched over us,
   For it began to rain.

Cf. "Shipwrecked Off Fairyland", *Collected Poetry*, Part II, pp. 204–206 and "Of the Dangers Attending Altruism on the High Seas", Part II, pp. 366–72.

The rain was pouring loud and long,
  The sea was fierce and dim.
A little fish was swimming there,
  Our Captain pitied him.

"How sad", he said, and dropt a tear
  Splash on the cabin roof,
"That we are gay: while he is there
  Without a waterproof."

"Let's take him on the ship at once,
    For science teaches me
That he'll be wet if he remains
    Much longer in the sea."

They fished him in: the first mate wept
    And came with Rugs and Ale,
The Boatswain brought him one golosh
    And fixed it on his tail.

But yet he never loved the ship,
    Against the mast he'd lean;
If spoken to he stammered
    And blushed a pallid green.

Though plied with hardbake, beef and beer,
  He showed no wish to sup—
The gayest riddles that they asked,
  He always gave them up.

A furrow lined his youthful cheek,
  One whisker grey he had,
The crew were grieved to look on one
  so lovely, yet so sad.

But soon they frowned: he never seemed
   When asked to smoke or sing
To really throw himself into
   The spirit of the thing.

They tried him by Court Martial
   —That fish of low degree;
They sentenced him to drowning
   And threw him in the sea.

Before he sank, one dazzling smile
　　Made every scale a gem,
And turning with a graceful bow
　　He kissed his fin to them.

MORAL

Princess, although the rain is sweet,
　Yet heed this tale of mine.
Do not be hopelessly depressed
　Because the day is fine.

If I can wile thy mournful soul
　From Melancholia's chain,
I kick my legs and I expire,
　I have not lived in vain.
　　　　　　　(Christmas, 1898)

HISTORY OF THE HUSBANDS OF RHODA

These suitors rolled upon the sand.
Asking for Rhoda's heart and hand.

(1) Professor Piff, whose 'Tuscan Rome"
Is loved in every English home;
Bits from his "British Trace in Gaul"
Bring down the house at the music hall.

(2) Roy Beauchamp, you observe to follow
A god, an artist, an Apollo—
What little cash, I am aware,
He had to spare, he did not spare.

(3) Sbolsky: an Anarchist, still alive,
Politically known as "5".
He blew up thousands, it was said;
Married and was blown up instead.

(4) Through Major Bumper's pleasant oaths,
Moustaches, and delightful clothes;
He was M. P. for Gallowglass
To represent the working class.

(5) Giles Rosethorn was an actor free,
Who with romantic mystery
Buttoned that cape about his throat
Because he had not got a coat

(6) And Mimmer! Music he in sum!
He played the fiddle, fife and drum;
He played the fool, when all was spent,
It was his favourite instrument.

(7) Good Captain Cubby then began,
A fine old country gentleman,
With him our Rhoda lived at ease,
Perpetually shelling peas.

(8) Then came the Rev. Ehud Boe
("The Battle-Blast of Pimlico").
He turned a Mormon later on
And married ten. But one had gone.

(9) Living with Phillip William Trevor,
One had no sentiments whatever.

. . . .

(10) Swarra NaGulosnaphyaptarwoedkz
Which, let me tell you, rhymes to "boots".
His ways were somewhat savage: he
Ate his papa ... but reverently.

(11) Of COLONEL BROWN—the writer begs
To utter nothing but the legs.

(ca. 1908)

The Husbands of Rhoda

III

POEMS OF THE EARLY
1900s

DARK BLUE

Science has sawed the timbers of time,
   The floor of the world has fallen away,
The sky is black as a bootless crime
   And heaven is redder than hell today.

It seems such a little while to pass
   Since Nature's beauty and all men's rights
The sages said should be cheap as grass,
   And Shelley played with the clouds like kites.

I do not mind if the stars be mire,
   If the suns that were lamps in Nature's hall
Are the idle sparks of a fruitless fire:
   I never worshipped the stars at all.

From my neck and under my shirt
   A wooden cross by a cord is hung.
I know it shall last when the world is gone,
   For I know it was best when the world was young.

Fast the arrows fall around us,
   On our body breaks the rod,
But we huddle in the darkness
   And we drink the blood of God.

                           (ca. 1900)

OLIVE

That sad old world that found the cross
   Was wiser than the world we see—
The men that brought us all to God
   Were wickeder than we.

They knew that whole of anarchy
   Whereof we grasp the gilded hem,
And these things that are new to us
   Were very old to them.

They knew how strange things turn to sad
   Under those evil ancient trees
When men are weary of green wine
   And sick of crimson seas.

They ever sought new worlds to rule,
   Cities of ivory, hills of gold.
What boots a man to conquer heaven
   If he be very old.

God gave them deserts old as heaven,
   Where fragments of gods were flung,
Deserts for hermits old and grey,
   And there the heart grew young.

                  (ca. 1900)

DARK GREEN

The sea was dark and evil,
The skies had not a spark,
But the wine we drank was darker,
And we drank it in the dark.

When we drank the stars grew paler
And the forests shrank and curled,
For we drained a secret fountain
Of the life-tide of the world.

We had neither bread nor fishes,
We had neither net nor line,
Yet the Kings of men pursued us;
Far they sought for the strange wine.

We got neither pence nor pity,
We are stark in our distress,
But the men that buy the mountains
Hate us for our happiness.

                  (ca. 1900)

VIOLET

Against heraldic sunsets scrawled
  With purple and fantastic gold
The heavy argosies were hauled,
  Crowned with Crusaders' crests of old.

Forgotten fathers, yours and mine,
  Rode down where Pagans watched for them,
And broke their breasts against the line,
  Their hearts against Jerusalem.

Oh long ago and dead they lie
  That roar and guard their master dead,
But human madness cannot die;
  We have our madness too, instead.

Our wise men sail to hells of snow
  And blindly die and sadly dare
To pass a line they cannot show
  And find a pole that is not there.

A perfect image of the day,
  We seek with all our pain of pride
A place more bare than Syria
  Where no man sure even died.

(ca. 1900)

[INSCRIPTION IN MRS. OLDERSHAW'S[1] COPY OF *POEMS AND BALLADS*]

I saw a poet, fair and frail,[2]
Gold-curled with painted cheeks and pale,
Clad soft in many a subtle silk,
Tawny as flame or white as milk.
Red and white roses round him fall
Calling young earth to carnival,
But in his eyes with wild lights shot
A loathing not to be forgot.

He chased the cherubim and powers
And pelted them with garden flowers,
He quenched the stars whereon he trod
And rent away the robe of God,
Showing a naked thorn-crowned Man
From whose red brow the red blood ran.

Then in voice womanish and wild
Cried out, "Lo man—clay's common child.
Thou that were God—what art thou now?"
The insulted reared his blood-red brow
And smiled, "Good friend—thou sayst true:
I was a man. But what are you?"

(ca. 1900)

---

[1] Frances Chesterton's sister Ethel, wife of Lucian Oldershaw.

[2] Algernon Charles Swinburne, author of *Poems and Ballads* (1866). Cf. "Inscription in *Poems and Ballads*", *Collected Poetry*, Part I, p. 55. For another parody of Swinburne see "The Ghost of the Great Suburban", p. 86.

[TO] VIOLET BOILEAU[1]
FROM GILBERT CHESTERTON

You will not like my picture of a pig
    For you have pigs of every shape and size
Who leap at your return and lick your hand
    And look up with their rapt seraphic eyes.

You will not like my Elephant at all,
    Although your scorn in pity may be sunk:
She who has passed the Belgian Custom House[2]
    Can pity anything that has a trunk.

You will not like my pictures or my rhymes,
    The scanty fruits of a disgusting mind.
There are three letters only you will like,
    Three letters that I leave to you to find.

                     (1900)

AN APOLOGY[1]

Another tattered rhymster in the ring,
With but the old plea to the sneering schools,
That on him too, some secret night in spring,
Came the old frenzy of a hundred fools
To make some thing; the old want dark and deep,
The thirst of men, the hunger of the stars,
Since first it tinged even the Eternal's sleep
With monstrous dreams of trees and towns and wars,

---

[1] GKC dedicated a copy of *Greybeards at Play* to Violet Boileau, the fiancée of Chesterton's friend E. C. Bentley and a lady whose family history is celebrated in a poem in that collection. See "Les Boileaux de Castelnau" in *Collected Poetry*, Part II, pp. 260–68 and "Ballade Des Boileaux", Part II, p. 388.

[2] The Boileau family had taken an extended vacation in Belgium.

[1] These are the introductory lines to the first edition of *The Wild Knight and Other Poems*. The title was only added to the poem in 1905 for the second edition.

When all He made for the first time He saw,
Scattering stars as misers shake their pelf,
Then in the last strange wrath broke His own law,
And made a graven image of Himself.

(1900)

THE FEAST OF SNOW

There is heard a hymn when the panes are dim,
  And never before or again,
When the nights are strong with a darkness long,
  And the dark is alive with rain.

Never we know but in sleet and in snow,
  The place where the great fires are,
That the midst of the earth is a raging mirth
  And the heart of the earth a star.

And at night we win to the ancient inn
  Where the Child in the frost is furled,
We follow the feet where all souls meet
  At the inn at the end of the world.

The gods lie dead where the leaves lie red,
  For the flame of the sun is flown,
The gods lie cold where the leaves lie gold,
  And a Child comes forth alone.

(from *Parents' Review*, vol. 11, 1900)

[CREATION]

Over and under
Splendour and wonder,
Sunshine and thunder,
Whirlwind and star;
Snows huge and hoary,
Sleet and sun-glory,
Fair is the story
Of all things that are.

(ca. 1901)

AN APOLOGY [II]

The dear dread days when first we met
Whate'er you think of them or me
Think not I said "Another song:
"Another blossom on the tree."

There were more terrors in your eyes,
O first of loves and last of friends,
I saw you: and my soul cried out
"Here all my idle story ends."

Nameless and gay my days have been,
Nameless and gay my life could pass,
Finding no trumpet, like the birds
No laurel greener than the grass.

But if I look but once again
Into that princely face and pale,
I lose my oldest liberty,
The peerless liberty to fail.

Two stanzas of "An Apology [II]" appear in *Collected Poetry*, Part I, p. 341. Here
we print the complete poem for the first time.

I looked again: I looked and knew
The hour was coming which has come,
When I should drop my idle pipe
To smite and shake the shuddering drum.

Dearest, I knew the thing I did;
I swore an oath on that last night
That I would love the lightning yet,
More than I ever loved the light,

That, I would hear the horns of war
As gladly as the birds of spring,
That I would fear your sacred face,
And after, fear not anything.

I am not he that roamed and wrote
Without a vision or a plan,
I am not he that dreamed a part;
Your love has made a better man.

And if, all dazed with a new din,
Things from my vaporous fancy fade,
Like God Himself, whose power you wear,
You must forgive the soul you made.

When in the dark of night my heart
Breaks up like water from its bands,
With pride as soft as all your hair,
And fear as tender as your hands,

I know my soul, to bless you, dear,
Grows soft and silver as your dress,
I know my rude and ragged thoughts
Grow open as the brow I bless.

There in that dark of night I know
God shall not sunder you and me,
Although He float the fish in heaven
And cast the stars into the sea.

(1901)

CREATION DAY [II]

Between the perfect marriage day
  And that fierce future proud, and furled,
I only stole six days—six days,
  Enough for God to make the world.

For us is a creation made,
  New moon by night, new sun by day,
That ancient elm that holds the heavens
  Sprang to its stature yesterday—

The old sad sun that saw our fears
  Lies with the old moon, shattered too,
New are our honours: yea, by God,
  If we have sins, they shall be new.

Dearest and first of all things free,
  Alone as bride and queen and friend,
Brute facts may come and bitter truths,
  But here all doubts shall have an end.

Straight bolts of doom shall smite us now,
  But no more fancies rent askew,
Hard war with hunger, hell and man,
  But never any war with you.

Never again shall tongue or soul
  Perplex with words, betray with breath;
We only deal with decent want,
  With cleanly pain and kindly death.

Never again wilh cloudy talk
  Shall life be tricked or faith undone.
The world is many and is made,
  But we are sane and we are one.

(1901)

"Creation Day [II]" was written either during or shortly after Chesterton's honeymoon. Cf. shorter version in *Collected Poetry*, Part I, pp. 344–45.

BALLADE OF REASONABLE INQUIRY [II]

Why is my head covered with curious hairs?
Why is the sun still rising in the East?
Oh! Why do stallions so often mate with mares?
And why is bread so often made with yeast?
When those Raid Wires were pawed about and pieced[1]
What is that one whose text has not transpired?
Now Chartereds have so painfully decreased[2]
I think an explanation is required.

Why noxious animals must hunt in pairs
Is not made clear by saying: Mark o' the Beast;
When Sergeant Sheridan sought balmier airs[3]
How were the wheels of his wild chariot greased?
"Hmm, Hmm." Yes, doubtless, as you say, the priest
Forced on a darkened world with fear, inspired
Wild explanations. But to say the least,
I think an explanation is required.

Envoi

Prince, now about this hare on which we feast,
Fitzsimmons swears you never even fired,
And Dick declares you never saw the beast:
I think an explanation is required.

(1904)

From *Father Brown on Chesterton*, London (Frederick Muller) 1937, pp. 24–25, in which Mgr. John O'Connor dates it to 1904. Cf. "Ballade of Reasonable Inquiry", *Collected Poetry*, Part II, pp. 445–46.

[1] The Jameson Raid was an attempt by Dr. L. S. Jameson to subvert the government of Paul Kruger in the Transvaal in 1875. Cecil Rhodes and Joseph Chamberlain, the British Colonial Secretary, were alleged to be involved, but vital evidence disappeared.

[2] Chartereds were a type of stock market bond.

[3] Sergeant Sheridan and other Irish police constables were dismissed in 1904 for giving perjured evidence to convict innocent men of cutting off cow's tails, a crime which Sheridan and his confederates had themselves done because they were fond of ox-tail soup. Sheridan himself became a fugitive.

THE QUEEN OF THE GREEN ELVES

CAST

Titania
Maid Marion
Robin Hood
King Stephen
King Henry
Spirit of England

(*Any tree, with any kind of rock or stone beside it, on which anybody can sit. Titania, in some sort of long dim robes, with a silver crown, enters.*)

Tit.   I am the Queen of the Green Elves,
I am the Soul of the Greenwood.
The saddest hind that drinks and delves
Has seen me when his dreams were good.
Under my green and gloaming wings—
This green and gloaming land shall be;
Before the oldest of its Kings—
    Forgotten Shakespeare sang to me.

This play was written and performed for Mr. and Mrs. Francis Steinthal. The Chestertons often spent short holidays in their home, St. John's, in Ilkley, Yorkshire, where they enjoyed walks upon the moors and discussions on cultural and philosophical topics. In the evenings the Steinthal's often entertained their guests with musical and theatrical performances.

Mrs. Steinthal had founded the Parents National Education Union, for which Frances Chesterton (nee Blogg) had worked as a secretary prior to her marriage. Friendship continued between the two couples, and it was in 1903, while staying at the Steinthal home, that GKC first met Father John O'Connor, who became the inspiration for his priest detective, Father Brown.

I poured your ancient laughter out
Through Chevy's fight and Chaucer's pen.[1]
I am the heart of the old rout,
I am the heart of English men.
Upon my folk for ever lay
The jolly witchcraft of the trees,
My dark was happier than day,
 My perils kindlier than peace.

Go spread your monstrous cities' girth
And fill the immortal sky with fumes.
Make the heavens fouler than the earth,
Your houses greyer than your tombs.
You shall not drown me deep in smoke,
You shall not drive me from my own;
I journey under elm and oak,
 And where I sit is England's throne (*Sits on the rock*).

This idle stone, this empty glade
I mark them with my seal and go,
And peer or peasant in its shade
Shall see my light and surely know.
The England of the Elves is old,
The England of the gods is good;
I am not bought; I am not sold,
I am the soul of the greenwood.
(*Disappears slowly into the wood.*)

(*Enter Maid Marion.*)

Mar. How sudden is the silence of this wood,
 How lean a line divideth peace and war.
 In that deep ravine below the hill

---

[1] Chevy Chase was a hunting incursion by the Percys into the territory of the Douglas family. Sometimes confused with the Battle of Otterburn. Geoffrey Chaucer (ca. 1345–1400) wrote *The Canterbury Tales*.

King Stephen and King Henry fight each other[2]
Asking the stars which shall be King of England.
As on the shining sands the small crabs crawl
Within an inch of the uproarious sea,
Robin and I walk idly on the hill
Like princes in a garden; and below
In that dark valley still the battle boils.

(*Enter Robin Hood.*)

Rob.   Have you been near the battle-field? Who wins?

Mar.   King Henry wins: King Stephen's arms go down.

Rob.   And Henry's arms go up. His arms go up
And legs go up, for all I know or care.

Mar.   I speak more sadly when I speak of war.

Rob.   Most seriously and most sadly, Marion,
I contemplate King Henry and King Stephen.
I estimate their banners; study well
Their coats of arms, their policies and claims,
And state, with tears, that I would see them all
Slung to the devil for a pot of ale.

Mar.   I am sorry for King Stephen: mortal man
Never fought better. When his host went down
And the whole howling foe went over it
He broke their passage like a brazen gate,
And his one sword was seven thunderbolts.

Rob.   I never knew a braver man. I knew
A ferret who was braver. His name was Bones.

Mar.   I have looked out again. The field still swirls,
The rout still quickens, and the King still stands
Like a tall ship amid the sea of spears,

[2] Stephen reigned 1135–1154. Henry II succeeded him and ruled until 1189.

And batters down the victors in their pride.
So brave a man might well be King of England.

Rob.   What does it matter who is King of England?
Stephen is brave: Henry is brave as well,
He heads the onset like a red-haired devil,
And I am brave and my dog, Spot, is brave;
And we are brave whoever's King of England,
And heaven is blue whoever's King of England,
And ale is brown whoever's King of England,
And I have only to sit down and sing
Here on this stone and I am king of England:

> The King that lives in London eats
>   A hundred cakes a day,
> He goes to bed for seven weeks
>   And no man says him nay,
> But long as blood and wine are red
>   And earth and ale are brown
> I care as much for the man in the moon
>   As the King in London town.
>
> The King that lives in London wears
>   A dozen coats at once
> And he can order twenty moons
>   And half a hundred suns,
> But ... .

(*Enter King Stephen, staggering into the glade, his sword drawn. His clothes, arms, etc. are torn and soiled, but he wears a crown and the gold leopards on his shield.*)

Mar.   Someone is coming here.

Rob.   Who are you?

Steph.   Stephen.
The King of England just an hour ago.
   (*Robin and Marion kneel.*)

You do not understand. An hour ago,
I said, I was King of England. So I was.
Now, my good sir, now I am Stephen of Blois,
A very impecunious gentleman. (*Flings away his shield.*)
What? Kneeling still? Kneeling to Stephen still?
Has he indeed two subjects still to rule?

Mar. Aye, you say right: Kneeling to Stephen still,
The hero of the battle in the valley.

Steph. Hero... battle ... valley ... then in God's name bring
The hero of the battle in the valley
Something to eat and drink. (*Stumbles and falls, half-fainting,
[to] the ground.*)

Mar. You fetch some wine here. I will bring the bread.
(*They rush out.*)

(*Enter Titania, while Stephen lies motionless.*)

Tit. (*sitting on the rock*).
Where I sit is England's throne,
And I sit upon this stone.
Four score yards from end to end
Is this glade that I befriend,
Yet this glade, whereof I sing,
Shall be England to the King.
It shall mean from tree to tree
Berwick to the Southern Sea.
In his woodland banishment
Stephen shall be quite content.
All he lost in his last fight
He shall gather here tonight.
Where I sit is England's throne,
And I sit upon this stone. (*Goes out.*)

(*Robin and Marion rush in, bringing food and wine.*)

Rob. He is still fainting. He is a fine fellow.

Mar.   Defeated people seem most beautiful.

Rob.   Defeated people are the bravest people.
       Till you are beaten, how can you be brave?

Mar.   You are right, Robin. Had he been King of England
       He might not ...

Rob.   He is wakening.

Steph. (*lifting himself*).   King at last.
       King! I am King of England. All I ask
       Is to be monarch of this glorious glade,
       Is to be monarch of this strip of trees.
       (*Staggers to his feet.*)
       Within this glade shall all my empire be.
       (*to Robin*) Since you bring wine, be you my cup-bearer,
       My Lord High Butler and Grand Wine-Merchant.
       (*to Marion*) Since you bring bread, be you my Bakeress
       And Lady Critic of all.
       (*to Robin*) Since you have bow and sword, be you my
                          army
       My generals, admirals, lines of all defence.
       (*to Marion*) Since you have round your neck a silver
                     cross,
       Be you my church. Since you have round your neck
       A string of beads, be you my school of arts.
       Since you bring help—be you my hospitals.
       I will be king and sit upon this rock,
       And where I sit, there is the throne of England.
          (*Sits on the rock.*)
       Lo, hear all men, all devils and all angels,
       I throw away the little throne of England
       And take the mighty throne of this one glade.
          (*Takes off his gold crown and flings it away.*)
       I fling this flashing English crown away.
       Give me a crown of leaves—a crown of leaves,
       For I am the one King of all this glade.

(*Marion twists a wreath of woodland boughs and hands
  it to him. He puts it on.*)
Lo, I am crowned the King of all this glade.
(*Throws away his sword.*)
I fling away my sword, my flaming sword,
My foolish sword that showed I was King of
England.
Bring me a bough of woods—a bough of the tree
To show I am monarch of this glade.
(*Robin hands him a bough from a tree.*)
A good green wreath and a good growing bough—
Has any King from Babylon to France
Such great regalia? Has any King
A living sceptre and a living crown?

Rob.   He is mad.

Mar.   It does not matter; he is happy.

Steph.   How glad I am King Henry rode me down.
How cramped I was when I was king of England!
(*Goes out at the back.*)

Mar.   Follow him, Robin; he has lost his wits.
He thinks this little wood is a great kingdom.

Rob.   Do you hear footsteps? Someone else comes here.

Mar.   Who is it?

Rob.   By St. Michael and All Angels,
I never thought of this!

Mar.   Who is it?

Rob.   Can it be?
How comes he straying far from his own camp?

Mar. (*furiously*).   Who is it?

Rob.   It is the victor.
It is Henry, King of England, comes.

Mar.   I hate him.

Rob.   Hate him? Why do you hate him, Marion?

Mar.   Because he has won. (*Goes out.*)

Rob.   And so here comes the victorious King, King Henry.
       Kings seem as common here as blackberries.
       We have seen one King beaten, he went mad.
       What will the conqueror do? (*Falls back into shadow.*)

       (*Enter King Henry. In strong contrast to King Stephen he is dressed
       in some rich and more or less peaceable garb. Anything with fur, feath-
       ers, etc. would do. He stands silent for some moments. As he does
       so, Titania passes across the back of the scene, lingers at the rock
       and goes out.*)

Hen.   Vanity, vanity and vexation of spirit.
       Kings have been good: Kings have been strong:
       But only one King ever was called wise
       And he said "Vanity of Vanities".
       I am victorious—Stephen is defeated—
       If Stephen is unhappier than I,
       Stephen is unhappier than the souls in hell.
       What is the use of having conquered England?
       I could rule easier this little glade
       Than I rule England. I could know much more
       Of this small place than I can know of England.
       I could be juster to the beetles here
       Than I can be to all the folk of England.
       Oh never pity men that are defeated,
       Keep all your pity for the conqueror—
       I wish I could be King of just this place,
       I wish I could sit on that rock and know
       That here at least no man would question me.
           (*Sits on the rock.*)
       No Parliament can dare, no Pope can dare
       Deny my right to sit upon this stone—
       This little quiet wood at least is mine.

(*Enter King Stephen, rushing in. He is a wild figure, crowned with leaves and armed with a club.*)

Steph.   Dog! Usurper! There
Upon my sacred throne?

Hen.   But who are you?

Steph.   The monarch of this forest. Quit my throne!
(*Rushes at him with the club. Henry catches up another club or heavy bough and fights him. They sway to and fro in fairly equal combat for some time. Then Stephen strikes Henry down.*)
Victory! Victory! Come up my subjects!
You saw King Henry beat me in the valley.
Now see me beat King Henry in the glade.
(*Robin Hood and Maid Marion rush in.*)
I do not mind his being King of England,
But King of this one space he shall not be.

Mar.   He is reviving.

Hen. (*lifting himself from the ground*).
Stephen has beaten me.
Stephen has beaten me after all. Are you
His court and army?

Rob.   We are his court and army,
His court and army who will die for him.

Hen.   Then I submit of course, your Majesty.

Steph.   And I take up my seat on England's throne.
                    (*Sits on the rock.*)
Capture the prisoner.
(*Robin and Marion seize K. Henry and force him to his knees.*)
I now pronounce your doom upon you, Henry.
Upon this place now wastes and woodlands stand;
Upon this place in after time shall stand
A splendid house that shall be called St. John's.
This glade of which I am King, this Yorkshire Vale,
Of this hereafter Steinthal shall be King.

> Here, on this barren glade on which we tread,
> Steinthal shall have a garden; possibly
> Children of Steinthal may herein enact
> The very battle between you and me
> Which now we end: I know not. But the doom
> Which I pronounce on you is terrible.
> Since you are king of England, you shall make
> All English homes as happy as St. John's.
> Since you are King of England, you shall make
> All English gardens fairer than St. John's.
> Since you are King of England, you shall build
> A House more beautiful than St. John's.
> Since you are King of England, you shall make
> All Englishmen as excellent as Steinthal.[3]

Hen. (*shuddering and grovelling*).
> No! no! I cannot do it! I cannot do it,
> The King of England cannot do such things.

> (*Enter Titania.*)

Tit.   The Queen of Fairyland can do such things,
> For she is mightier than English Kings.
> I see into the future like a glass,
> I see them now, these things that come to pass
> Before me; carven with its stone and bronze
> I seem to see the house that's called St. John's.

Steph.   The fairy dreams; we cannot see these things.

Tit.   But I am even cleverer than Kings.
> Do you not see the great house standing there?
> (*Pointing.*)

Mar.   No, no indeed. We see the empty air.

---

[3] Francis Steinthal. He and his wife often hosted the Chestertons in their home in Yorkshire.

Tit.   I see prophetic things. I seem to see
        This desert peopled with more folk than we.
        With eyes imaginative, wild and rare,
        I see a Steinthal sitting in that chair.
           (*Points to Mr. S.*)

Mar.   No, no, she raves. There is no Steinthal here.

Tit.   In some 800 years he shall appear.
        I do invoke the spirit of England now
        To bring great garlands for that future brow.
        For I have sat upon this garden throne
        Supreme: and where I sit is England's throne.
        (*Spirit of England appears at back, white-robed, with the cross of St. George. Procession, to some sort of music. First Marion, then Robin, then the two kings, then England, then Titania.*)

                          (August 1904)

THE NOTTING HILL ANTHEM

When the world was in the balance, there was night on Notting Hill,
(There was night on Notting Hill): it was nobler than the day;
On the cities where the lights are and the firesides glow,
From the seas and from the deserts came the thing we did not know,
Came the darkness, came the darkness, came the darkness on our foe,
      And the old guard of God turned to bay.

For the old guard of God turns to bay, turns to bay,
And the stars fall down before it ere its banners fall to-day:
For when armies were around us as a howling and a horde,
When falling was the citadel and broken was the sword,
The darkness came upon them like the Dragon of the Lord,
      When the old guard of God turned to bay.

           (from *The Napoleon of Notting Hill*, 1904)

THE SONG OF THE SHIP

Come: we have played with shells and sand
Enough: this year at least shall be
Bearer of something new besides
The sullen level of the sea.

Something at least shall sound beside
The foolish breaking of the foam,
Build up the beacon, watch the west—
This year—this year—our ship comes home.

If it come red with weary wars,
Or laden like the ships long gone
That brought the cedar and the gold
To build the house of Solomon?

Heed not the darkness and the rain,
There grows a passion in the gloam
There speeds a purpose through the seas—
Our ship comes home! Our ship comes home.

Within my living soul I know
Our ship shall save us once for all,
But should it split on rock or reef
Beseiged with breakers: let it fall

As fits the ship of a man's soul,
Heaped with the slain and wrecked and red,
But flying flags at every spar,
And on the prow a woman's head.

(1904)

Inscribed in a copy of *The Napoleon of Notting Hill* given to Mrs Grace (Daisy) Saxon Mills, who had refused any payment for typing out the copy for the printer. She was a neighbor at Overstrand Mansions who became a life-long friend.

To V. G.

Lines written in great haste immediately on receipt of an admirable lyric on Modern Manners, and now dispatched after long delay, reluctance and shame, in their original form, but in a decayed and disreputable condition. G.K.C.

THE GHOST OF THE GREAT SUBURBAN

> *The thunderous nameless love that makes*
> *Hell's iron gin*
> *Shut on you like a trap that breaks*
> *The soul, Faustine.*
> ["Faustine", Algernon Charles Swinburne]

When that I was the Pagan of Putney,
    A Pickle deluded in brine,
And Watts-Dunton permitted me chutney[1]
    If I rose not too red out of wine,*
Wild villas deflowered and deflected
    Ran mad to one murderous kiss—
But really we never expected
    Behaviour like this.
*And love was the pearl of his oyster
And Venus rose red out of wine.* ["Dolores", Swinburne]

"The Ghost of the Great Suburban", written to GKC's cousin Vera Grosjean, is a satire on Algernon Charles Swinburne (1837–1909) and his poem "Dolores" ("Notre-Dame des Sept Douleurs"), an ode to the Lady of Pain, the daughter of lust and death who is both adored and reviled with sacrilegious allusions to the Blessed Virgin Mary. GKC also lampooned "Dolores" elsewhere; see "Our Lady of Wain", *Collected Poetry*, Part II, p. 137, and "Dolores Replies to Swinburne" in this Part III, p. 333. See p. 68 for a caricature of Swinburne in "[Inscription in Mrs. Oldershaw's Copy of *Poems and Ballads*]".

[1] Swinburne's excessive drinking nearly destroyed his health, and in 1879 Walter Theodore Watts-Dunton (1832–1914), his friend and literary agent, took the poet into his home in suburban Putney in order to wean him from alcohol.

No doubt many solid suburbans
    Having read half a line of my verse
Rushed off to be tyrants in turbans,
    Turned out to be Heros or worse:
Clerks towered where great Tauit had towered,
    Prone brokers saw Ashtaroth's face,
But nothing, believe me, that lowered
    The tone of the place.[2]

Well, well, there are Pagans and Pagans,
    And hierarchies even in hells:
More fish in the sea than are Dagon's,
    More dragons on Earth than are Bel's:
And if these be the shames that unshape us,
    And this tree ten times barren can grow,
What's the matter with poor old Priapus?
    I'm damned if I know.[3]

Cry aloud on the Red God of Gardens
    And the Lust never sundered from Life,
Though of Christ we go crippled with pardons
    When the Woman is less than the Wife.
When the Woman is less than the Woman,
    We are less than rank thickets that thrive,
And Priapus looks down on things human,
    And death is alive.

Cry aloud: for the old world is broken:
    Cry aloud for the Phrygian is priest
And rears not the bountiful token
    And spreads not the fatherly feast.

[2] Much of Swinburne's poetry exalted pagan religion. Heros is GKC's spelling of Eros. Tauit could be connected with the Tau cross that was used in pagan initiation rites. The Phoenician goddess Ashtaroth, a counterpart to Aphrodite, is named in *Dolores*.

[3] Dagon was the half-man, half-fish god worshipped by, among others, the Philistines. Bel is another name for the Babylonian god Baal. Priapus, the lustful garden god who was worshipped in the Greek countryside, is the father of Swinburne's Lady of Pain.

From Lesbos—from notably shady
  Recesses that murmur at morn,*
They have brought a remarkable lady,
  And Nothing is born.[4]
*From the midmost of Ida from shady
  Recesses that murmured at morn. ["Dolores"]

(ca. 1905)

QUATRAIN FROM A COMIC OPERA ON CHRISTIAN SCIENCE[1]

'Tis a pale old world, a stale old world,
  And it must renew its youth,
So don't coddle up, but toddle up
  And tumble to the truth.

(ca. 1906)

[THE ANCIENT QUEERNESS OF THE WORLD]

If I could turn the moon to blood,
  A lamp-post to a luggage van,
And Dr. Clifford to a cat,[1]
And Dr. Haeckel to a man,[2]

[4] Phrygia is the region where the cult of Priapus originated. It was also the locus of devotion to Cybele, whom Swinburne conflates with his Lady of Pain. Cybele's priestesses were eunuchs in women's clothing who led their followers in frenzied, violent orgies. Chesterton replaces Ida, the supposed birthplace of Cybele, with Lesbos, the Greek island from which lesbianism takes its name.

[1] Monsignor John O'Connor quotes this in *Father Brown on Chesterton*. Any news of the missing text would be welcomed by the editor.

[1] The Rev. John Clifford (1836–1923) was a Baptist minister much involved in writing to newspapers to attack legislation passing through the British parliament.

[2] Ernst Heinrich Haeckel (1834–1919) was a German zoologist, a proponent of evolutionary transformism, and a believer in inferior races.

I think that I would break my wand
And bid my figured scrolls be furled,
Lest my small meddling magic spoilt
The ancient queerness of the world.

It is the powers we cannot change
That are our wizards and our betters—
The moon still pouring deathless beams
On Dr. Clifford writing letters.
So lightly judge the headless man,
Lady, that doth your pages mar—
I know that he is badly drawn,
But so the real people are.

We could not make Man funnier
If he were made as I've done him,
Nor laugh, if Perks took off his head,
As God laughed when He put it on him.
To Fairyland we shall not come
To see the goblins and the elves,
For Fleet Street is in fairyland,
And all the goblins are ourselves.

We keep the elfin gravity,
And only yester[day I saw]
A pair of small and moth-like wings
Grow on the back [of . . .].
And airy fairy Furnival
Is dancing where in the [clover]
The sylph-like figure [of]. . . .
Swings on a swing of gossamer.

                              (ca. 1906)

BALLADE OF WEDDING PRESENTS

What wedding gifts I could command
  Were all mislaid or all misled.
The Golden Firescreen blocked the Strand,
  They smashed the Alabaster Bed,
The Ten Prize Ostriches have fled
  And eaten all the Diamond Rings,
I fear the Nubian Slaves are dead—
  But we will hope for better things.

These books I cannot understand;
  I shove them on to you instead,
And though the tales be poorly planned
  I will not mock the thing I said—
He who is with you knew and led
  Such battle in our boyish springs,
The feeble say the faith is fled,
  But we will hope for better things.

The baser powers about you stand,
  In whom the pen and sword are wed,
Though little doubts devour the land,
  Let the dead wise dissect the dead;
Let the new knowledge, void and dread,
  Arise with sickness in its wings,
Let dons eat fossils and be fed,
  But we will hope for better things.

Inscribed in a copy of *The Man Who Was Thursday* given to Lucy Lyttleton on the occasion of her marriage to Charles Masterman. Remembered Lyttleton: "I was married in Henry VII chapel and I seem to remember Gilbert sitting on one of the chairs in the empty [Westminster] Abbey nave busy with my father's fountain pen, which he borrowed for the purpose and never returned." See "An Invitation", p. 90.

Envoy

Princess, convert this book unread
To pipe-lights or to paper strings,
Or chuck the thing at Charlie's head
(But we will hope for better things).
(June 2, 1908)

AN INVITATION

To a tune of Tom Moore, to a metre unsteady[1]
I seek yet again all her merits to range,
Nor know how to name her, whose name is already,
As poets have put it, in peril of change.

But my heart's in the grave of the old English glories,
And my Radical soul finds no food in the new,
And I love the great songs of the Whigs and the Tories[2]
Who fought with Napoleon and Wellington too.

The songs where the moon was the favourite planet
And roses the only permissible flowers—
And the maidens turned Greek after Byron began it,[3]
And the sexes had nothing but bumpers and bowers.

Inscribed in a copy of *The Napoleon of Notting Hill* presented to Charles Master-man on his wedding day. See "Ballade of Wedding Presents", p. 89.

[1] Thomas Moore (1779–1852), Ireland's national poet, author of "The Minstrel Boy" and "The Last Rose of Summer", among many other well-known songs.

[2] Whig—a name (originally meaning Presbyterian rebels) applied to politicians opposed to the policies of Charles II and intent on excluding James II from the throne. The Whig Party gradually developed until it became the Liberal Party in the nineteenth century. Tory—a name (originally meaning Irish outlaw or cattle rustler) applied to the monarchist, pro Church of England and anti-reformist politicians who eventually developed into the Conservative Party in the nineteenth century. In 1908 both Masterman and Chesterton were Liberal Party supporters.

[3] George Gordon (1788–1824), Lord Byron, English Romantic poet.

You have not a Bower; yet will I have a Bumper[4]
To life that was old and the love that is true,
To the Man of West Ham, to the thinker and thumper,[5]
To England, to Honour, to Friendship and You.

(June 2, 1908)

THE TWO NOISES[1]

They say the sun is on your knees,
 A lamp to light your lands from harm,
They say you turn the seven seas
 To little brooks about your farm.
I hear the sea and the new song
That calls you empress all day long.

(O fallen and fouled! O you that lie
Dying in swamps—you shall not die,
Your rich have secrets, and strange lust,
Your poor are chased about like dust,
Emptied of anger and surprise—
And God is gone out of their eyes,
Your cohorts break—your captains lie,
I say to you, you shall not die.)

I know the bright baptismal rains,
 I love your tender troubled skies,
I know your little climbing lanes.
 Are peering into Paradise,

[4] A Bumper was a large glass, usually of champagne, with which to drink a toast.
[5] In 1906 Charles Masterman was elected as Liberal Party Member of Parliament for the constituency of West Ham in the East End of London.

[1] During "the worst assault at night on a seaside parade where the sea smote on the doors of England with the hammers of earthquake", Chesterton found an undaunted brass band playing imperialistic songs. This put two tunes into his mind and, reported Chesterton, "I did a foolish thing. As I could not express my meaning in an article, I tried to express it in a poem—a bad one." It formed part of an essay of the same name in the *Daily News*, August 29, 1908, and in *Tremendous Trifles* in 1909.

From open hearth to orchard cool,
How bountiful and beautiful.

(O throttled and without a cry,
O strangled and stabbed, you shall not die,
The frightful word is on your walls,
The east sea to the west sea calls,
The stars are dying in the sky,
You shall not die; you shall not die.)

I see you how you smile in state
   Straight from the Peak to Plymouth Bar,
You need not tell me you are great,
   I know how more than great you are.
I know what spirit Chaucer was,
I have seen Gainsborough and the grass.[2]

(O given to believe a lie,
O my mad mother, do not die,
Whose eyes turn all ways but within,
Whose sin is innocence of sin,
Whose eyes, blinded with beams at noon,
Can see the motes upon the moon,
You shall your lover still pursue.
To what last madhouse shelters you
I will uphold you, even I.
You that are dead. You shall not die).
                   (1908)

---

[2] Geoffrey Chaucer (ca. 1345–1400), poet best known for *The Canterbury Tales*. Gainsborough is a market town in Lincolnshire.

THE BROAD-MINDED CHILD'S RELIGIOUS AND PHILOSOPHICAL ALPHABET

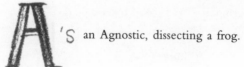's   an Agnostic, dissecting a frog.

was a Buddhist (who had been a dog).

C is a Christian (A Christist, I mean).

was the dog that the Buddhist had been.

is for Ethics, which grow upon trees.

is St. Francis, who preached to the Fleas.

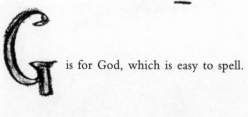 is for God, which is easy to spell.

is for Hegel: and also for Hell.[1]

[1] Georg Wilhelm Friedrich Hegel (1770–1831) German philosopher whose theory of history formed the foundation for Karl Marx's view of progress. In another version, H is for Ernst Heinrich Haeckel (1834–1919), a proponent of evolutionary transformism and a believer in inferior races.

I is the Incas; now most of them dead.

is a Jesuit under the bed.

K is the letter for Benjamin Kidd.[2] The angels and devils cried "Don't." But he did.

[2] Benjamin Kidd (1858–1916), English sociologist and evolutionist.

L is Louis IX, who (unlike the XIth) was a much better man than King Edward the Seventh.[3]

[3] St. Louis, the Crusader King of France.

is for Man. By the way, what is man?

N is for Nunquam, who'll learn if he can.[4]

[4] Nunquam was the pseudonym used by Robert Blatchford (1851–1943) when he was a reporter for the *Sunday Chronicle* and criticized the living conditions of the poor.

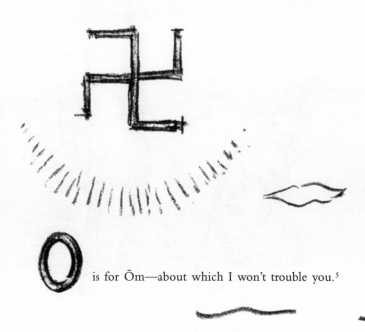

is for Ōm—about which I won't trouble you.[5]

---

[5] The ancient swastika is a symbol used in both Buddhism and Hinduism, which teach that the sound "om" underlies all existence.

P is the Pope and P.W.W.[6]

[6] P. W. Wilson was a journalist colleague of Chesterton on the *Daily News*.

is for Quaker, quiescent in Quod.

R is for reason, a primitive God.

is the Superman, harmless, but fat.

T, a Theosophist, losing his hat.

U the Upanishads—clever, but slight.[7]

[7] Ancient Hindu scriptures.

V is the Virtuous Man, killing Beit.[8]

[8] Alfred Beit (1853–1906), German-born diamond merchant and financier whom Chesterton held responsible for the intrigues that led to the Boer War.

W is Wesley, who banged with his fist.[9]

[9]John Wesley (1703–1791), Anglican cleric who founded the Methodist movement, which later became the Methodist Church.

X   is King Xerxes, a Monotheist.[10]

[10] King of Persia (485–65 B.C.) whose fleet lost the decisive Battle of Salamis against the Greeks. He was a Zoroastrian, as was his Father, Darius I.

is for You, who inane as you are, are the theme of all sages, the Lord of a star.[11]

[11] The figure is a caricature of friend Hilaire Belloc, for whose children the alphabet was created.

's Zarathrustra, who couldn't drink stout. He made war on the weak and they banged him about.[12] (From *The New Age*, October 29, 1908).

[12] Friedrich Nietzsche's *Thus Spoke Zarathrustra* argues that Christian morality, with its care for the weak, holds back the development of superior men.

FUTURISTS' SONG

"We will sing the praises of man holding the flywheel of which the
ideal steering-post traverses the earth impelled itself around the cir-
cuit of its own orbit"

— Declaration of Futurism

A notion came into my head as new as it was bright
That poems might be written on the subject of a fight;
No praise was given to Lancelot, Achilles, Nap or Corbett,[1]
But we will sing the praises of man holding the flywheel of
    which the ideal steering-post traverses the earth impelled
    itself around the circuit of its own orbit.

My fathers scaled the mountains in their pilgrimages far,
But I feel full of energy while sitting in a car;
And petrol is the perfect wine, I lick it and absorb it,
So we will sing the praises of man holding the flywheel of
    which the ideal steering-post traverses the earth impelled
    itself around the circuit of its own orbit.

(from *Daily News*, November 13, 1909)

THE GOLDEN TREASURY OF ENGLISH VERSE
IN ARTIFICIAL METRES

EXERCISE I: THE TRIOLET

I give this book to Marjory,
Though it belongs to her already.
Without decrease of £.s.d.
I give this book to Marjory.
I show my generosity,
Along the lines of Mrs. Eddy[1];
I give this book to Marjory,
Though it belongs to her already.

---

[1] Nap is for Napoleon Buonaparte (1769–1821). James John Corbett (1866–1933),
better known as Gentleman Jim Corbett, one of the best heavyweight boxers of all time.

[1] Mary Baker Eddy (1821–1910), founder of Christian Science.

EXERCISE II: THE ROUNDEL

To Marjory Biggs I offer a book that is bosh,
O Sages, O Terrible Tories and Wonderful Whigs!
Explain why I offer such totally evident tosh
                        To Marjory Biggs—?

If I were as rich as the Marquis of Farintosh,
I would buy her "Assyrian Rambles" by Adelaide Higgs,
And Shuffleby's "Gradual Growth of the Modern Golosh".
And "Ethics" by Pisch also "Super-Ethics" by Posch,
And Bink's "Evolution of Aviation for Pigs",
And Harnack on Protestant Gospel—But *that* will not wash
                        With Marjory Biggs.

EXERCISE III: THE BALLADE

When turning cartwheels half a mile
Rehearse it with a chosen few;
Finding the sources of the Nile
Requires a little practice too,
To mend the Milo's[1] arms with glue
And draw Leviathan with a hook,
Are far from easy things to do,
But anyone can write a book.

Essay not, with an easy smile,
The Prussian Army to review,
Or play in Paderewski's[2] style
Or rival Roberts[3] with a cue,

[1] Venus de Milo statue.

[2] Ignacy Jan Paderewski (1860–1941) was a Polish virtuoso pianist, composer and politician.

[3] John Roberts, Jr., was a champion billiards player.

Or find another and a new
North Pole unknown to Dr. Cook;[4]
But spill the ink till all is blue—
For anyone can write a book.

If you have failed and lost your pile
And find your uncle is a Jew[5]
Who will do nothing but revile
Some crimes that you were led into:
Mentioning, with malice ever new,
That silver tea-pot that you took,
I know the very job for you
For anyone can write a book.

Envoy

Princess, with an indulgent view
Upon these foolish pages look.
'Tis hard to write a verse to you,
But anyone can write a book.
            (from Marjorie Biggs's copy of
                Tremendous Trifles, 1909)

[4] Frederick A. Cook (1865–1940), an American polar explorer, claimed to have reached the North Pole on April 21, 1908, a year before Robert Peary.
[5] Until quite recently a common usage as a synonym for stingy or mean.

THE DISCOVERY OF PINE
— AN EPIC —

The First Canto—describing how Cousin Ticklets and Cousin Booklets were asked by Mr. Slelly to go and look for the Buslus and how they did so.
To be continued in later issues

The booklet *The Discovery of Pine* was written and illustrated between 1909 and 1913 for the amusement of Charles and Stephen Johnson, the sons of GKC's cousin Reginald (Rex) Brimley Johnson. Apart from some sketches, the continuation of the story has not survived.

Charles Heaton Johnson recalled, "It was rapture for either of us to be able to sit on Gilbert's knee and ask him to draw whatever we liked. We invented a complex mythology including many characters who lived in a world with a geography of its own. There was a strange animal known as a Buslus and a soldier called Ticklets, who began life as a ticket collector on the railway but was later engaged in a military career, becoming ultimately Prince Ticklets. There was Mr. Slelly who lived in a tower and wore a round hat that was in prosaic fact the lid of mother's work basket. By wearing it one became an entirely different person."

THE AUTHOR WRITING.

THE DISCOVERY OF PINE.—

Beyond the last strange hills forlorn
Where the old sunsets, soiled and torn
Sleep: in this turret of white stone
Dwelt Mr Skelly, all alone. —

— He filled it, though he was not fat
The roof consisted of his hat
Their sizes did not coincide;
Two tufts of hair were left outside

Birds from all regions of the air
Made nests on those two tufts of hair
And mosses all the turret bind
But Mr Skelly did not mind

For in the dark, through years & phases
He thought & thought a thought like blazes
And once in every nineteen years
His large head suddenly appears
To all the stars observing this
"I WONDER WHAT A BUSBUS IS".

"The best authorities are vague";
"The learned Dr Bock (of Prague)
Writes "Totally unlike a rat . . . . "
I cannot & argue much from that.

Pottinger says "Its knobs are round:"
"See Beeswax": I have also found
This doubtful note of Dr Moon.
"Delightful in the afternoon."

Count Poskly writes (in joke, I hope)
"Coughs rather like an antelope."
And what can Jupp of Cambridge mean
By saying "Kindness turns it green"?

"Some say a Buslus is a bird.
And some a science: I have heard
It talked of a club, a pigeon
A tool, a fish and a religion"

"For many an age; for many an hour
I've sat & wondered in this town.
O stars, O seas, O all that is
I wonder what a Buslus is!"

Beyond the sunsets trailed & torn
Thus did immortal Shelly mourn,
Till looking down, once on a while
He smiled a more than Shellic smile.

He smiled a smile so large & sweet
The very birds were moved by it
And blew him kisses from their bills
And wept and put him in their wills

He saw two funny little boys,
So far they seemed as small as toys
One bore a book & one a sword
Oh need I name them by a word?

What world of love that has not known
BOOKLETS! — what battle-trumpets' tone
Has not cried TICKLETS till we heard —
TICKLETS — tremendous, mellow word!

THE AUTHOR RESTING

THE DISCOVERY OF PINE[1]

Beyond the last strange hills forlorn
Where the old sunsets, soiled and torn
Sleep: in this turret of white stone
Dwelt Mr. Slelly, all alone.

He filled it, though he was not fat
The roof consisted of his hat
Their sizes did not coincide,
Two tufts of hair were left outside.

Birds from all regions of the air
Made nests on those two tufts of hair
And mosses all the turret bind
But Mr Slelly did not mind.

For in the dark through years and phases
He thought and thought and thought like blazes
And once in every nineteen years
His large head suddenly appears
To all the stars observing this
"I WONDER WHAT A BUSLUS IS".

"The best authorities are vague:
The learned Dr. Bock (of Prague)
Writes 'Totally unlike a rat...'
I cannot argue much from that.

Pottiger says 'Its knobs are round:
See Beeswax.' I have also found
This doubtful note of Dr. Moon.
'Delightful in the afternoon.'

Count Posky writes (in joke, I hope)
'Coughs rather like an antelope.'

[1] See footnote on p. 122.

And what can Jupp of Cambridge mean
By saying 'Kindness turns it green'?

Some say a Buslus is a bird
And some a science: I have heard
It talked of as a club, a pigeon
A tool, a fish and a religion

For many an age, for many an hour
I've sat and wondered in this tower
O stars, O seas, O all that is
I wonder what a Buslus is!"

Beyond the sunsets trailed and torn
Thus did immortal Slelly mourn,
Till looking down, once in a while
He smiled a more than Slellic smile.

He smiled a smile so large and sweet
The very birds were moved by it,
And blew him kisses from their bills
And wept and put him in their wills.

He saw two funny little boys,
So far they seemed as small as toys,
One bore a book and one a sword;
Oh need I name them by a word?

What world of lore that has not known
BOOKLETS!—what battle-trumpet's tone
Has not cried TICKLETS till we heard—
TICKLETS—tremendous, mellow word!

They reached him with a ladder-high
They swore "By yon undying sky
The great world we will travel through
And bring a BUSLUS back to you."

End of First Canto. To be continued.

                                    (ca. 1910)

ST. DAVID'S DAY [1]

My eyes are void with vision; I sing but I cannot speak;
I hide in the vaporous caverns like a creature wild and weak;
But for ever my harps are tuned and for ever my songs are sung,
And I answer my tyrants ever in an unknown tongue.

When the blue men broke in the battle with the Roman or the
    Dane,
In the cracks of my ghastly uplands they gathered like ghosts again.
Some say I am still a Druid, some say my spirit shows
Catholic, Puritan, Pagan; but no man knows.

Mother of God's good witches, of all white mystery,
Whatever else I am seeking, I seek for thee.
For the old harp better fitted and swung on a stronger thong,
We, that shall sing for ever; O hear our song!

(1911)

LEPANTO [II]
[An earlier variation or fragment]

Mahound is in his paradise above the evening star, [1]
(*Don John of Austria is going to the war*.) [2]
He moves a mighty turban on the houri's golden knees,
His turban that is coloured with the sunset and the seas.
He shakes the peacock gardens as he rises from his ease,
And he strides among the tree-tops and is taller than the trees,

[1] Presumably an early version of "The Queen of Seven Swords". Cf. pp. 364–80.

Cf. "Lepanto", *Collected Poetry*, Part I, pp. 548–52.

A crucial sea battle between Christian and Ottoman Turkish fleets was fought in the Gulf of Lepanto (Naupaklos) in Greece on Oct. 7, 1571. The Christians prevailed, preventing Muslim control over the Mediterranean Sea and their intended attack on Italy.

[1] Mahound is an older form of Muhammad.

[2] Don John of Austria (1547–78) was the bastard son of Holy Roman Emperor Charles V and half-brother to King Philip II of Spain.

And his voice through all the garden is a thunder sent to bring
Black Azrael and Ariel and Ammon on the wing,[3]
Giants and the Genii, all the shapeless shapes that fly
With many a wing and many an eye,
Whose strong obedience broke the sky
When Solomon was king;
Some from sea deeps dripping with the green oils of the sea
And bearded with the sea-forests, a fearful sight to see;
Some from the black caverns where the wordless rites are done,
One-eyed and black and groping, the haters of the sun;
Some pushing red and purple from the red clouds of the morn,
And the temples where the yellow gods have shut their eyes in scorn:
And he bade them reach the sea-board and he bade them shake the
    sand
And the red-silver deserts to sift them in the hand,
And to ask the locusts flying by the fortress of St. John,[4]
And to stop the sparkling lizard in the gates of Ascalon,[5]
For he heard gongs grinding and he heard guns jar.
Don John of Austria is gone by Alcalar.[6]

St. Michael's on his Mountain in the sea-roads of the north[7]
(*Don John of Austria is girt and going forth*)
Where the grey seas glitter and the sharp tides shift,
And the fish-folk labour and the red sails lift.
He shakes his lance of iron and he claps his wings of stone;
The noise is gone through Normandy; the noise is gone alone;
Through Britain and through Germany, in Flanders and in France
They hear no more the mighty wing that clashes like the lance;

[3] In Islam, Azreal is the angel of death. Ariel is a spirit. Ammon is another form of Amun, an Egyptian god.

[4] Fortress of St. John, built by the Knights of St. John on the island of Malta.

[5] Ascalon, a town in Israel once held by the Crusaders and destroyed by Muslim forces in 1270.

[6] Alcalar could be Alcalá de Gudaira, once a Moorish stronghold.

[7] "St. Michael's on his Mountain" refers to Mont St. Michel, a fortified abbey on an islet off the coast of Normandy and dedicated to God's champion.

And Christian slayeth Christian in a narrow dusty room,
And Christian dreadeth Christ that hath a newer face of doom,
And Christian hateth Mary that God kissed in Galilee,
But Don John of Austria is riding to the sea[8]

The Pope is in his chapel with the Latin on his lips;
(*Don John of Austria looks out upon the ships.*)
He strove to stay the conquest, he had found it weary work,
He thrust his desperate galleys to the timber for the Turk.
The world was weak and warring: the Cross was snapt in twain,
And lies had loosened Italy, and pride had stiffened Spain,
And every king of Christendom was bent above his gold,
And every church in Christendom stood empty and grown cold,
And brutish the rebellion was and cruel the decree,
But Don John of Austria is standing on the quay.

King Philip's in his closet, with the Fleece about his neck,[9]
(*Don John of Austria is going upon deck.*)
The halls are hung with velvet all as black and soft as sin,
And little dwarfs creep out of it and little dwarfs creep in.
He holds a crystal phial that has colours like the moon,[10]
He turns it and he touches it, but leaves it idle very soon.
His face is white like fishes in the lost parts of the sea,
For hate has taken hold there like strong white leprosy,
And death is in the phial, and the end of noble work,
But Don John of Austria has fired upon the Turk.

(ca. 1911)

---

[8] Allusions to Christians in conflict with other Christians refer to the Protestant Reformation.

[9] King Philip II of Spain was a member of the Order of the Golden Fleece established in 1430 to commemorate the union of Flanders and Burgandy, which became Hapsburg dominions.

[10] "He holds a crystal phial"; it was alleged that Philip II later had Don John, of whom he was always jealous, poisoned.

IV

THE BALLAD OF THE
WHITE HORSE

1911

DEDICATION

Of great limbs gone to chaos,
    A great face turned to night—
Why bend above a shapeless shroud
Seeking in such archaic cloud
    Sight of strong lords and light?

Where seven sunken Englands[1]
    Lie buried one by one,
Why should one idle spade, I wonder,
Shake up the dust of thanes like thunder
    To smoke and choke the sun?

In cloud of clay so cast to heaven
    What shape shall man discern?
These lords may light the mystery
Of mastery or victory,
And these ride high in history,
    But these shall not return.

Gored on the Norman gonfalon
    The Golden Dragon died:[2]
We shall not wake with ballad strings
The good time of the smaller things,
We shall not see the holy kings
    Ride down by Severn side.

Stiff, strange, and quaintly coloured
    As the broidery of Bayeux[3]
The England of that dawn remains,
And this of Alfred and the Danes[4]

---

[1] Seven periods of English history.

[2] Golden Dragon, the banner of the Anglo-Saxons, who were conquered by the Normans.

[3] The Bayeux Tapestry that depicts the Norman victory at the Battle of Hastings in 1066.

[4] King Alfred the Great (849–899), who defeated the Danish invaders in 878.

Seems like the tales a whole tribe feigns
   Too English to be true.

Of a good king on an island
   That ruled once on a time;
And as he walked by an apple tree
There came green devils out of the sea
With sea-plants trailing heavily
   And tracks of opal slime.

Yet Alfred is no fairy tale;
   His days as our days ran,
He also looked forth for an hour
On peopled plains and skies that lower,
From those few windows in the tower
   That is the head of a man.

But who shall look from Alfred's hood
   Or breathe his breath alive?
His century like a small dark cloud
Drifts far; it is an eyeless crowd,
Where the tortured trumpets scream aloud
   And the dense arrows drive.

Lady, by one light only
   We look from Alfred's eyes,
We know he saw athwart the wreck
The sign that hangs about your neck,
Where One more than Melchizedek
   Is dead and never dies.

Therefore I bring these rhymes to you.
   Who brought the cross to me,[5]
Since on you flaming without flaw

---

[5] GKC dedicates this work to Frances Chesterton, his wife, who brought him to Anglican observance.

I saw the sign that Guthrum saw[6]
When he let break his ships of awe,
   And laid peace on the sea.

Do you remember when we went
   Under a dragon moon,
And 'mid volcanic tints of night
Walked where they fought the unknown fight
And saw black trees on the battle-height,
   Black thorn on Ethandune?[7]

And I thought, "I will go with you,
   As man with God has gone,
And wander with a wandering star,
The wandering heart of things that are,
The fiery cross of love and war
   That like yourself, goes on."

O go you onward; where you are
   Shall honour and laughter be,
Past purpled forest and pearled foam,
God's winged pavilion free to roam,
Your face, that is a wandering home.
   A flying home for me.

Ride through the silent earthquake lands,
   Wide as a waste is wide,
Across these days like deserts, when
Pride and a little scratching pen
Have dried and split the hearts of men,
   Heart of the heroes, ride.

Up through an empty house of stars,
   Being what heart you are,
Up the inhuman steeps of space

[6] Gunthrum, King of Denmark, converted to Christianity by Alfred.
[7] Ethandune, site of the decisive battle between Alfred and Guthrum.

As on a staircase go in grace,
Carrying the firelight on your face
    Beyond the loneliest star.

Take these; in memory of the hour
    We strayed a space from home
And saw the smoke-hued hamlets, quaint
With Westland king and Westland saint,
And watched the western glory faint
    Along the road to Frome.[8]

BOOK I
THE VISION OF THE KING

Before the gods that made the gods
    Had seen their sunrise pass,
The White Horse of the White Horse Vale[9]
    Was cut out of the grass.

Before the gods that made the gods
    Had drunk at dawn their fill,
The White Horse of the White Horse Vale
    Was hoary on the hill.

Age beyond age on British land,
    Æons on æons gone,
Was peace and war in western hills,
    And the White Horse looked on.

---

[8] Gilbert and Frances toured the area in Wessex where many of the events in the poem take place. Frome is a town in Somersetshire.

[9] The White Horse of the White Horse Vale—the White Horse of Uffington in Berkshire is cut into the hillside overlooking the Vale of the White Horse, and being some 350 feet from nose to tail is visible from a considerable distance. There have been numerous legends concerning its origin, but scientific tests date it to be 3,000 years old. It is pure co-incidence that the Saxon badge was that of a white horse.

For the White Horse knew England
　　When there was none to know;
He saw the first oar break or bend,
He saw heaven fall and the world end,
　　O God, how long ago.

For the end of the world was long ago—
　　And all we dwell to-day
As children of some second birth,
Like a strange people left on earth
　　After a judgment day.

For the end of the world was long ago,
　　When the ends of the world waxed free,
When Rome was sunk in a waste of slaves,
　　And the sun drowned in the sea.

When Cæsar's sun fell out of the sky
　　And whoso hearkened right
Could only hear the plunging
　　Of the nations in the night.

When the ends of the earth came marching in
　　To torch and cresset gleam.
And the roads of the world that lead to Rome
Were filled with faces that moved like foam,
　　Like faces in a dream.

And men rode out of the eastern lands,
　　Broad river and burning plain;
Trees that are Titan flowers to see,
And tiger skies, striped horribly,
　　With tints of tropic rain.

Where Ind's enamelled peaks arise[10]
　　Around that inmost one,
Where ancient eagles on its brink,

[10] Ind is India.

Vast as archangels, gather and drink
    The sacrament of the sun.

And men brake out of the northern lands,
    Enormous lands alone,
Where a spell is laid upon life and lust
And the rain is changed to a silver dust
    And the sea to a great green stone.

And a Shape that moveth murkily
    In mirrors of ice and night,
Hath blanched with fear all beasts and birds,
As death and a shock of evil words
    Blast a man's hair with white.

And the cry of the palms and the purple moons,
    Or the cry of the frost and foam,
Swept ever around an inmost place,
And the din of distant race on race
    Cried and replied round Rome.

And there was death on the Emperor
    And night upon the Pope:
And Alfred, hiding in deep grass,
    Hardened his heart with hope.

A sea-folk blinder than the sea
    Broke all about his land,
But Alfred up against them bare
And gripped the ground and grasped the air,
    Staggered, and strove to stand.

He bent them back with spear and spade,
    With desperate dyke and wall,
With foemen leaning on his shield
And roaring on him when he reeled;
    And no help came at all.

He broke them with a broken sword
   A little towards the sea,
And for one hour of panting peace,
Ringed with a roar that would not cease,
With golden crown and girded fleece
   Made laws under a tree.

.   .   .   .   .

The Northmen came about our land
   A Christless chivalry:
Who knew not of the arch or pen,
Great, beautiful half-witted men
   From the sunrise and the sea.

Misshapen ships stood on the deep
   Full of strange gold and fire,
And hairy men, as huge as sin
With hornèd heads, came wading in
   Through the long, low sea-mire.

Our towns were shaken of tall kings
   With scarlet beards like blood:
The world turned empty where they trod,
They took the kindly cross of God
   And cut it up for wood.

Their souls were drifting as the sea,
   And all good towns and lands
They only saw with heavy eyes,
   And broke with heavy hands.

Their gods were sadder than the sea,
   Gods of a wandering will,
Who cried for blood like beasts at night,
   Sadly, from hill to hill.

They seemed as trees walking the earth,
   As witless and as tall,

Yet they took hold upon the heavens
    And no help came at all.

They bred like birds in English woods,
    They rooted like the rose,
When Alfred came to Athelney[11]
    To hide him from their bows.

There was not English armour left,
    Nor any English thing,
When Alfred came to Athelney
    To be an English king.

For earthquake swallowing earthquake
    Uprent the Wessex tree;[12]
The whirlpool of the pagan sway
Had swirled his sires as sticks away
    When a flood smites the sea.

And the great kings of Wessex
    Wearied and sank in gore,
And even their ghosts in that great stress
Grew greyer and greyer, less and less,
With the lords that died in Lyonesse
    And the king that comes no more.[13]

And the God of the Golden Dragon
    Was dumb upon his throne,
And the lord of the Golden Dragon
    Ran in the woods alone.

And if ever he climbed the crest of luck
    And set the flag before,
Returning as a wheel returns,
Came ruin and the rain that burns,
    And all began once more.

[11] Athelney in the marshes of Somerset is where Alfred built his fort.
[12] Alfred was the only remaining son of the House of Wessex.
[13] The legendary Arthur is the "king that comes no more".

And naught was left King Alfred
  But shameful tears of rage,
In the island in the river
  In the end of all his age.

In the island in the river
  He was broken to his knee:
And he read, writ with an iron pen,
That God had wearied of Wessex men
And given their country, field and fen,
  To the devils of the sea.

And he saw in a little picture,
  Tiny and far away,
His mother sitting in Egbert's hall,[14]
And a book she showed him, very small,
Where a sapphire Mary sat in stall
  With a golden Christ at play.

It was wrought in the monk's slow manner,
  From silver and sanguine shell,
Where the scenes are little and terrible,
  Keyholes of heaven and hell.

In the river island of Athelney,
  With the river running past,
In colours of such simple creed
All things sprang at him, sun and weed,
Till the grass grew to be grass indeed
  And the tree was a tree at last.

Fearfully plain the flowers grew,
  Like the child's book to read,
Or like a friend's face seen in a glass;
He looked; and there Our Lady was,
She stood and stroked the tall live grass
  As a man strokes his steed.

[14] Egbert, an ancestor of King Alfred.

Her face was like an open word
    When brave men speak and choose,
The very colours of her coat
    Were better than good news.

She spoke not, nor turned not,
    Nor any sign she cast,
Only she stood up straight and free,
Between the flowers in Athelney,
    And the river running past.

One dim ancestral jewel hung[15]
    On his ruined armour grey,
He rent and cast it at her feet:
Where, after centuries, with slow feet,
Men came from hall and school and street
    And found it where it lay.

"Mother of God," the wanderer said,
    "I am but a common king,
Nor will I ask what saints may ask,
    To see a secret thing.

"The gates of heaven are fearful gates
    Worse than the gates of hell;
Not I would break the splendours barred
Or seek to know the thing they guard,
    Which is too good to tell.

"But for this earth most pitiful,
    This little land I know,
If that which is for ever is,
Or if our hearts shall break with bliss,
    Seeing the stranger go?

"When our last bow is broken, Queen,
    And our last javelin cast,

[15] Alfred's Jewel, found at Athelney in 1693, is a miniature enamelled portrait that
bears his name.

Under some sad, green evening sky,
Holding a ruined cross on high,
Under warm westland grass to lie,
　　Shall we come home at last?"

And a voice came human but high up,
　　Like a cottage climbed among
The clouds; or a serf of hut and croft
That sits by his hovel fire as oft,
But hears on his old bare roof aloft
　　A belfry burst in song.

"The gates of heaven are lightly locked.
　　We do not guard our gain,
The heaviest hind may easily
Come silently and suddenly
　　Upon me in a lane.

"And any little maid that walks
　　In good thoughts apart,
May break the guard of the Three Kings
And see the dear and dreadful things
　　I hid within my heart.

"The meanest man in grey fields gone
　　Behind the set of sun,
Heareth between star and other star,
Through the door of the darkness fallen ajar,
The council, eldest of things that are,
　　The talk of the Three in One.

"The gates of heaven are lightly locked,
　　We do not guard our gold,
Men may uproot where worlds begin,
Or read the name of the nameless sin;
But if he fail or if he win
　　To no good man is told.

"The men of the East may spell the stars,
　　And times and triumphs mark,

But the men signed of the cross of Christ
　　Go gaily in the dark.

"The men of the East may search the scrolls
　　For sure fates and fame,
But the men that drink the blood of God
　　Go singing to their shame.

"The wise men know what wicked things
　　Are written on the sky,
They trim sad lamps, they touch sad strings,
Hearing the heavy purple wings,
Where the forgotten seraph kings
　　Still plot how God shall die.

"The wise men know all evil things
　　Under the twisted trees,
Where the perverse in pleasure pine
And men are weary of green wine
　　And sick of crimson seas.

"But you and all the kind of Christ
　　Are ignorant and brave,
And you have wars you hardly win
　　And souls you hardly save.

"I tell you naught for your comfort,
　　Yea, naught for your desire,
Save that the sky grows darker yet
　　And the sea rises higher.

"Night shall be thrice night over you,
　　And heaven an iron cope.
Do you have joy without a cause,
　　Yea, faith without a hope?"

Even as she spoke she was not,
　　Nor any word said he,
He only heard, still as he stood
Under the old night's nodding hood,

The sea-folk breaking down the wood
  Like a high tide from sea.

He only heard the heathen men,
  Whose eyes are blue and bleak,
Singing about some cruel thing
Done by a great and smiling king
  In daylight on a deck.

He only heard the heathen men,
  Whose eyes are blue and blind,
Singing what shameful things are done
Between the sunlit sea and the sun
  When the land is left behind.

BOOK II
THE GATHERING OF THE CHIEFS

Up across windy wastes and up
  Went Alfred over the shaws,
Shaken of the joy of giants,
  The joy without a cause.

In the slopes away to the western bays,
  Where blows not ever a tree,
He washed his soul in the west wind
  And his body in the sea.

And he set to rhyme his ale-measures,
  And he sang aloud his laws,
Because of the joy of the giants,
  The joy without a cause.

For the King went gathering Wessex men,
  As grain out of the chaff
The few that were alive to die,
Laughing, as littered skulls that lie

After lost battles turn to the sky
    An everlasting laugh.

The King went gathering Christian men,
    As wheat out of the husk;
Eldred, the Franklin by the sea,
And Mark, the man from Italy,
And Colan of the Sacred Tree,
    From the old tribe on Usk.

The rook croaked homeward heavily,
    The west was clear and warm,
The smoke of evening food and ease
Rose like a blue tree in the trees
    When he came to Eldred's farm.

But Eldred's farm was fallen awry,
    Like an old cripple's bones,
And Eldred's tools were red with rust,
And on his well was a green crust,
And purple thistles upward thrust,
    Between the kitchen stones.

But smoke of some good feasting
    Went upwards evermore,
And Eldred's doors stood wide apart
For loitering foot or labouring cart,
And Eldred's great and foolish heart
    Stood open like his door.

A mighty man was Eldred,
    A bulk for casks to fill,
His face a dreaming furnace,
    His body a walking hill.

In the old wars of Wessex
    His sword had sunken deep,
But all his friends, he sighed and said,
Were broken about Ethelred;

And between the deep drink and the dead
  He had fallen upon sleep.

"Come not to me, King Alfred,
  Save always for the ale:
Why should my harmless hinds be slain
Because the chiefs cry once again,
As in all fights, that we shall gain,
  And in all fights we fail?

"Your scalds still thunder and prophesy
  That crown that never comes;
Friend, I will watch the certain things,
Swine, and slow moons like silver rings,
  And the ripening of the plums."

And Alfred answered, drinking,
  And gravely, without blame,
"Nor bear I boast of scald or king,
The thing I bear is a lesser thing,
  But comes in a better name.

"Out of the mouth of the Mother of God,
  More than the doors of doom,
I call the muster of Wessex men
From grassy hamlet or ditch or den,
To break and be broken, God knows when,
  But I have seen for whom.

"Out of the mouth of the Mother of God
  Like a little word come I;
For I go gathering Christian men
From sunken paving and ford and fen,
To die in a battle, God knows when,
  By God, but I know why.

"And this is the word of Mary,
  The word of the world's desire:
'No more of comfort shall ye get,

Save that the sky grows darker yet
  And the sea rises higher.' "

Then silence sank. And slowly
  Arose the sea-land lord,
Like some vast beast for mystery,
He filled the room and porch and sky,
And from a cobwebbed nail on high
  Unhooked his heavy sword.

Up on the shrill sea-downs and up
  Went Alfred all alone,
Turning but once e'er the door was shut,
Shouting to Eldred over his butt,
That he bring all spears to the woodman's hut
  Hewn under Egbert's Stone.

And he turned his back and broke the fern,
  And fought the moths of dusk,
And went on his way for other friends,
Friends fallen of all the wide world's ends,
From Rome that wrath and pardon sends
  And the grey tribes on Usk.

He saw gigantic tracks of death
  And many a shape of doom,
Good steadings to grey ashes gone
And a monk's house white like a skeleton
  In the green crypt of the combe.

And in many a Roman villa
  Earth and her ivies eat,
Saw coloured pavements sink and fade
In flowers, and the windy colonnade
  Like the spectre of a street.

But the cold stars clustered
  Among the cold pines
Ere he was half on his pilgrimage
  Over the western lines.

And the white dawn widened
  Ere he came to the last pine,
Where Mark, the man from Italy,
  Still made the Christian sign.

The long farm lay on the large hill-side,
  Flat like a painted plan,
And by the side the low white house,
  Where dwelt the southland man.

A bronzed man, with a bird's bright eye,
  And a strong bird's beak and brow,
His skin was brown like buried gold,
And of certain of his sires was told
That they came in the shining ship of old,
  With Caesar in the prow.

His fruit trees stood like soldiers
  Drilled in a straight line,
His strange, stiff olives did not fail,
And all the kings of the earth drank ale,
  But he drank wine.

Wide over wasted British plains
  Stood never an arch or dome,
Only the trees to toss and reel,
The tribes to bicker, the beasts to squeal;
But the eyes in his head were strong like steel,
  And his soul remembered Rome.

Then Alfred of the lonely spear
  Lifted his lion head;
And fronted with the Italian's eye,
Asking him of his whence and why,
  King Alfred stood and said:

"I am that oft-defeated King
  Whose failure fills the land,
Who fled before the Danes of old,
Who chaffered with the Danes with gold,

Who now upon the Wessex wold
   Hardly has feet to stand.

"But out of the mouth of the Mother of God
   I have seen the truth like fire,
This—that the sky grows darker yet
   And the sea rises higher."

Long looked the Roman on the land;
   The trees as golden crowns
Blazed, drenched with dawn and dew-empearled
While faintlier coloured, freshlier curled,
The clouds from underneath the world
   Stood up over the downs.

"These vines be ropes that drag me hard,"
   He said. "I go not far;
Where would you meet? For you must hold
Half Wiltshire and the White Horse wold,
And the Thames bank to Owsenfold,
   If Wessex goes to war.

"Guthrum sits strong on either bank
   And you must press his lines
Inwards, and eastward drive him down;
I doubt if you shall take the crown
Till you have taken London town.
   For me, I have the vines."

"If each man on the Judgment Day
   Meet God on a plain alone,"
Said Alfred, "I will speak for you
As for myself, and call it true
That you brought all fighting folk you knew
   Lined under Egbert's Stone.

"Though I be in the dust ere then,
   I know where you will be."
And shouldering suddenly his spear
He faded like some elfin fear,

Where the tall pines ran up, tier on tier.
    Tree overtoppling tree.

He shouldered his spear at morning
    And laughed to lay it on,
But he leaned on his spear as on a staff,
With might and little mood to laugh,
Or ever he sighted chick or calf
    Of Colan of Caerleon.[16]

For the man dwelt in a lost land
    Of boulders and broken men,
In a great grey cave far off to the south
Where a thick green forest stopped the mouth,
    Giving darkness in his den.

And the man was come like a shadow,
    From the shadow of Druid trees,
Where Usk, with mighty murmurings,
Past Caerleon of the fallen kings,
    Goes out to ghostly seas.

Last of a race in ruin—
    He spoke the speech of the Gaels;
His kin were in holy Ireland,
    Or up in the crags of Wales.

But his soul stood with his mother's folk,
    That were of the rain-wrapped isle,
Where Patrick and Brandan westerly
Looked out at last on a landless sea
    And the sun's last smile.

His harp was carved and cunning,
    As the Celtic craftsman makes,
Graven all over with twisting shapes
    Like many headless snakes.

His harp was carved and cunning,
    His sword prompt and sharp,

[16] Carleon-on-Usk, the legendary residence of King Arthur.

And he was gay when he held the sword,
  Sad when he held the harp.

For the great Gaels of Ireland
  Are the men that God made mad,
For all their wars are merry,
  And all their songs are sad.

He kept the Roman order,
  He made the Christian sign;
But his eyes grew often blind and bright,
And the sea that rose in the rocks at night
  Rose to his head like wine.

He made the sign of the cross of God,
  He knew the Roman prayer,
But he had unreason in his heart
  Because of the gods that were.

Even they that walked on the high cliffs,
  High as the clouds were then,
Gods of unbearable beauty,
  That broke the hearts of men.

And whether in seat or saddle,
  Whether with frown or smile,
Whether at feast or fight was he,
He heard the noise of a nameless sea
  On an undiscovered isle.

Lifting the great green ivy
  And the great spear lowering,
One said, "I am Alfred of Wessex,
  And I am a conquered king."

And the man of the cave made answer,
  And his eyes were stars of scorn,
"And better kings were conquered
  Or ever your sires were born.

"What goddess was your mother,
　　What fay your breed begot,
That you should not die with Uther
　　And Arthur and Lancelot?[17]

"But when you win you brag and blow,
　　And when you lose you rail,
Army of eastland yokels
　　Not strong enough to fail."

"I bring not boast or railing,"
　　Spake Alfred not in ire.
"I bring of Our Lady a lesson set,
This—that the sky grows darker yet
　　And the sea rises higher."

Then Colan of the Sacred Tree
　　Tossed his black mane on high,
And cried, as rigidly he rose,
"And if the sea and sky be foes,
　　We will tame the sea and sky."

Smiled Alfred, "Seek ye a fable
　　More dizzy and more dread
Than all your mad barbarian tales
　　Where the sky stands on its head?

"A tale where a man looks down on the sky
　　That has long looked down on him;
A tale where a man can swallow a sea
　　That might swallow the seraphim.

"Bring to the hut by Egbert's Stone
　　All bills and bows ye have."
And Alfred strode off rapidly,
And Colan of the Sacred Tree
　　Went slowly to his cave.

[17] Uther Pendragon, King of Britain and father of King Arthur. Sir Lancelot of the Round Table who was raised by the Lady of the Lake.

BOOK III
THE HARP OF ALFRED

In a tree that yawned and twisted
   The King's few goods were flung,
A mass-book mildewed, line by line,
And weapons and a skin of wine,
   And an old harp unstrung.

By the yawning tree in the twilight
   The King unbound his sword,
Severed the harp of all his goods,
And there in the cool and soundless woods
   Sounded a single chord.

Then laughed; and watched the finches flash,
   The sullen flies in swarm,
And went unarmed over the hills,
   With the harp upon his arm,

Until he came to the White Horse Vale
   And saw across the plains,
In the twilight high and far and fell,
Like the fiery terraces of hell,
   The camp fires of the Danes—

The fires of the Great Army
   That was made of iron men,
Whose lights of sacrilege and scorn
Ran around England red as morn,
Fires over Glastonbury Thorn—[18]
   Fires out on Ely Fen.[19]

---

[18] Glastonbury Thorn—Glastonbury is an ancient town and abbey in Somerset on the spot reputed to be where Joseph of Arimathea plunged his staff into the ground where it took root and budded. Joseph supposedly brought the Christian faith together with the Holy Grail in 64 AD. The Glastonbury Thorn, a variety of hawthorn, flowers every Christmas in honour of Christ's birth.

[19] Ely Fen—the fen land surrounding the Isle of Ely was largely drained by Dutch engineers in the eighteenth century, but in King Alfred's days it was still a tract of water.

And as he went by White Horse Vale
    He saw lie wan and wide
The old horse graven, God knows when,
By gods or beasts or what things then
Walked a new world instead of men
    And scrawled on the hill-side.

And when he came to White Horse Down
    The great White Horse was grey,
For it was ill scoured of the weed,
And lichen and thorn could crawl and feed,
Since the foes of settled house and creed
    Had swept old works away.

King Alfred gazed all sorrowful
    At thistle and mosses grey,
Till a rally of Danes with shield and bill
Rolled drunk over the dome of the hill,
And, hearing of his harp and skill,
    They dragged him to their play.

And as they went through the high green grass
    They roared like the great green sea;
But when they came to the red camp fire
    They were silent suddenly.

And as they went up the wastes away
    They went reeling to and fro;
But when they came to the red camp fire
    They stood all in a row.

For golden in the firelight,
    With a smile carved on his lips,
And a beard curled right cunningly,
Was Guthrum of the Northern Sea,
    The emperor of the ships—

With three great earls King Guthrum
    Went the rounds from fire to fire,
With Harold, nephew of the King,

And Ogier of the Stone and Sling,
And Elf, whose gold lute had a string
   That sighed like all desire.

The Earls of the Great Army
   That no men born could tire,
Whose flames anear him or aloof
Took hold of towers or walls of proof,
Fire over Glastonbury roof
   And out on Ely, fire.

And Guthrum heard the soldiers' tale
   And bade the stranger play;
Not harshly, but as one on high,
On a marble pillar in the sky,
Who sees all folk that live and die—
   Pigmy and far away.

And Alfred, King of Wessex,
   Looked on his conqueror—
And his hands hardened; but he played,
And leaving all later hates unsaid,
He sang of some old British raid
   On the wild west march of yore.

He sang of war in the warm wet shires,
   Where rain nor fruitage fails,
Where England of the motley states
Deepens like a garden to the gates
   In the purple walls of Wales.

He sang of the seas of savage heads
   And the seas and seas of spears,
Boiling all over Offa's Dyke,[20]
What time a Wessex club could strike
   The kings of the mountaineers.

---

[20] Offa's Dyke—a defensive earthwork built by King Offa of Mercia (784–96) to mark the boundary between his lands and Wales. The Dyke stretches from Prestatyn in North Wales down to the River Wye in Monmouthshire in South Wales.

Till Harold laughed and snatched the harp,
  The kinsman of the King,
A big youth, beardless like a child,
Whom the new wine of war sent wild,
  Smote, and began to sing—

And he cried of the ships as eagles
  That circle fiercely and fly,
And sweep the seas and strike the towns
  From Cyprus round to Skye.[21]

How swiftly and with peril
  They gather all good things,
The high horns of the forest beasts,
  Or the secret stones of kings.

"For Rome was given to rule the world,
  And gat of it little joy—
But we, but we shall enjoy the world,
  The whole huge world a toy.

"Great wine like blood from Burgundy,
  Cloaks like the clouds from Tyre,
And marble like solid moonlight,
  And gold like frozen fire.

"Smells that a man might swill in a cup,
  Stones that a man might eat,
And the great smooth women like ivory
  That the Turks sell in the street."

He sang the song of the thief of the world,
  And the gods that love the thief;
And he yelled aloud at the cloister-yards,
  Where men go gathering grief.

"Well have you sung, O stranger,
  Of death on the dyke in Wales,

[21] From Cyprus round to Skye—The range of the Northmen's voyages was even
wider, taking in Newfoundland in North America and perhaps beyond.

Your chief was a bracelet-giver;
But the red unbroken river
Of a race runs not for ever,
    But suddenly it fails.

"Doubtless your sires were sword-swingers
    When they waded fresh from foam,
Before they were turned to women
    By the god of the nails from Rome;

"But since you bent to the shaven men,
    Who neither lust nor smite,
Thunder of Thor,[22] we hunt you
    A hare on the mountain height."

King Guthrum smiled a little,
    And said, "It is enough,
Nephew, let Elf retune the string;
A boy must needs like bellowing,
But the old ears of a careful king
    Are glad of songs less rough."

Blue-eyed was Elf the minstrel,
    With womanish hair and ring,
Yet heavy was his hand on sword,
    Though light upon the string.

And as he stirred the strings of the harp
    To notes but four or five,
The heart of each man moved in him
    Like a babe buried alive.

And they felt the land of the folk-songs
    Spread southward of the Dane,
And they heard the good Rhine flowing
    In the heart of all Allemagne.

They felt the land of the folk-songs,
    Where the gifts hang on the tree,

---

[22] Thor—Norse god of Thunder and of War, son of Odin.

Where the girls give ale at morning
    And the tears come easily.

The mighty people, womanlike,
    That have pleasure in their pain
As he sang of Balder beautiful,[23]
    Whom the heavens loved in vain.

As he sang of Balder beautiful,
    Whom the heavens could not save,
Till the world was like a sea of tears
    And every soul a wave.

"There is always a thing forgotten
    When all the world goes well;
A thing forgotten, as long ago,
When the gods forgot the mistletoe,
And soundless as an arrow of snow
    The arrow of anguish fell.

"The thing on the blind side of the heart,
    On the wrong side of the door,
The green plant groweth, menacing
Almighty lovers in the spring;
There is always a forgotten thing,
    And love is not secure."

And all that sat by the fire were sad,
    Save Ogier,[24] who was stern,
And his eyes hardened, even to stones,
    As he took the harp in turn;

Earl Ogier of the Stone and Sling
    Was odd to ear and sight,
Old he was, but his locks were red,
And jests were all the words he said,

---

[23] Balder—Norse god of Light, son of Odin and Frigg.
[24] Ogier—not the medieval hero, one of Charlemagne's paladins, although he has some of his attributes.

Yet he was sad at board and bed
　　And savage in the fight.

"You sing of the young gods easily
　　In the days when you are young;
But I go smelling yew and sods,
And I know there are gods behind the gods,
　　Gods that are best unsung.

"And a man grows ugly for women,
　　And a man grows dull with ale,
Well if he find in his soul at last
　　Fury, that does not fail.

"The wrath of the gods behind the gods
　　Who would rend all gods and men,
Well if the old man's heart hath still
Wheels sped of rage and roaring will,
Like cataracts to break down and kill,
　　Well for the old man then—

"While there is one tall shrine to shake,
　　Or one live man to rend;
For the wrath of the gods behind the gods
　　Who are weary to make an end.

"There lives one moment for a man
　　When the door at his shoulder shakes,
When the taut rope parts under the pull,
And the barest branch is beautiful
　　One moment, while it breaks.

"So rides my soul upon the sea
　　That drinks the howling ships,
Though in black jest it bows and nods
Under the moons with silver rods,
I know it is roaring at the gods,
　　Waiting the last eclipse.

"And in the last eclipse the sea
　Shall stand up like a tower,
Above all moons made dark and riven,
Hold up its foaming head in heaven,
　And laugh, knowing its hour.

"And the high ones in the happy town
　Propped of the planets seven,
Shall know a new light in the mind,
A noise about them and behind,
Shall hear an awful voice, and find
　Foam in the courts of heaven.

"And you that sit by the fire are young,
　And true love waits for you;
But the king and I grow old, grow old,
　And hate alone is true."

And Guthrum shook his head but smiled,
　For he was a mighty clerk,
And had read lines in the Latin books
　When all the north was dark.

He said, "I am older than you, Ogier;
　Not all things would I rend,
For whether life be bad or good
　It is best to abide the end."

He took the great harp wearily,
　Even Guthrum of the Danes,
With wide eyes bright as the one long day
　On the long polar plains.

For he sang of a wheel returning,
　And the mire trod back to mire,
And how red hells and golden heavens
　Are castles in the fire.

"It is good to sit where the good tales go,
　To sit as our fathers sat;

But the hour shall come after his youth,
When a man shall know not tales but truth,
　　And his heart fail thereat.

"When he shall read what is written
　　So plain in clouds and clods,
When he shall hunger without hope
　　Even for evil gods.

For this is a heavy matter,
　　And the truth is cold to tell;
Do we not know, have we not heard,
The soul is like a lost bird,
　　The body a broken shell.

"And a man hopes, being ignorant,
　　Till in white woods apart
He finds at last the lost bird dead:
And a man may still lift up his head
　　But never more his heart.

"There comes no noise but weeping
　　Out of the ancient sky,
And a tear is in the tiniest flower
　　Because the gods must die.

"The little brooks are very sweet,
　　Like a girl's ribbons curled,
But the great sea is bitter
　　That washes all the world.

"Strong are the Roman roses,
　　Or the free flowers of the heath,
But every flower, like a flower of the sea,
　　Smelleth with the salt of death.

"And the heart of the locked battle
　　Is the happiest place for men;
When shrieking souls as shafts go by
And many have died and all may die;

Though this word be a mystery,
    Death is most distant then.

"Death blazes bright above the cup,
    And clear above the crown;
But in that dream of battle
    We seem to tread it down.

"Wherefore I am a great king,
    And waste the world in vain,
Because man hath not other power,
Save that in dealing death for dower,
He may forget it for an hour
    To remember it again."

And slowly his hands and thoughtfully
    Fell from the lifted lyre,
And the owls moaned from the mighty trees
Till Alfred caught it to his knees
    And smote it as in ire.

He heaved the head of the harp on high
    And swept the framework barred,
And his stroke had all the rattle and spark
    Of horses flying hard.

"When God put man in a garden
    He girt him with a sword,
And sent him forth a free knight
    That might betray his lord;

"He brake Him and betrayed Him,
    And fast and far he fell,
Till you and I may stretch our necks
    And burn our beards in hell.

"But though I lie on the floor of the world,
    With the seven sins for rods,
I would rather fall with Adam
    Than rise with all your gods.

"What have the strong gods given?
  Where have the glad gods led?
When Guthrum sits on a hero's throne
  And asks if he is dead?

"Sirs, I am but a nameless man,
  A rhymester without home,
Yet since I come of the Wessex clay
  And carry the cross of Rome,

"I will even answer the mighty earl
  That asked of Wessex men
Why they be meek and monkish folk,
And bow to the White Lord's broken yoke;
What sign have we save blood and smoke?
  Here is my answer then.

"That on you is fallen the shadow,
And not upon the Name;
That though we scatter and though we fly,
And you hang over us like the sky,
You are more tired of victory,
  Than we are tired of shame.

"That though you hunt the Christian man
  Like a hare on the hill-side,
The hare has still more heart to run
  Than you have heart to ride.

"That though all lances split on you,
  All swords be heaved in vain,
We have more lust again to lose
  Than you to win again.

"Your lord sits high in the saddle,
  A broken-hearted king,
But our king Alfred, lost from fame,
Fallen among foes or bonds of shame,
In I know not what mean trade or name.
  Has still some song to sing;

Our monks go robed in rain and snow,
　　But the heart of flame therein,
But you go clothed in feasts and flames,
　　When all is ice within;

"Nor shall all iron dooms make dumb
　　Men wondering ceaselessly,
If it be not better to fast for joy
　　Than feast for misery.

"Nor monkish order only
　　Slides down, as field to fen,
All things achieved and chosen pass,
As the White Horse fades in the grass.
　　No work of Christian men.

"Ere the sad gods that made your gods
　　Saw their sad sunrise pass,
The White Horse of the White Horse Vale,
That you have left to darken and fail,
　　Was cut out of the grass.

"Therefore your end is on you,
　　Is on you and your kings,
Not for a fire in Ely fen,
Not that your gods are nine or ten,
But because it is only Christian men
　　Guard even heathen things.

"For our God hath blessed creation,
　　Calling it good. I know
What spirit with whom you blindly band
Hath blessed destruction with his hand;
Yet by God's death the stars shall stand
　　And the small apples grow."

And the King, with harp on shoulder,
　　Stood up and ceased his song;
And the owls moaned from the mighty trees,
　　And the Danes laughed loud and long.

BOOK IV
THE WOMAN IN THE FOREST

Thick thunder of the snorting swine.
    Enormous in the gloam,
Rending among all roots that cling,
And the wild horses whinnying,
Were the night's noises when the King
    Shouldering his harp, went home.

With eyes of owl and feet of fox,
    Full of all thoughts he went;
He marked the tilt of the pagan camp,
The paling of pine, the sentries' tramp,
And the one great stolen altar-lamp
    Over Guthrum in his tent.

By scrub and thorn in Ethandune
    That night the foe had lain;
Whence ran across the heather grey
The old stones of a Roman way;
And in a wood not far away
    The pale road split in twain.

He marked the wood and the cloven ways
    With an old captain's eyes,
And he thought how many a time had he
Sought to see Doom he could not see;
How ruin had come and victory,
    And both were a surprise.

Even so he had watched and wondered
    Under Ashdown from the plains;[25]
With Ethelred praying in his tent,[26]
Till the white hawthorn swung and bent.
As Alfred rushed his spears and rent
    The shield-wall of the Danes.

[25] Ashdown—an area and battlefield now in Berkshire.
[26] Ethelred—Aethelred I (?–871), not the later Aethelred II the Unready.

Even so he had watched and wondered,
  Knowing neither less nor more,
Till all his lords lay dying,
And axes on axes plying,
Flung him, and drove him flying
  Like a pirate to the shore.

Wise he had been before defeat,
  And wise before success;
Wise in both hours and ignorant,
  Knowing neither more nor less.

As he went down to the river-hut
  He knew a night-shade scent,
Owls did as evil cherubs rise,
With little wings and lantern eyes,
As though he sank through the under-skies;
  But down and down he went.

As he went down to the river-hut
  He went as one that fell;
Seeing the high forest domes and spars.
Dim green or torn with golden scars,
As the proud look up at the evil stars,
  In the red heavens of hell.

For he must meet by the river-hut
  Them he had bidden to arm,
Mark from the towers of Italy,
And Colan of the Sacred Tree,
And Eldred who beside the sea
  Held heavily his farm.

The roof leaned gaping to the grass,
  As a monstrous mushroom lies;
Echoing and empty seemed the place;
But opened in a little space
A great grey woman with scarred face
  And strong and humbled eyes.

King Alfred was but a meagre man,
  Bright eyed, but lean and pale:
And swordless, with his harp and rags,
He seemed a beggar, such as lags
  Looking for crusts and ale.

And the woman, with a woman's eyes
  Of pity at once and ire,
Said, when that she had glared a span,
"There is a cake for any man
  If he will watch the fire."

And Alfred, bowing heavily,
  Sat down the fire to stir,
And even as the woman pitied him
  So did he pity her.

Saying, "O great heart in the night,
  O best cast forth for worst,
Twilight shall melt and morning stir,
And no kind thing shall come to her,
Till God shall turn the world over
  And all the last are first.

"And well may God with the serving-folk
  Cast in His dreadful lot;
Is not He too a servant,
  And is not He forgot?

"For was not God my gardener
  And silent like a slave;
That opened oaks on the uplands
  Or thicket in graveyard gave?

"And was not God my armourer,
  All patient and unpaid,
That sealed my skull as a helmet,
  And ribs for hauberk made?

"Did not a great grey servant
  Of all my sires and me,

Build this pavilion of the pines,
   And herd the fowls and fill the vines,
And labour and pass and leave no signs
   Save mercy and mystery?

"For God is a great servant,
   And rose before the day,
From some primordial slumber torn;
But all we living later born
Sleep on, and rise after the morn,
   And the Lord has gone away.

"On things half sprung from sleeping,
   All sleepy suns have shone,
They stretch stiff arms, the yawning trees,
The beasts blink upon hands and knees,
Man is awake and does and sees—
   But Heaven has done and gone.

"For who shall guess the good riddle
   Or speak of the Holiest,
Save in faint figures and failing words,
Who loves, yet laughs among the swords,
   Labours, and is at rest?

"But some see God like Guthrum,
   Crowned, with a great beard curled,
But I see God like a good giant,
   That, labouring, lifts the world.

"Wherefore was God in Golgotha,
   Slain as a serf is slain;[27]
And hate He had of prince and peer,
And love He had and made good cheer,
Of them that, like this woman here,
   Go powerfully in pain.

"But in this grey morn of man's life,
   Cometh sometime to the mind

[27] Jesus was crucified on Golgotha, the place of the skull.

A little light that leaps and flies,
    Like a star blown on the wind.

"A star of nowhere, a nameless star,
    A light that spins and swirls,
And cries that even in hedge and hill.
Even on earth, it may go ill
    At last with the evil earls.

"A dancing sparkle, a doubtful star,
    On the waste wind whirled and driven;
But it seems to sing of a wilder worth,
A time discrowned of doom and birth,
And the kingdom of the poor on earth
    Come, as it is in heaven.

"But even though such days endure,
    How shall it profit her?
Who shall go groaning to the grave,
With many a meek and mighty slave,
Field-breaker and fisher on the wave,
    And woodman and waggoner.

"Bake ye the big world all again
    A cake with kinder leaven;
Yet these are sorry evermore—
Unless there be a little door,
    A little door in heaven."

And as he wept for the woman
    He let her business be,
And like his royal oath and rash
The good food fell upon the ash
    And blackened instantly.

Screaming, the woman caught a cake
    Yet burning from the bar,
And struck him suddenly on the face,
    Leaving a scarlet scar.

King Alfred stood up wordless,
  A man dead with surprise,
And torture stood and the evil things
That are in the childish hearts of kings
  An instant in his eyes.

And even as he stood and stared
  Drew round him in the dusk
Those friends creeping from far-off farms,
Marcus with all his slaves in arms,
And the strange spears hung with ancient charms
  Of Colan of the Usk.

With one whole farm marching afoot
  The trampled road resounds,
Farm-hands and farm-beasts blundering by
And jars of mead and stores of rye,
Where Eldred strode above his high
  And thunder-throated hounds.

And grey cattle and silver lowed
  Against the unlifted morn,
And straw clung to the spear-shafts tall.
And a boy went before them all
  Blowing a ram's horn.

As mocking such rude revelry,
  The dim clan of the Gael
Came like a bad king's burial-end,
With dismal robes that drop and rend
  And demon pipes that wail—

In long, outlandish garments,
  Torn, though of antique worth,
With Druid beards and Druid spears.
As a resurrected race appears
  Out of an elder earth.

And though the King had called them forth
 And knew them for his own,
So still each eye stood like a gem,
So spectral hung each broidered hem,
Grey carven men he fancied them,
 Hewn in an age of stone.

And the two wild peoples of the north
 Stood fronting in the gloam,
And heard and knew each in its mind
The third great thunder on the wind,
The living walls that hedge mankind,
 The walking walls of Rome.

Mark's were the mixed tribes of the west,
 Of many a hue and strain,
Gurth, with rank hair like yellow grass,
And the Cornish fisher, Gorlias,
And Halmer, come from his first mass,
 Lately baptized, a Dane.

But like one man in armour
 Those hundreds trod the field,
From red Arabia to the Tyne
The earth had heard that marching-line,
Since the cry on the hill Capitoline,[28]
 And the fall of the golden shield.

And the earth shook and the King stood still
 Under the greenwood bough,
And the smoking cake lay at his feet
 And the blow was on his brow.

Then Alfred laughed out suddenly,
 Like thunder in the spring,
Till shook aloud the lintel-beams,

[28] Capitoline Hill was the centre of social, political and religious life in ancient Rome.

And the squirrels stirred in dusty dreams,
And the startled birds went up in streams,
   For the laughter of the King.

And the beasts of the earth and the birds looked down,
   In a wild solemnity,
On a stranger sight than a sylph or elf,
On one man laughing at himself
   Under the greenwood tree—

The giant laughter of Christian men
   That roars through a thousand tales,
Where greed is an ape and pride is an ass,
And Jack's away with his master's lass,
And the miser is banged with all his brass,
   The farmer with all his flails;

Tales that tumble and tales that trick,
   Yet end not all in scorning—
Of kings and clowns in a merry plight,
And the clock gone wrong and the world gone right,
That the mummers sing upon Christmas night
   And Christmas Day in the morning.

"Now here is a good warrant,"
   Cried Alfred, "by my sword;
For he that is struck for an ill servant
   Should be a kind lord.

"He that has been a servant
   Knows more than priests and kings,
But he that has been an ill servant,
   He knows all earthly things.

"Pride flings frail palaces at the sky,
   As a man flings up sand,
But the firm feet of humility
   Take hold of heavy land.

"Pride juggles with her toppling towers,
    They strike the sun and cease,
But the firm feet of humility
    They grip the ground like trees.

"He that hath failed in a little thing
    Hath a sign upon the brow;
And the Earls of the Great Army
    Have no such seal to show.

"The red print on my forehead,
    Small flame for a red star,
In the van of the violent marching, then
When the sky is torn of the trumpets ten,
And the hands of the happy howling men
    Fling wide the gates of war.

"This blow that I return not
    Ten times will I return
On kings and earls of all degree,
And armies wide as empires be
Shall slide like landslips to the sea
    If the red star burn.

"One man shall drive a hundred,
    As the dead kings drave;
Before me rocking hosts be riven,
And battering cohorts backwards driven,
For I am the first king known of Heaven
    That has been struck like a slave.

"Up on the old white road, brothers,
    Up on the Roman walls!
For this is the night of the drawing of swords,
And the tainted tower of the heathen hordes
Leans to our hammers, fires and cords,
    Leans a little and falls.

"Follow the star that lives and leaps,
    Follow the sword that sings,

For we go gathering heathen men,
A terrible harvest, ten by ten,
As the wrath of the last red autumn—then
　　When Christ reaps down the kings.

"Follow a light that leaps and spins,
　　Follow the fire unfurled!
For riseth up against realm and rod,
A thing forgotten, a thing downtrod,
The last lost giant, even God,
　　Is risen against the world."

Roaring they went o'er the Roman wall,
　　And roaring up the lane,
Their torches tossed, a ladder of fire,
Higher their hymn was heard and higher,
More sweet for hate and for heart's desire,
And up in the northern scrub and brier,
　　They fell upon the Dane.

BOOK V
ETHANDUNE: THE FIRST STROKE

King Guthrum was a dread king,
　　Like death out of the north;
Shrines without name or number
He rent and rolled as lumber,
From Chester to the Humber
　　He drove his foemen forth.

The Roman villas heard him
　　In the valley of the Thames,
Come over the hills roaring
Above their roofs, and pouring
On spire and stair and flooring
　　Brimstone and pitch and flames.

Sheer o'er the great chalk uplands
   And the hill of the Horse went he,
Till high on Hampshire beacons[29]
   He saw the southern sea.

High on the heights of Wessex
   He saw the southern brine,
And turned him to a conquered land,
And where the northern thornwoods stand,
And the road parts on either hand,
   There came to him a sign.

King Guthrum was a war-chief,
   A wise man in the field,
And though he prospered well, and knew
How Alfred's folk were sad and few,
Not less with weighty care he drew
   Long lines for pike and shield.

King Guthrum lay on the upper land,
   On a single road at gaze,
And his foe must come with lean array,
Up the left arm of the cloven way,
   To the meeting of the ways.

And long ere the noise of armour,
   An hour ere the break of light,
The woods awoke with crash and cry,
And the birds sprang clamouring harsh and high,
And the rabbits ran like an elves' army
   Ere Alfred came in sight.

The live wood came at Guthrum,
   On foot and claw and wing,
The nests were noisy overhead,
For Alfred and the star of red,
All life went forth, and the forest fled
   Before the face of the King.

[29] Some of the hilltops along the South Downs in Hampshire are named beacons
for the practice long ago of lighting signal fires.

But halted in the woodways
   Christ's few were grim and grey,
And each with a small, far, bird-like sight
Saw the high folly of the fight;
And though strange joys had grown in the night,
   Despair grew with the day.

And when white dawn crawled through the wood,
   Like cold foam of a flood,
Then weakened every warrior's mood,
In hope, though not in hardihood;
And each man sorrowed as he stood
   In the fashion of his blood.

For the Saxon Franklin sorrowed
   For the things that had been fair;
For the dear dead woman, crimson-clad,
And the great feasts and the friends he had;
But the Celtic prince's soul was sad
   For the things that never were.

In the eyes Italian all things
   But a black laughter died;
And Alfred flung his shield to earth
   And smote his breast and cried—

"I wronged a man to his slaying,
   And a woman to her shame,
And once I looked on a sworn maid
   That was wed to the Holy Name.

"And once I took my neighbour's wife,
   That was bound to an eastland man,
In the starkness of my evil youth,
   Before my griefs began.

"People, if you have any prayers,
   Say prayers for me:
And lay me under a Christian stone
In that lost land I thought my own,

To wait till the holy horn is blown,
　　And all poor men are free."

Then Eldred of the idle farm
　　Leaned on his ancient sword,
As fell his heavy words and few;
And his eyes were of such alien blue
As gleams where the Northman saileth new
　　Into an unknown fiord.

"I was a fool and wasted ale—
　　My slaves found it sweet;
I was a fool and wasted bread,
　　And the birds had bread to eat.

"The kings go up and the kings go down.
　　And who knows who shall rule;
Next night a king may starve or sleep,
But men and birds and beasts shall weep
　　At the burial of a fool.

"O, drunkards in my cellar,
　　Boys in my apple tree,
The world grows stern and strange and new,
And wise men shall govern you,
　　And you shall weep for me.

"But yoke me my own oxen,
　　Down to my own farm;
My own dog will whine for me,
My own friends will bend the knee,
And the foes I slew openly
　　Have never wished me harm."

And all were moved a little,
　　But Colan stood apart,
Having first pity, and after
Hearing, like rat in rafter,

That little worm of laughter
  That eats the Irish heart.

And his grey-green eyes were cruel,
  And the smile of his mouth waxed hard,
And he said, "And when did Britain
  Become your burying-yard?

"Before the Romans lit the land,
  When schools and monks were none,
We reared such stones to the sun-god
  As might put out the sun.

"The tall trees of Britain
  We worshipped and were wise,
But you shall raid the whole land through
And never a tree shall talk to you,
Though every leaf is a tongue taught true
  And the forest is full of eyes.

"On one round hill to the seaward
  The trees grow tall and grey
And the trees talk together
  When all men are away.

"O'er a few round hills forgotten
  The trees grow tall in rings,
And the trees talk together
  Of many pagan things.

"Yet I could lie and listen
  With a cross upon my clay,
And hear unhurt for ever
  What the trees of Britain say."

A proud man was the Roman,
  His speech a single one,
But his eyes were like an eagle's eyes
  That is staring at the sun.

"Dig for me where I die," he said,
  "If first or last I fall—
Dead on the fell at the first charge,
  Or dead by Wantage[30] wall;

"Lift not my head from bloody ground,
  Bear not my body home,
For all the earth is Roman earth
  And I shall die in Rome."

Then Alfred, King of England,
  Bade blow the horns of war,
And fling the Golden Dragon out,
With crackle and acclaim and shout,
  Scrolled and aflame and far.

And under the Golden Dragon
  Went Wessex all along,
Past the sharp point of the cloven ways,
Out from the black wood into the blaze
  Of sun and steel and song.

And when they came to the open land
  They wheeled, deployed, and stood;
Midmost were Marcus and the King,
And Eldred on the right-hand wing,
And leftwards Colan darkling,
  In the last shade of the wood.

But the Earls of the Great Army
  Lay like a long half moon,
Ten poles before their palisades,
With wide-winged helms and runic blades
Red giants of an age of raids,
  In the thornland of Ethandune.

Midmost the saddles rose and swayed,
  And a stir of horses' manes,

[30] Wantage: the birthplace of King Alfred.

Where Guthrum and a few rode high
On horses seized in victory;
But Ogier went on foot to die,
  In the old way of the Danes.

Far to the King's left Elf the bard
  Led on the eastern wing
With songs and spells that change the blood;
And on the King's right Harold stood,
  The kinsman of the King.

Young Harold, coarse, with colours gay,
  Smoking with oil and musk,
And the pleasant violence of the young,
Pushed through his people, giving tongue
Foewards, where, grey as cobwebs, hung
  The banners of the Usk.

But as he came before his line
  A little space along,
His beardless face broke into mirth,
And he cried: "What broken bits of earth
Are here? For what their clothes are worth
  I would sell them for a song."

For Colan was hung with raiment
  Tattered like autumn leaves,
And his men were all as thin as saints,
  And all as poor as thieves.

No bows nor slings nor bolts they bore,
  But bills and pikes ill-made;
And none but Colan bore a sword,
  And rusty was its blade.

And Colan's eyes with mystery
  And iron laughter stirred,
And he spoke aloud, but lightly
  Not labouring to be heard.

"Oh, truly we be broken hearts,
  For that cause, it is said,
We light our candles to that Lord
  That broke Himself for bread.

"But though we hold but bitterly
  What land the Saxon leaves,
Though Ireland be but a land of saints,
  And Wales a land of thieves,

"I say you yet shall weary
  Of the working of your word,
That stricken spirits never strike
  Nor lean hands hold a sword.

"And if ever ye ride in Ireland,
  The jest may yet be said,
There is the land of broken hearts,
  And the land of broken heads."

Not less barbarian laughter
  Choked Harold like a flood,
"And shall I fight with scarecrows
  That am of Guthrum's blood?

"Meeting may be of war-men,
  Where the best war-man wins;
But all this carrion a man shoots
  Before the fight begins."

And stopping in his onward strides,
  He snatched a bow in scorn
From some mean slave, and bent it on
Colan, whose doom grew dark; and shone
Stars evil over Caerleon,
  In the place where he was born.

For Colan had not bow nor sling,
  On a lonely sword leaned he,

Like Arthur on Excalibur
  In the battle by the sea.

To his great gold ear-ring Harold
  Tugged back the feathered tail,
And swift had sprung the arrow,
  But swifter sprang the Gael.

Whirling the one sword round his head,
  A great wheel in the sun,
He sent it splendid through the sky,
Flying before the shaft could fly—
It smote Earl Harold over the eye,
  And blood began to run.

Colan stood bare and weaponless,
  Earl Harold, as in pain,
Strove for a smile, put hand to head,
Stumbled and suddenly fell dead;
And the small white daisies all waxed red
  With blood out of his brain.

And all at that marvel of the sword,
  Cast like a stone to slay,
Cried out. Said Alfred: "Who would see
Signs, must give all things. Verily
Man shall not taste of victory
  Till he throws his sword away."

Then Alfred, prince of England,
  And all the Christian earls,
Unhooked their swords and held them up.
Each offered to Colan, like a cup
  Of chrysolite and pearls.

And the King said, "Do thou take my sword
  Who have done this deed of fire,
For this is the manner of Christian men,
Whether of steel or priestly pen,

That they cast their hearts out of their ken
   To get their heart's desire.

"And whether ye swear a hive of monks,
   Or one fair wife to friend,
This is the manner of Christian men,
   That their oath endures the end.

"For love, our Lord, at the end of the world,
   Sits a red horse like a throne,
With a brazen helm and an iron bow,
   But one arrow alone.

"Love with the shield of the Broken Heart
   Ever his bow doth bend,
With a single shaft for a single prize,
And the ultimate bolt that parts and flies
Comes with a thunder of split skies,
   And a sound of souls that rend.

"So shall you earn a king's sword,
   Who cast your sword away."
And the King took, with a random eye,
A rude axe from a hind hard by
   And turned him to the fray.

For the swords of the Earls of Daneland
   Flamed round the fallen lord.
The first blood woke the trumpet-tune,
As in monk's rhyme or wizard's rune,
Beginneth the battle of Ethandune
   With the throwing of the sword.

BOOK VI
ETHANDUNE: THE SLAYING OF THE CHIEFS

As the sea flooding the flat sands
   Flew on the sea-born horde,
The two hosts shocked with dust and din,
Left of the Latin paladin,
Clanged all Prince Harold's howling kin
   On Colan and the sword.

Crashed in the midst on Marcus,
   Ogier with Guthrum by,
And eastward of such central stir,
Far to the right and faintlier,
The house of Elf the harp-player.
   Struck Eldred's with a cry.

The centre swat[31] for weariness,
   Stemming the screaming horde,
And wearily went Colan's hands
   That swung King Alfred's sword.

But like a cloud of morning
   To eastward easily,
Tall Eldred broke the sea of spears
   As a tall ship breaks the sea.

His face like a sanguine sunset,
   His shoulder a Wessex down,
His hand like a windy hammer-stroke;
Men could not count the crests he broke,
   So fast the crests went down.

As the tall white devil of the Plague
   Moves out of Asian skies,
With his foot on a waste of cities
   And his head in a cloud of flies;

---

[31] Swat, an archaic form of "sweated".

Or purple and peacock skies grow dark
　　With a moving locust-tower;
Or tawny sand-winds tall and dry,
Like hell's red banners beat and fly,
When death comes out of Araby,
　　Was Eldred in his hour.

But while he moved like a massacre
　　He murmured as in sleep,
And his words were all of low hedges
　　And little fields and sheep.

Even as he strode like a pestilence,
　　That strides from Rhine to Rome,
He thought how tall his beans might be
　　If ever he went home.

Spoke some stiff piece of childish prayer,
　　Dull as the distant chimes,
That thanked our God for good eating
　　And corn and quiet times—

Till on the helm of a high chief
　　Fell shatteringly his brand,
And the helm broke and the bone broke
　　And the sword broke in his hand.

Then from the yelling Northmen
　　Driven splintering on him ran
Full seven spears, and the seventh
　　Was never made by man.

Seven spears, and the seventh
　　Was wrought as the faerie blades,
And given to Elf the minstrel
　　By the monstrous water-maids;

By them that dwell where luridly
　　Lost waters of the Rhine

Move among roots of nations,
  Being sunken for a sign.

Under all graves they murmur,
  They murmur and rebel,
Down to the buried kingdoms creep,
And like a lost rain roar and weep
  O'er the red heavens of hell.

Thrice drowned was Elf the minstrel,
  And washed as dead on sand;
And the third time men found him
  The spear was in his hand.

Seven spears went about Eldred,
  Like stays about a mast;
But there was sorrow by the sea
  For the driving of the last.

Six spears thrust upon Eldred
  Were splintered while he laughed;
One spear thrust into Eldred,
  Three feet of blade and shaft.

And from the great heart grievously
  Came forth the shaft and blade,
And he stood with the face of a dead man,
  Stood a little, and swayed—

Then fell, as falls a battle-tower,
  On smashed and struggling spears.
Cast down from some unconquered town
That, rushing earthward, carries down
Loads of live men of all renown—
  Archers and engineers.

And a great clamour of Christian men
  Went up in agony,

Crying, "Fallen is the tower of Wessex
   That stood beside the sea."

Centre and right the Wessex guard
   Grew pale for doubt and fear,
And the flank failed at the advance,
For the death-light on the wizard lance—
   The star of the evil spear.

"Stand like an oak," cried Marcus,
   "Stand like a Roman wall!
Eldred the Good is fallen—
   Are you too good to fall?

"When we were wan and bloodless
   He gave you ale enow;
The pirates deal with him as dung,
   God! are you bloodless now?"

"Grip, Wulf and Gorlias, grip the ash!
   Slaves, and I make you free?
Stamp, Hildred hard in English land,
Stand Gurth, stand Gorlias, Gawen stand!
Hold, Halfgar, with the other hand,
   Halmer, hold up on knee!

"The lamps are dying in your homes,
   The fruits upon your bough;
Even now your old thatch smoulders, Gurth,
Now is the judgment of the earth,
   Now is the death-grip, now!"

For thunder of the captain,
   Not less the Wessex line,
Leaned back and reeled a space to rear
As Elf charged with the Rhine maids' spear,
   And roaring like the Rhine.

For the men were borne by the waving walls
   Of woods and clouds that pass,

By dizzy plains and drifting sea,
And they mixed God with glamoury,
God with the gods of the burning tree
    And the wizard's tower and glass.

But Mark was come of the glittering towns
    Where hot white details show,
Where men can number and expound,
And his faith grew in a hard ground
Of doubt and reason and falsehood found,
    Where no faith else could grow.

Belief that grew of all beliefs
    One moment back was blown
And belief that stood on unbelief
    Stood up iron and alone.

The Wessex crescent backwards
    Crushed, as with bloody spear
Went Elf roaring and routing,
And Mark against Elf yet shouting,
    Shocked, in his mid-career.

Right on the Roman shield and sword
    Did spear of the Rhine maids run;
But the shield shifted never,
The sword rang down to sever,
The great Rhine sang for ever,
    And the songs of Elf were done.

And a great thunder of Christian men
    Went up against the sky,
Saying, "God hath broken the evil spear
    Ere the good man's blood was dry."

"Spears at the charge!" yelled Mark amain,
    "Death on the gods of death!
Over the thrones of doom and blood
Goeth God that is a craftsman good,

And gold and iron, earth and wood,
   Loveth and laboureth.

"The fruits leap up in all your farms,
   The lamps in each abode;
God of all good things done on earth,
All wheels or webs of any worth,
The God that makes the roof, Gurth,
   The God that makes the road.

"The God that heweth kings in oak
   Writeth songs on vellum,
God of gold and flaming glass,
Confregit potentias
Arcuum, scutum, Gorlias,
   Gladium et bellum." [32]

Steel and lightning broke about him.
   Battle-bays and palm,
All the sea-kings swayed among
Woods of the Wessex arms upflung,
The trumpet of the Roman tongue,
   The thunder of the psalm.

And midmost of that rolling field
   Ran Ogier ragingly,
Lashing at Mark, who turned his blow,
And brake the helm about his brow,
   And broke him to his knee.

Then Ogier heaved over his head
   His huge round shield of proof;
But Mark set one foot on the shield,
One on some sundered rock upheeled,
And towered above the tossing field,
   A statue on a roof.

[32] *Confregit potentias arcuum, scutum … gladium et bellum*—Psalm 75:4 in Saint Jerome's Latin Vulgate version: "He has broken the powers of the bow, shield, sword and war."

Dealing far blows about the fight,
　Like thunder-bolts a-roam,
Like birds about the battle-field,
While Ogier writhed under his shield
　Like a tortoise in his dome.

But hate in the buried Ogier
　Was strong as pain in hell,
With bare brute hand from the inside
He burst the shield of brass and hide,
And a death-stroke to the Roman's side
　Sent suddenly and well.

Then the great statue on the shield
　Looked his last look around
With level and imperial eye;
And Mark, the man from Italy,
Fell in the sea of agony,
　And died without a sound.

And Ogier, leaping up alive,
　Hurled his huge shield away
Flying, as when a juggler flings
　A whizzing plate in play.

And held two arms up rigidly,
　And roared to all the Danes:
"Fallen is Rome, yea, fallen
　The city of the plains!

"Shall no man born remember,
　That breaketh wood or weald,
How long she stood on the roof of the world
　As he stood on my shield.

"The new wild world forgetteth her
　As foam fades on the sea,
How long she stood with her foot on Man
　As he with his foot on me.

"No more shall the brown men of the south
 Move like the ants in lines,
To quiet men with olives
 Or madden men with vines.

"No more shall the white towns of the south,
 Where Tiber and Nilus run,
Sitting around a secret sea
 Worship a secret sun.

"The blind gods roar for Rome fallen,
 And forum and garland gone,
For the ice of the north is broken,
 And the sea of the north comes on.

"The blind gods roar and rave and dream
 Of all cities under the sea,
For the heart of the north is broken,
 And the blood of the north is free.

"Down from the dome of the world we come,
 Rivers on rivers down,
Under us swirl the sects and hordes
 And the high dooms we drown.

"Down from the dome of the world and down,
 Struck flying as a skiff
On a river in spate is spun and swirled
Until we come to the end of the world
 That breaks short, like a cliff.

"And when we come to the end of the world
 For me, I count it fit
To take the leap like a good river,
 Shot shrieking over it.

"But whatso hap at the end of the world,
 Where Nothing is struck and sounds,
It is not, by Thor, these monkish men
 These humbled Wessex hounds—

"Not this pale line of Christian hinds,
    This one white string of men,
Shall keep us back from the end of the world,
    And the things that happen then.

"It is not Alfred's dwarfish sword,
    Nor Egbert's pigmy crown,[33]
Shall stay us now that descend in thunder,
Rending the realms and the realms thereunder,
    Down through the world and down."

There was that in the wild men back of him,
    There was that in his own wild song,
A dizzy throbbing, a drunkard smoke,
That dazed to death all Wessex folk,
    And swept their spears along.

Vainly the sword of Colan
    And the axe of Alfred plied—
The Danes poured in like a brainless plague,
    And knew not when they died.

Prince Colan slew a score of them,
    And was stricken to his knee;
King Alfred slew a score and seven
    And was borne back on a tree.

Back to the black gate of the woods,
    Back up the single way,
Back by the place of the parting ways
    Christ's knights were whirled away.

And when they came to the parting ways
    Doom's heaviest hammer fell,
For the King was beaten, blind, at bay,
Down the right lane with his array,
But Colan swept the other way,
    Where he smote great strokes and fell.

[33] The crown of Wessex.

The thorn-woods over Ethandune
 Stand sharp and thick as spears,
By night and furze and forest-harms
Far sundered were the friends in arms;
The loud lost blows, the last alarms,
 Came not to Alfred's ears.

The thorn-woods over Ethandune
 Stand stiff as spikes in mail;
As to the Haut King came at morn
Dead Roland on a doubtful horn,[34]
Seemed unto Alfred lightly borne
 The last cry of the Gael.

BOOK VII
ETHANDUNE: THE LAST CHARGE

Away in the waste of White Horse Down
 An idle child alone
Played some small game through hours that pass,
And patiently would pluck the grass,
 Patiently push the stone.

On the lean, green edge for ever,
 Where the blank chalk touched the turf,
The child played on, alone, divine,
As a child plays on the last line
 That sunders sand and surf.

For he dwelleth in high divisions
 Too simple to understand,
Seeing on what morn of mystery
The Uncreated rent the sea
 With roarings, from the land.

---

[34] Haut King is Charlemagne, whose champion Roland blew his horn for reinforcements too late to save himself and his men from the Moors.

Through the long infant hours like days
  He built one tower in vain—
Piled up small stones to make a town,
And evermore the stones fell down,
  And he piled them up again.

And crimson kings on battle-towers,
  And saints on Gothic spires,
And hermits on their peaks of snow,
  And heroes on their pyres,

And patriots riding royally,
  That rush the rocking town,
Stretch hands, and hunger and aspire,
Seeking to mount where high and higher,
The child whom Time can never tire,
  Sings over White Horse Down.

And this was the might of Alfred,
  At the ending of the way;
That of such smiters, wise or wild,
He was least distant from the child,
  Piling the stones all day.

For Eldred fought like a frank hunter
  That killeth and goeth home;
And Mark had fought because all arms
  Rang like the name of Rome.

And Colan fought with a double mind,
  Moody and madly gay;
But Alfred fought as gravely
  As a good child at play.

He saw wheels break and work run back
  And all things as they were;
And his heart was orbed like victory
  And simple like despair.

Therefore is Mark forgotten,
 That was wise with his tongue and brave:
And the cairn over Colan crumbled,
 And the cross on Eldred's grave.

Their great souls went on a wind away,
 And they have not tale or tomb;
And Alfred born in Wantage
 Rules England till the doom.

Because in the forest of all fears
 Like a strange fresh gust from sea,
Struck him that ancient innocence
 That is more than mastery.

And as a child whose bricks fall down
 Re-piles them o'er and o'er,
Came ruin and the rain that burns,
Returning as a wheel returns,
And crouching in the furze and ferns
 He began his life once more.

He took his ivory horn unslung
 And smiled, but not in scorn:
"Endeth the Battle of Elthandune
 With the blowing of a horn."

On a dark horse at the double way
 He saw great Guthrum ride,
Heard roar of brass and ring of steel,
The laughter and the trumpet peal,
 The pagan in his pride.

And Ogier's red and hated head
 Moved in some talk or task;
But the men seemed scattered in the brier,
And some of them had lit a fire,
 And one had broached a cask.

And waggons one or two stood up,
 Like tall ships in sight,

As if an outpost were encamped
  At the cloven ways for night.

And joyous of the sudden stay
  Of Alfred's routed few,
Sat one upon a stone to sigh,
And some slipped up the road to fly,
Till Alfred in the fern hard by
  Set horn to mouth and blew.

And they all abode like statues—
  One sitting on the stone,
One half-way through the thorn hedge tall,
One with a leg across a wall,
And one looked backwards, very small,
  Far up the road, alone.

Grey twilight and a yellow star
  Hung over thorn and hill;
Two spears and a cloven war-shield lay
Loose on the road as cast away,
The horn died faint in the forest grey,
  And the fleeing men stood still.

"Brothers at arms," said Alfred,
  "On this side lies the foe;
Are slavery and starvation flowers,
  That you should pluck them so?

"For whether is it better
  To be prodded with Danish poles,
Having hewn a chamber in a ditch,
And hounded like a howling witch,
  Or smoked to death in holes?

"Or that before the red cock crow
  All we, a thousand strong,
Go down the dark road to God's house,
  Singing a Wessex song?

"To sweat a slave to a race of slaves,
    To drink up infamy?
No, brothers, by your leave, I think
Death is a better ale to drink,
And by all the stars of Christ that sink,
    The Danes shall drink with me.

"To grow old cowed in a conquered land.
    With the sun itself discrowned,
To see trees crouch and cattle slink—
Death is a better ale to drink,
And by high Death on the fell brink,
    That flagon shall go round.

"Though dead are all the paladins
    Whom glory had in ken,
Though all your thunder-sworded thanes
With proud hearts died among the Danes,
While a man remains, great war remains:
    Now is a war of men.

"The men that tear the furrows,
    The men that fell the trees,
When all their lords be lost and dead
The bondsmen of the earth shall tread
    The tyrants of the seas.

"The wheel of the roaring stillness
    Of all labours under the sun,
Speed the wild work as well at least
    As the whole world's work is done.

"Let Hildred hack the shield-wall
    Clean as he hacks the hedge;
Let Gurth the fowler stand as cool
    As he stands on the chasm's edge;

"Let Gorlias ride the sea-kings
    As Gorlias rides the sea,
Then let all hell and Denmark drive,

Yelling to all its fiends alive,
  And not a rag care we."

When Alfred's word was ended
  Stood firm that feeble line,
Each in his place with club or spear,
And fury deeper than deep fear,
  And smiles as sour as brine.

And the King held up the horn and said,
  "See ye my father's horn,
That Egbert blew in his empery,
Once, when he rode out commonly,
Twice when he rode for venery,
  And thrice on the battle-morn.

"But heavier fates have fallen
  The horn of the Wessex kings,
And I blew once, the riding sign,
To call you to the fighting line
  And glory and all good things.

"And now two blasts, the hunting sign,
  Because we turn to bay;
But I will not blow the three blasts,
  Till we be lost or they.

"And now I blow the hunting sign,
  Charge some by rule and rod;
But when I blow the battle sign,
  Charge all and go to God."

Wild stared the Danes at the double ways
  Where they loitered, all at large,
As that dark line for the last time
  Doubled the knee to charge—

And caught their weapons clumsily,
  And marvelled how and why—
In such degree, by rule and rod,

The people of the peace of God
   Went roaring down to die.

And when the last arrow
   Was fitted and was flown,
When the broken shield hung on the breast,
And the hopeless lance was laid in rest,
   And the hopeless horn blown,

The King looked up, and what he saw
   Was a great light like death,
For Our Lady stood on the standards rent,
As lonely and as innocent
As when between white walls she went
   And the lilies of Nazareth.

One instant in a still light
   He saw Our Lady then,
Her dress was soft as western sky,
And she was a queen most womanly—
   But she was a queen of men.

Over the iron forest
   He saw Our Lady stand,
Her eyes were sad withouten art,
And seven swords were in her heart—
   But one was in her hand.

Then the last charge went blindly,
   And all too lost for fear:
The Danes closed round, a roaring ring,
And twenty clubs rose o'er the King,
Four Danes hewed at him, halloing,
And Ogier of the Stone and Sling
   Drove at him with a spear.

But the Danes were wild with laughter,
   And the great spear swung wide,
The point stuck to a straggling tree,

And either host cried suddenly,
    As Alfred leapt aside.

Short time had shaggy Ogier
    To pull his lance in line—
He knew King Alfred's axe on high,
    He heard it rushing through the sky,

He cowered beneath it with a cry—
    It split him to the spine:
And Alfred sprang over him dead,
    And blew the battle sign.

Then bursting all and blasting
    Came Christendom like death,
Kicked of such catapults of will,
The staves shiver, the barrels spill,
The waggons waver and crash and kill
    The waggoners beneath.

Barriers go backwards, banners rend,
    Great shields groan like a gong—
Horses like horns of nightmare
    Neigh horribly and long.

Horses ramp high and rock and boil
    And break their golden reins,
And slide on carnage clamorously,
Down where the bitter blood doth lie,
Where Ogier went on foot to die,
    In the old way of the Danes.

"The high tide!" King Alfred cried.
    "The high tide and the turn!
As a tide turns on the tall grey seas,
See how they waver in the trees,
How stray their spears, how knock their knees.
    How wild their watchfires burn!

"The Mother of God goes over them,
    Walking on wind and flame,
And the storm-cloud drifts from city and dale,
And the White Horse stamps in the White Horse Vale,
And we all shall yet drink Christian ale
    In the village of our name.

"The Mother of God goes over them,
    On dreadful cherubs borne;
And the psalm is roaring above the rune,
And the Cross goes over the sun and moon,
Endeth the battle of Ethandune
    With the blowing of a horn."

For back indeed disorderly
    The Danes went clamouring,
Too worn to take anew the tale,
Or dazed with insolence and ale,
Or stunned of heaven, or stricken pale
    Before the face of the King.

For dire was Alfred in his hour
    The pale scribe witnesseth,
More mighty in defeat was he
Then all men else in victory,
And behind, his men came murderously,
    Dry-throated, drinking death.

And Edgar of the Golden Ship
    He slew with his own hand,
Took Ludwig from his lady's bower,
And smote down Harmar in his hour,
And vain and lonely stood the tower—
    The tower in Guelderland,[35]

And Torr out of his tiny boat,
    Whose eyes beheld the Nile,

[35] Guelderland, a province of the Netherlands.

Wulf with his war-cry on his lips,
And Harco born in the eclipse,
Who blocked the Seine with battleships
    Round Paris on the Isle.

And Hacon of the Harvest-Song,
    And Dirck from the Elbe he slew,
And Cnut that melted Durham bell
And Fulk and fiery Oscar fell,
And Goderic and Sigael,
    And Uriel of the Yew.

And highest sang the slaughter,
    And fastest fell the slain,
When from the wood-road's blackening throat
A crowning and crashing wonder smote
    The rear-guard of the Dane.

For the dregs of Colan's company—
    Lost down the other road—
Had gathered and grown and heard the din,
And with wild yells came pouring in,
Naked as their old British kin,
    And bright with blood for woad.

And bare and bloody and aloft
    They bore before their band
The body of their mighty lord,
Colan of Caerleon and its horde,
That bore King Alfred's battle-sword
    Broken in his left hand.

And a strange music went with him,
    Loud and yet strangely far;
The wild pipes of the western land,
Too keen for the ear to understand,
Sang high and deathly on each hand
    When the dead man went to war.

Blocked between ghost and buccaneer,
  Brave men have dropped and died;
And the wild sea-lords well might quail
As the ghastly war-pipes of the Gael
Called to the horns of White Horse Vale,
  And all the horns replied.

And Hildred the poor hedger
  Cut down four captains dead,
And Halmar laid three others low,
And the great earls wavered to and fro
  For the living and the dead.

And Gorlias grasped the great flag,
  The Raven of Odin, torn;
And the eyes of Guthrum altered,
  For the first time since morn.

As a turn of the wheel of tempest
  Tilts up the whole sky tall,
And cliffs of wan cloud luminous
Lean out like great walls over us,
  As if the heavens might fall.

As such a tall and tilted sky
  Sends certain snow or light,
So did the eyes of Guthrum change,
And the turn was more certain and more strange
  Than a thousand men in flight.

For not till the floor of the skies is split,
  And hell-fire shines through the sea,
Or the stars look up through the rent earth's knees,
Cometh such rending of certainties,
As when one wise man truly sees
  What is more wise than he.

He set his horse in the battle-breech
  Even Guthrum of the Dane,

And as ever had fallen fell his brand,
A falling tower o'er many a land,
But Gurth the fowler laid one hand
   Upon this bridle rein.

King Guthrum was a great lord,
   And higher than his gods—
He put the popes to laughter,
   He chid the saints with rods,

He took this hollow world of ours
   For a cup to hold his wine;
In the parting of the woodways
   There came to him a sign.

In Wessex in the forest,
   In the breaking of the spears.
We set a sign on Guthrum
   To blaze a thousand years.

Where the high saddles jostle
   And the horse-tails toss,
There rose to the birds flying
A roar of dead and dying;
In deafness and strong crying
   We signed him with the cross.

Far out to the winding river
   The blood ran down for days,
When we put the cross on Guthrum
   In the parting of the ways.

BOOK VIII
THE SCOURING OF THE HORSE

In the years of the peace of Wessex,
   When the good King sat at home;
Years following on that bloody boon
When she that stands above the moon
Stood above death at Ethandune
   And saw his kingdom come—

When the pagan people of the sea
   Fled to their palisades,
Nailed there with javelins to cling
And wonder smote the pirate king,
And brought him to his christening
   And the end of all his raids.

(For not till the night's blue slate is wiped
   Of its last star utterly,
And fierce new signs writ there to read,
Shall eyes with such amazement heed,
As when a great man knows indeed
   A greater thing than he.)

And there came to his chrism-loosing
   Lords of all lands afar,
And a line was drawn north-westerly[36]
That set King Egbert's empire free,
Giving all lands by the northern sea
   To the sons of the northern star.

In the days of the rest of Alfred,
   When all these things were done,
And Wessex lay in a patch of peace,
   Like a dog in a patch of sun—

[36] The line separating lands under the Danes and lands under Alfred ran roughly
from London to Chester.

The King sat in his orchard,
  Among apples green and red,
With the little book in his bosom
  And the sunshine on his head.

And he gathered the songs of simple men
  That swing with helm and hod,
And the alms he gave as a Christian
Like a river alive with fishes ran;
And he made gifts to a beggar man
  As to a wandering god.

And he gat good laws of the ancient kings,
  Like treasure out of the tombs;
And many a thief in thorny nook,
Or noble in sea-stained turret shook,
For the opening of his iron book,
  And the gathering of the dooms.

Then men would come from the ends of the earth,
  Whom the King sat welcoming,
And men would go to the ends of the earth[37]
  Because of the word of the King.

For folk came in to Alfred's face
  Whose javelins had been hurled
On monsters that make boil the sea,
Crakens and coils of mystery.[38]
Or thrust in ancient snows that be
  The white hair of the world.

And some had knocked at the northern gates
  Of the ultimate icy floor,
Where the fish freeze and the foam turns black,
And the wide world narrows to a track,

[37] King Alfred is credited with founding the English navy.
[38] Krakens, fabulous sea monsters reported off the Norwegian coast, possibly giant squid.

And the other sea at the world's back
  Cries through a closed door.

And men went forth from Alfred's face,
  Even great gift-bearing lords,
Not to Rome only, but more bold,
Out to the high hot courts of old,
Of negroes clad in cloth of gold,
  Silence, and crooked swords,

Scrawled screens and secret gardens
  And insect-laden skies—
Where fiery plains stretch on and on
To the purple country of Prester John[39]
  And the walls of Paradise.

And he knew the might of the Terre Majeure,[40]
  Where kings began to reign;
Where in a night-rout, without name,
Of gloomy Goths and Gauls there came
White, above candles all aflame,
  Like a vision, Charlemagne.

And men, seeing such embassies,
  Spake with the King and said:
"The steel that sang so sweet a tune
On Ashdown and on Ethandune,
Why hangs it scabbarded so soon,
  All heavily like lead?

"Why dwell the Danes in North England,
  And up to the river ride?
Three more such marches like thine own

[39] Prester John, a legendary Christian emperor who reigned in Asia or Abyssinia. Marco Polo reported him to be King of the Tartars, leader of a people converted to Christianity by Saint Thomas the Apostle.

[40] Terre Majeure, in some ways the mainland of Europe but more especially the area of what became known as the Holy Roman Empire under Charlemagne, with whom King Alfred established diplomatic relations.

Would end them; and the Pict should own[41]
Our sway; and our feet climb the throne
    In the mountains of Strathclyde." [42]

And Alfred in the orchard,
    Among apples green and red,
With the little book in his bosom,
    Looked at green leaves and said:

"When all philosophies shall fail,
    This word alone shall fit;
That a sage feels too small for life,
    And a fool too large for it.

"Asia and all imperial plains
    Are too little for a fool;
But for one man whose eyes can see
The little island of Athelney
    Is too large a land to rule.

"Haply it had been better
    When I built my fortress there,
Out in the reedy waters wide,
I had stood on my mud wall and cried:
'Take England all, from tide to tide—
    Be Athelney my share.'

"Those madmen of the throne-scramble—
    Oppressors and oppressed—
Had lined the banks by Athelney,
And waved and wailed unceasingly,
Where the river turned to the broad sea,
    By an island of the blest.

"An island like a little book
    Full of a hundred tales,
Like the gilt page the good monks pen,

[41] The Picts were the original inhabitants of Scotland.
[42] Strathclyde was a Celtic kingdom in the 6th and 7th centuries bridging Scotland and England.

That is all smaller than a wren,
Yet hath high towns, meteors, and men,
 And suns and spouting whales;

"A land having a light on it
 In the river dark and fast,
An isle with utter clearness lit,
Because a saint had stood in it;
Where flowers are flowers indeed and fit,
 And trees are trees at last.

"So were the island of a saint;
 But I am a common king,
And I will make my fences tough
From Wantage Town to Plymouth Bluff,
Because I am not wise enough
 To rule so small a thing."

And it fell in the days of Alfred,
 In the days of his repose,
That as old customs in his sight
Were a straight road and a steady light,
He bade them keep the White Horse white
 As the first plume of the snows.

And right to the red torchlight,
 From the trouble of morning grey,
They stripped the White Horse of the grass
 As they strip it to this day.

And under the red torchlight
 He went dreaming as though dull,
Of his old companions slain like kings,
And the rich irrevocable things
Of a heart that hath not openings,
 But is shut fast, being full.

And the torchlight touched the pale hair
 Where silver clouded gold,
And the frame of his face was made of cords,

And a young lord turned among the lords
   And said: "The King is old."

And even as he said it
   A post ran in amain,
Crying: "Arm, Lord King, the hamlets arm,
In the horror and the shade of harm,
They have burnt Brand of Aynger's farm—
   The Danes are come again!

"Danes drive the white East Angles
   In six fights on the plains,
Danes waste the world about the Thames,
   Danes to the eastward—Danes!"

And as he stumbled on one knee,
   The thanes broke out in ire,
Crying: "Ill the watchmen watch, and ill
   The sheriffs keep the shire."

But the young earl said: "Ill the saints,
   The saints of England, guard
The land wherein we pledge them gold;
The dykes decay, the King grows old,
   And surely this is hard,

"That we be never quit of them;
   That when his head is hoar
He cannot say to them he smote,
And spared with a hand hard at the throat,
   'Go, and return no more.'"

Then Alfred smiled. And the smile of him
   Was like the sun for power.
But he only pointed: bade them heed
Those peasants of the Berkshire breed,
Who plucked the old Horse of the weed
   As they pluck it to this hour.

"Will ye part with the weeds for ever?
   Or show daisies to the door?

Or will you bid the bold grass
   Go, and return no more?

"So ceaseless and so secret
   Thrive terror and theft set free;
Treason and shame shall come to pass
While one weed flowers in a morass;
And like the stillness of stiff grass
   The stillness of tyranny.

"Over our white souls also
   Wild heresies and high
Wave prouder than the plumes of grass,
   And sadder than their sigh.

"And I go riding against the raid,
   And ye know not where I am;
But ye shall know in a day or year,
When one green star of grass grows here;
Chaos has charged you, charger and spear,
   Battle-axe and battering-ram.

"And though skies alter and empires melt,
   This word shall still be true:
If we would have the horse of old,
   Scour ye the horse anew.

"One time I followed a dancing star
   That seemed to sing and nod,
And ring upon earth all evil's knell;
But now I wot if ye scour not well
Red rust shall grow on God's great bell
   And grass in the streets of God."

Ceased Alfred; and above his head
   The grand green domes, the Downs,
Showed the first legions of the press,
Marching in haste and bitterness
   For Christ's sake and the crown's.

Beyond the cavern of Colan,
   Past Eldred's by the sea,
Rose men that owned King Alfred's rod,
From the windy wastes of Exe[43] untrod,
Or where the thorn of the grave of God
   Burns over Glastonbury.

Far northward and far westward
   The distant tribes drew nigh,
Plains beyond plains, fell beyond fell,
That a man at sunset sees so well,
And the tiny coloured towns that dwell
   In the corners of the sky.

But dark and thick as thronged the host.
   With drum and torch and blade,
The still-eyed King sat pondering,
As one that watches a live thing,
   The scoured chalk; and he said,

"Though I give this land to Our Lady,
   That helped me in Athelney,
Though lordlier trees and lustier sod
And happier hills hath no flesh trod
Than the garden of the Mother of God
   Between Thames side and the sea,

"I know that weeds shall grow in it
   Faster than men can burn;
And though they scatter now and go,
In some far century, sad and slow,
I have a vision, and I know
   The heathen shall return.

"They shall not come with warships,
   They shall not waste with brands,

---

[43] Exe is the river that drains Exmoor.

But books be all their eating,
   And ink be on their hands.

"Not with the humour of hunters
   Or savage skill in war,
But ordering all things with dead words,
Strings shall they make of beasts and birds,
   And wheels of wind and star.

"They shall come mild as monkish clerks,
   With many a scroll and pen;
And backward shall ye turn and gaze,
Desiring one of Alfred's days,
   When pagans still were men.

"The dear sun dwarfed of dreadful suns,
   Like fiercer flowers on stalk,
Earth lost and little like a pea
In high heaven's towering forestry,
—These be the small weeds ye shall see
   Crawl, covering the chalk.

"But though they bridge St. Mary's sea,
   Or steal St. Michael's wing—
Though they rear marvels over us,
Greater than great Vergilius[44]
   Wrought for the Roman king;

"By this sign you shall know them,
   The breaking of the sword,
And man no more a free knight,
   That loves or hates his lord.

"Yea, this shall be the sign of them,
   The sign of the dying fire;
And Man made like a half-wit,
   That knows not of his sire.

[44] The poet Virgil, whose epic *Aeneid* was written for Caesar Augustus. He was later viewed as a sorcerer.

"What though they come with scroll and pen,
  And grave as a shaven clerk,
By this sign you shall know them,
  That they ruin and make dark;

"By all men bond to Nothing,
  Being slaves without a lord,
By one blind idiot world obeyed,
  Too blind to be abhorred;

"By terror and the cruel tales
  Of curse in bone and kin,
By weird and weakness winning,
Accursed from the beginning,
By detail of the sinning,
  And denial of the sin;

"By thought a crawling ruin,
  By life a leaping mire,
By a broken heart in the breast of the world,
  And the end of the world's desire;

"By God and man dishonoured,
  By death and life made vain,
Know ye the old barbarian,
  The barbarian come again—

"When is great talk of trend and tide,
  And wisdom and destiny,
Hail that undying heathen
  That is sadder than the sea.

"In what wise men shall smite him.
  Or the Cross stand up again,
Or charity or chivalry,
My vision saith not; and I see
No more; but now ride doubtfully
  To the battle of the plain."

And the grass-edge of the great down
  Was cut clean as a lawn,

While the levies thronged from near and far,
From the warm woods of the western star,
And the King went out to his last war
   On a tall grey horse at dawn.

And news of his far-off fighting
   Came slowly and brokenly
From the land of the East Saxons,[45]
   From the sunrise and the sea.

From the plains of the white sunrise,
   And sad St. Edmund's crown,[46]
Where the pools of Essex pale and gleam
   Out beyond London Town—

In mighty and doubtful fragments,
   Like faint or fabled wars,
Climbed the old hills of his renown,
Where the bald brow of White Horse Down
   Is close to the cold stars.

But away in the eastern places
   The wind of death walked high,
And a raid was driven athwart the raid,
The sky reddened and the smoke swayed,
   And the tall grey horse went by.

The gates of the great river
   Were breached as with a barge,
The walls sank crowded, say the scribes,
And high towers populous with tribes
   Seemed leaning from the charge.

Smoke like rebellious heavens rolled
   Curled over coloured flames,
Mirrored in monstrous purple dreams
   In the mighty pools of Thames.

[45] Essex.
[46] St. Edmund's crown is East Anglia centered on Bury St. Edmunds.

Loud was the war on London wall,
   And loud in London gates,
And loud the sea-kings in the cloud
Broke through their dreaming gods, and loud
   Cried on their dreadful Fates.

And all the while on White Horse Hill
   The horse lay long and wan,
The turf crawled and the fungus crept,
And the little sorrel, while all men slept,
   Unwrought the work of man.

With velvet finger, velvet foot,
   The fierce soft mosses then
Crept on the large white commonweal
All folk had striven to strip and peel,
And the grass, like a great green witch's wheel,
   Unwound the toils of men.

And clover and silent thistle throve,
   And buds burst silently,
With little care for the Thames Valley
   Or what things there might be—

That away on the widening river,
   In the eastern plains for crown
Stood up in the pale purple sky
One turret of smoke like ivory;
And the smoke changed and the wind went by,
   And the King took London Town.[47]

---

[47] London Town was taken in A.D. 886.

V

SONGS FROM
THE FLYING INN
1912–1914

SONGS FROM THE FLYING INN (PLAY)

[THE TURK'S FIRST SONG]

La Illa, lalla la,
The words you know so well.
Not the trumpets of the Tartars
Or the hollow Christian bell.
Like the coffin of the Prophet
Swinging between God and Tophet.[1]
Even the voice of Man immortal
Crying between heaven and hell.
La Illa, lalla la,
The words you know so well.

OLD MARNE'S SONG
(A vivid picture of life in Buckingham Palace)

The king he lives in London Town,
I hope they will defend his crown,
And Bonyparte be quite put down
    On Christmas Day in the morning.

The king has servants three or four,
Three or four, or even more,
And he never opens his own front door
    On Christmas Day in the morning.

The songs from *The Flying Inn* would seem to have been written in 1912 for inclusion in a musical play. Chesterton later developed his play into a novel which appeared in 1914. In the meantime thirteen of the songs were given titles and contributed to "Songs of the Simple Life", a series of poems in Cecil Chesterton's *The New Witness* in 1912–1913. A fourth bite at the cherry was taken in 1915 when sixteen but not all were collected in *Wine, Water and Song* under new titles by which they are now best known. Finally in the late 1920s there was an attempt to use *The Flying Inn* as a libretto for an opera, a project which seems to have foundered after the stock-market crash of 1929.

[1] The Hell of the ancient Hebrews.

He wears a golden crown like fire
All round his hat as he may require
So he never need touch his hat to the squire
   On Christmas Day in the morning.

He drinks his cider and beer galore
And however he spills it on the floor
He can bang on the counter and call for more
   On Christmas Day in the morning

(*Chorus, sung by all with loud bangs on the table*)

He can bang on the counter and call for more
He can bang on the counter and call for more
He can bang on the counter and call for more
   On Christmas Day in the morning.

[THE SONG OF THE SIMPLE SOULS]
(Lady Enid's Song)

Whoever has come to the cloudless land
Where the good things grow like grass,
Where the folk stand up like the virgin trees
And their eyes are clean as glass;
Whoever has come through the crack of the world,
Whoever has known, we know
He has never come back, he has never come back
From the place where the good things grow.

Whoever has climbed to the cloudless place
Where the good things grow on trees,
Where the hare and the hunter play together
And Honour can dwell with Ease,
And the hole in the heart is stuffed at last
And pleasure is what we please;
Ah, that is a folly will never be found
Till good things grow on trees.

THE DUCHESS'S SONG

Is our ugliness utterly, utterly lovely,
Can we hair-split our hells?
Is it worse to grow sick of green noises
Or be torn by triangular smells,
To be deafened by daylight
Or throttled with bells?

Is toothache as truly as purple
As Tuesday is pink?
Can we choose between dung and dried hair—
Can we think? Can we think? Can we think?
Is it worse, the weak whisper of thunder,
Or the snigger of ink?

[THE TURK'S SECOND SONG]

Who shall ride after me; I am the Thunderbolt.
Who shall take hold on me; I am the flame.
Burning the world to the dust of the deserts,
Naming for ever the Name and the name.
            God is God
        On the gongs of the ages,
Sand and the sword and the song are the same.

Who shall make walls for me; I am the Wilderness.
Who shall lift shields for me; I am the Sun.
Seeing from of old in the height and the hollow
Doom that is written and all things done.
            God is God
        The immortal monotony
Words and the Word and the World are One.

GARGE'S SONG

My Uncle Green was a rare Old Bean
But he might have looked like a might-have-been
For he hadn't a bean, the dear old bean,
But he wasn't one of the grousers.
There was always a lot of us pinching grub
Or going on tick at the Ten Pin Pub,
And sucking up gin at the Temperance Club
There were bally old big carousers.
                    (*emphatically*)
But they weren't the patch of a patch on the patch
On the patch on Uncle's trousers!

When Uncle Garge had gone to the Race
There was nothing left but a hole in space
Of the empty pouch and the pushed-in face
Of the Bookie that Uncle laid for;
There was always a lot of them spry and keen
At begging a brown[1] from the Rooshin Queen
Or slipping a bob from the gas machine[2]
Which is what machines is made for—
But they 'adn't not 'arf of the 'arf-and 'arfs
That Uncle never paid for.

(*Chorus with thundering sympathy from the back.*)

But they 'adn't not 'arf of the 'arf-and-'arfs
That Uncle never paid for.

[1] A ten-shilling note.
[2] Stealing a shilling from the gas meter.

THE DUCHESS'S SECOND SONG

The days are dogs,
Black, bleeding, bloody dogs that dog
And drink the blood of the bourgeoisie.

The dogs are days,
Hot, screaming, scorching, scarlet days
That devour everything,
And establish the dominion of the International Proletariat.

[JOAN BRETT'S SONG]

The Men go down to the sea in ships
And the ships of men go down;
And it's woe for the long and laughing days
In the large forgetful town.
For the broad oblivious blank tomorrow
Where the sorriest sight is to see no sorrow,
Nor the thoughtless think how the nameless fares;
And nobody knows and nobody cares
When Nobody's ship goes down.

But it's woe and woe for the shining hour
When all our ships come home—
To a strange harbour and a strange town
The feet of strangers come.
And left in the tavern and lost in the throng
Are the more than dead that have lived too long;
And a new house stands and a stranger stares;
And nobody knows and nobody cares
When Nobody's ship comes home.

DALROY'S SERENADE

Lady, the light is dying in the skies,
Lady, and let us die when honour dies;
Your dear, dropped glove was like a gauntlet flung
    When you and I were young,
For something more than splendour stood; and
    ease was not the only good,
About the woods in Ivywood, when you and I were young.

Lady, the stars are falling pale and small,
Lady, we will not live if life be all,
Forgetting those good stars in heaven hung,
    When all the world was young;
For more than gold was in a ring, and love was
    not a little thing,
Between the trees in Ivywood, when all the world was young.

                              (ca. 1912)

SONGS FROM THE FLYING INN (NOVEL)

[MACAULAY IN *VERS LIBRE*]

While flows the sacred river,
While stands the sacred hill,
The proud old pantaloons and nincompoops
Who yawn at the very length of their own lies
In that accursed sanhedrim where
People put each other's hats on in a poisonous room
With no more windows than hell,
Shall have such honour still.

The following songs from *The Flying Inn* novel appear in *Collected Poetry*, Part I: "The Englishman", p. 435, "The Good Rich Man", p. 498, "The Logical Vegetarian", p. 451, "Me Heart", p. 454, "Pioneers, O Pioneers", p. 458, "The Road to Roundabout", p. 465, "The Rolling English Road", p. 467, "The Saracen's Head", p. 468, "The Song against Grocers", p. 470, "The Song against Songs", p. 474, "The Song of Right and Wrong", p. 475, "The Song of the Dog Quoodle", p. 477, "The Song of the Oak", p. 479, "Wine and Water", p. 490.

[THE ROAD]

The road turned first towards the left
Where Pinker's quarry made the cleft;
The path turned next towards the right,
Because the mastiff used to bite,
Then left, because of Slippery Height,
And then again towards the right—
We could not take the left because
It would have been against the laws:
Squire closed it in King William's day
Because it was a Right of Way.
Still right; to dodge the ridge of chalk
Where Parson's Ghost it used to walk,
Till some one Parson used to know
Met him blind drunk in Callao.
Then left, a long way round, to skirt
The good land, where old Doggy Burt
Was owner of the "Crown and Cup",
And would not give his freehold up;
Right, missing the old river-bed,
They tried to make him take instead
Right, since they say Sir Gregory
Went mad and let the Gipsies be,
And so they have their camp secure:
And though not honest, they are poor;
And that is something; then along
And first to right—no, I am wrong!
Second to right of course; the first
Is what the holy sisters cursed,
And none defy their awful oaths
Since the policeman lost his clothes
Because of fairies; right again
What used to be High Toby Lane,
Left by the double larch and right
Until the milestone is in sight,

Because the road is firm and good
From past the milestone to the wood.
And I was told by Dr. Lowe,
Whom Mr. Wimpole's aunt would know,
Who lives at Oxford writing books,
And ain't so silly as he looks,
The Romans did that little bit
And we've done all the rest of it,
By which we hardly seem to score.
Left and then forward as before
To where they nearly hanged Miss Browne,
Who told them not to cut her down,
But loose the rope or let her swing
Because it was a waste of string;
Left once again by Hunker's Cleft
And right beyond the elm, and left
By Pills's, right by Nineteen Nicks
And left——

(1914)

VI

POEMS 1912–1914

[GLITTER]

All is gold that glitters—
   Tree and tower of brass;
Rolls the golden evening air
   Down the golden grass.
Kick the cry to Jericho,
   How yellow mud is sold;
All is gold that glitters,
   For the glitter is the gold.
     (from *Manalive*, 1912)

[OUR ANGEL, MICHAEL]
"Michael Angelorum dux in bellis primus ac
clarissimus a domo tamen coelesti diu abest"
    —St. Thomas Aquinas,
     Summa Contra Gentes[1]

Translation (by a Person of Quality)

Our Angel, Michael,[2] is a warrior good
And kicks the ball about as angels should,
But somewhat is he given to linger and roam,
And come in late to his quite heavenly home.
Those hours come round, when next the youth is seen,
Like angels' visits few and far between.

          (ca. 1912)

---

[1] "Michael of the angels is the first and most brilliant leader in wars; however, he is for a long time absent from the heavenly home." Quote does not seem to exist as such in *Summa Contra Gentes*.

[2] Michael Braybrooke was a young cousin of Frances Chesterton. After the Braybrooke marriage ran into difficulties he was semi-adopted by the Chestertons and lived with them in Beaconsfield until he left school to join the Royal Naval Air Service during the course of the First World War. Later his medical studies were funded by Chesterton.

[I AM FOND OF JEWS]

I am fond of Jews;
Jews are fond of money:
Never mind of whose,
I am fond of Jews.
Oh, but when they lose,
Damn it all, it's funny.
[I am fond of Jews,
Jews are fond of money.]
(ca. 1912)

About 1912 Dr. Pocock of Beaconsfield was attending GKC who had broken his arm. The doctor "told him at a certain stage to write something—anything—to see if he could use a pen again. After an instant's thought, Gilbert headed his paper with the name of a prominent Jew and wrote: *I am fond of Jews. . . .* The name at the head (which wild horses would not drag from me) is the key to this impromptu." (Maisie Ward, *Gilbert Keith Chesterton*, London and New York (Sheed and Ward) 1944.

It would seem that Dr. Pocock had kept the original piece and handed it to either Dorothy Collins or Maisie Ward. Unfortunately, the paper was either lost in the London blitz when Sheed and Ward's offices were hit by a bomb or was thrown away once it had been published in the biography (there is some evidence to suggest that this may have been common practice). The lines are in the form of a defective Triolet, so it is possible that the two missing lines were also cut by Maisie Ward at Miss Collins's insistence. We have made good the two lines omitted by following the usual pattern of the triolet form, but it is possible, even probable, that the original lines identified the man who had lost money.

A CIDER SONG
To J. S. M.

(Extract from a Romance which is not yet written and probably never will be)

The wine they drink in Paradise
They make in Haute Lorraine;
God brought it burning from the sod
To be a sign and signal rod
That they that drink the blood of God
Shall never thirst again.

The wine they praise in Paradise
They make in Ponterey,
The purple wine of Paradise,
But we have better at the price;
It's wine they praise in Paradise,
It's cider that they pray.

The wine they want in Paradise
They find in Plodder's End,
The apple wine of Hereford,
Of Hafod Hill and Hereford,
Where woods went down to Hereford,
And there I had a friend.

The soft feet of the blessed go
In the soft western vales,
The road the silent saints accord,
The road from heaven to Hereford,
Where the apple wood of Hereford
Goes all the way to Wales.

(from *Odd Volume*, 1912)

J. S. M. was probably John Saxon Mills (d. 1929), a friend and neighbor of GKC when he and Frances lived in Overstrand Mansions in Battersea. He later moved and took a job in Herefordshire, which is known for its cider.

ANTICHRIST, OR THE REUNION
OF CHRISTENDOM: AN ODE
(Lines to F. E. Smith)
"A bill which has shocked the conscience of every
Christian community in Europe."
— Mr. F. E. Smith,
on the Welsh Disestablishment Bill

Are they clinging to their crosses,
            F. E. Smith,[1]
Where the Breton boat-fleet tosses,
            Are they, Smith?
Do they, fasting, trembling, bleeding,
    Wait the news from this our city?
Groaning "That's the Second Reading!"
    Hissing "There is still Committee!"
If the voice of Cecil falters,
    If McKenna's point has pith,
Do they tremble for their altars?
            Do they, Smith?

Russian peasants round their pope
            Huddled, Smith,
Hear about it all, I hope,
            Don't they, Smith?
In the mountain hamlets clothing
    Peaks beyond Caucasian pales,
Where Establishment means nothing
    And they never heard of Wales,
Do they read it all in Hansard[2]
    With a crib to read it with—

---

[1] F.E. Smith (1872–1930), later 1st Earl of Birkenhead, was a brilliant advocate in court, but on this occasion had gone over the top with his rhetoric. The Welsh Disestablishment Bill was passed, disestablishing the Church of Wales as the official church in a country which was largely Non-Conformist. A year later Smith prosecuted Cecil Chesterton in the Marconi trial.

[2] The daily record of proceedings in the British parliament, named after its first editor.

"Welsh Tithes: Dr. Clifford[3] Answered."
                    Really, Smith?

In the lands where Christians were,
                    F. E. Smith,
In the little lands laid bare,
                    Smith, O Smith!
Where the Turkish bands are busy,
    And the Tory name is blessed
Since they hailed the Cross of Dizzy[4]
    On the banners from the West!
Men don't think it half so hard if
    Islam burns their kin and kith,
Since a curate lives in Cardiff
                    Saved by Smith.

It would greatly, I must own,
                    Soothe me, Smith!
If you left this theme alone,
                    Holy Smith!
For your legal cause or civil
    You fight well and get your fee:
For your God or dream or devil
    You will answer, not to me.
Talk about the pews and steeples
    And the Cash that goes therewith!
But the souls of Christian peoples ...
                    Chuck it, Smith!
(from *The Eye Witness*, May 30, 1912)

[3] The Rev. John Clifford, M.A., L.L.B., D.D. (1836–1923), a Baptist minister much involved in attacking various bills passing through the British parliament.

[4] Dizzy—Benjamin Disraeli (1804–81), Lord Beaconsfield, Leader of the British Conservative Party and Prime Minister on several occasions, was also known as a novelist.

MARCH OF THE BLACK MOUNTAIN

What will there be to remember
   Of us in the days to be?
Whose faith was a trodden ember
   And even our doubts not free;
Parliaments built of paper,
   And the soft swords of gold
That twist like a waxen taper
   In the weak aggressor's hold;
A hush around Hunger, slaying
   A city of serfs unfed;
What shall we leave for a saying
   To praise us when we are dead?
But men shall remember the Mountain
   That broke its forest chains,
And men shall remember the Mountain
   When it arches against the plains:
And christen their children from it
   And season and ship and street,
When the Mountain came to Mahomet
   And looked small before his feet.

His head was as high as the crescent
   Of the moon that seemed his crown,
And on glory of past and present
   The light of his eyes looked down;
One hand went out to the morning
   Over Brahmin and Buddhist slain,
And one to the west in scorning
   To point at the scars of Spain:
One foot on the hills for warden
   By the little Mountain trod;
And one was in a garden
   And stood on the grave of God.
But men shall remember the Mountain,
   Though it fall down like a tree,

They shall see the sign of the Mountain
   Faith cast into the sea;
Though the crooked swords overcome it
   And the Crooked Moon ride free,
When the Mountain comes to Mahomet
   It has more life than he.

But what will there be to remember
   Or what will there be to see—
Though our towns through a long November
   Abide to the end and be?
Strength of slave and mechanic
   Whose iron is ruled by gold,
Peace of immortal panic,
   Love that is hate grown cold—
Are these a bribe or a warning
   That we turn not to the sun,
Nor look on the lands of morning
   Where deeds at last are done?
Where men shall remember the Mountain
   When truth forgets the plain—
And walk in the way of the Mountain
   That did not fail in vain;
Death and eclipse and comet,
   Thunder and seals that rend:
When the Mountain came to Mahomet;
   Because it was the end.
       (from *Daily News*, October 31, 1912)

WHEN I CAME BACK TO FLEET STREET

When I came back to Fleet Street,[1]
    Through a sunset nook at night,
And saw the old Green Dragon[2]
    With the windows all alight,
And hailed the old Green Dragon
    And the Cock[3] I used to know,
Where all good fellows were my friends
    A little while ago;

I had been long in meadows,
    And the trees took hold of me,
And the still towns in the beech-woods,
    Where men were meant to be.
But old things held; the laughter,
    The long unnatural night,
And all the truth they talk in hell,
    And all the lies they write.

For I came back to Fleet Street,
    And not in peace I came;
A cloven pride was in my heart,
    And half my love was shame.
I came to fight in fairy tale,
    Whose end shall no man know
To fight the old Green Dragon
    Until the Cock shall crow!

Under the broad bright windows
    Of men I serve no more,

Cf. a shorter version in *Collected Poetry*, Part I, p. 489.

[1] A London thoroughfare running from the end of the Strand down to Ludgate Circus below St. Paul's; its name was once synonymous with newspaper offices, printing works and journalism.

[2] The site of an historic inn at 56 South Fleet Street.

[3] The Olde Cock, a tavern at 22 Fleet Street.

The groaning of the old great wheels
　　Thickened to a throttled roar:
All buried things broke upward;
　　And peered from its retreat,
Ugly and silent, like an elf,
　　The secret of the street.[4]

They did not break the padlocks,
　　Or clear the wall away.
The men in debt that drank of old
　　Still drink in debt today;
Chained to the rich by ruin,
　　Cheerful in chains, as then
When old unbroken Pickwick[5] walked
　　Among the broken men.

Still he that dreams and rambles
　　Through his own elfin air,
Knows that the street's a prison,
　　Knows that the gates are there:
Still he that scorns or struggles
　　Sees, frightful and afar,
All that they leave of rebels
　　Rot high on Temple Bar.[6]

All that I loved and hated,
　　All that I shunned and knew,

[4] It had long been the site of a prison, latterly a debtor's prison.

[5] In Charles Dickens' *Pickwick Papers* kind-hearted Mr. Samuel Pickwick finds the jaunty rogue Alfred Jingle sick and imprisoned in the Fleet and redeems his debts.

[6] Former Gate of the City of London where the heads of executed criminals were displayed. It stood at the junction of the Strand and of Fleet Street by the present Law Courts until, judged to be a bottleneck for traffic, it was dismantled in January 1878 and then rebuilt in Theobalds Park in Cheshunt, Hertfordshire. A campaign for its return to the City of London finally saw success on November 10, 2004 when it was reconstructed on a site next to St. Paul's Cathedral.

Clears in broad battle lightning,
Where they, and I, and you,
Run high the barricade that breaks
The barriers of the street,
And shout to them that shrink within,
The Prisoners of the Fleet.[7]
(from *The New Witness*, March 13, 1913.)

THE HYGIENIST IN HEAVEN[1]

If all the schoolgirls' heads were shaved
Karl Busch believed we might be saved.
No doubt the task was steep and slow;
For hair was started long ago
And still keeps growing everywhere,
But give him beans and filtered air,
The Vacuum Bed of Dr. Funcke,
No labourers—and no liquids—drunk,
No Bibles and no babies kissed,
And—well, he was an optimist.

While he reviled, in writings wroth,
The "Kissing of the Gospel" oath
(For, quite apart from microbes, this
Was the last thing he wished to kiss).

[7] The Fleet Prison once stood east of Farringdon Street on the site now occupied by the Memorial Hall until it was demolished in 1845–1846. Its name was taken from the River Fleet, a waterway once navigable as far as Holborn but now long culverted as a sewer until it joins the Thames at Blackfriars Bridge. Chesterton insinuates that journalists are in thrall to the newspaper moguls of his day.

[1] GKC wrote a number of poems, including this one, for a "Rhymes for the Times" series in *The Eye-Witness*. Among these were "The Shakespeare Memorial", "The Horrible History of Jones", "The Orator of the Opposition" and "The New Free Thinker", all of which are included in *Collected Poetry*, Part I.

Tired with his own entrancing prose
He chanced to fall into a doze;
And by some very strange device
Supposed himself in Paradise,
Or such a Paradise as he
Had heard of from his family;
Where on a cloudland cold and flat
The god of all his fathers sat.
He thought the gold and glassy sea
Was dangerously slippery;
He thought the windy blazonings
Of feathers in the seraphs' wings
That swayed like wheels about their heads
As perilous as feather-beds.
But though he feared the plumes and seas,
And feared to breathe or blink or sneeze,
And feared to walk or stand or fall,
He did not fear his god at all.
"I know you what you are," he said,
"Some tribal seer or chief long dead,
A man at least, a common birth,
Science has hunted you to earth.
You that were God, what are you now?"

The insulted reared his thunderous brow
And, smiling dreadfully, said, "True,
I was a man. But what are you?"
(from the *Eye-Witness*, October 31, 1913)

A SONG OF GIFTS TO GOD

When the first Christmas presents came, the straw where Christ was
   rolled
Smelt sweeter than their frankincense, burnt brighter than their gold,
And a wise man said, "We will not give; the thanks would be but cold."

"Nay," said the next. "To all new gifts, to this gift or another,
Bends the high gratitude of God; even as He now, my brother,
Who had a Father for all time, yet thanks Him for a Mother.

"Yet scarce for Him this yellow stone or prickly smells and sparse,
Who holds the gold heart of the sun that fed these timber bars,
Nor any scentless lily lives for One that smells the stars."

Then spake the third of the Wise Men, the wisest of the three;
"We may not with the widest lives enlarge His liberty,
Whose wings are wider than the world. It is not He, but we.

"We say He has more to gain, but we have less to lose.
Less gold shall go astray, we say, less gold, if thus we choose,
Go to make harlots of the Greeks and hucksters of the Jews.

"Less clouds before colossal feet redden in the underlight,
To the blind gods from Babylon less incense burn to-night,
To the high beasts of Babylon, whose mouths make mock of right."

Babe of the thousand birthdays, we that are young yet grey,
White with the centuries, still can find no better thing to say,
We that with sects and whims and wars have wasted Christmas Day.

Light Thou Thy censer to Thyself, for all our fires are dim,
Stamp Thou Thine image on our coins, for Caesar's face grows grim,
And a dumb devil of pride and greed has taken hold of him.

We bring Thee back great Christendom, churches and towns and
   towers,
And if our hands are glad, O God, to cast them down like flowers,
'Tis not that they enrich Thine hands, but they are saved from ours.

                  (from *Pall Mall Magazine*, December 1913)

A CHRISTMAS SONG FOR THREE GUILDS
(To be sung a long time ago—or hence)

The Carpenters

St. Joseph to the Carpenters said on a Christmas Day:
"The master shall have patience and the 'prentice shall obey;
And your word unto your women shall be nowise hard or wild:
For the sake of me, your master, who have worshipped Wife and Child.
But softly you shall frame the fence, and softly carve the door,
And softly plane the table—as to spread it for the poor,
And all your thoughts be soft and white as the wood of the white tree.
But if they tear the Charter, let the tocsin speak for me!
Let the wooden sign above your shop be prouder to be scarred
Than the lion-shield of Lancelot that hung at Joyous Garde."

The Shoemakers

St. Crispin to the shoemakers said on a Christmastide:
"Who fashions at another's feet will get no good of pride.
They were bleeding on the Mountain, the feet that brought good news,
The latchet of whose shoes we were not worthy to unloose.
See that your feet offend not, nor lightly lift your head,
Tread softly on the sunlit roads the bright dust of the dead.
Let your own feet be shod with peace; be lowly all your lives.
But if they touch the Charter, ye shall nail it with your knives.
And the bill-blades of the commons drive in all as dense array
As once a crash of arrows came, upon St. Crispin's Day."

The Painters

St. Luke unto the painters on Christmas Day he said:
"See that the robes are white you dare to dip in gold and red;
For only gold the kings can give, and only blood the saints.
And his high task grows perilous that mixes them in paints.
Keep you the ancient order; follow the men that knew
The labyrinth of black and white, the maze of green and blue;
Paint mighty things, paint paltry things, paint silly things or sweet,
But if men break the Charter, you may slay them in the street.

And if you paint one post for them, then ... but you know it well,
You paint a harlot's face to drag all heroes down to hell."

All together

Almighty God to all mankind on Christmas Day said he:
"I rent you from the old red hills and, rending, made you free.
There was charter, there was challenge; in a blast of breath I gave;
You can be all things other; you cannot be a slave.
You shall be tired and tolerant of fancies as they fade,
But if men doubt the Charter, ye shall call on the Crusade—
Trumpet and torch and catapult, cannon and bow and blade,
Because it was My challenge to all the things I made."

(from *The New Witness*, December 25, 1913)

[A THANK-YOU FOR A GIFT OF CIGARETTES]

Your cigarettes have long ago
Laid the presumptuous Post low.[1]
Quoodle has smoked the cigarettes
And has been taken to the vet's.

(ca. 1913)

BREAKING GLASS[1]

Prince, when I took your goblet tall,
And smashed it with inebriate care,
I knew not how from Rome and Gaul
You gained it; I was unaware
It stood by Charlemagne's great chair
And served St. Peter at High Mass
... I'm sorry if the thing was rare,
I like the noise of breaking glass.

(ca. 1913–1914)

[1] Post was one of the Chestertons' cats. Quoodle was their Scottish Highland terrier, the successor to Winkle.

[1] Chesterton's apology for breaking a wine-glass at Auberon Herbert's dinner table.

TO LORD CLAUD HAMILTON AND ANOTHER

"General Botha is a man. Such men are wanted in the
    United Kingdom." —Lord Claud Hamilton.[1]
"Botha is a man of firmness." —*Unionist Evening Paper*

He is a man. Rich and arresting thought.
His nose, I hear, sticks forward; it ought,
Having indeed no other way to stick.
Lord Claud, whose passion is arithmetic,
Counts and recounts the legs and counts anew,
And always brings it out that there are two.
B. is not covered (as was said) with scales.
He has *not* eight, or indeed any, tails.
He has no horns. A Devil may have two,
But he is not a devil. Strange, but true.

Alas, my lord, and was there not a time
Some of us call glory, some of [us] crime,
When he showed more of manhood than he needs
To fling away poor weedy serfs like weeds?
When Englishmen had horses they might ride,
When all the guns were not on Botha's side,
When stricken of storm from heaven or light from hell,
Ruin or dawn, awhile [his] republic fell;
When through the Laud of Lies he blindly spurred,
The man might have been grateful for the word,
When all your jackals cursed with grinning jaws
A brainless stiffness in a hopeless cause,
Could they not then have said, as foemen can,
"He loves his land; a man is but a man."
When his own farmstead turned his heavens red,
Fired by the stranger, could they not have said

---

[1] Lord Claud Hamilton (1843–1925) was Second Lord of The Treasury in the
Balfour government of 1902–06. General Louis Botha (1862–1919) was the youngest
general in the Boer forces during the South African War. He became the first prime
minister of the Union of South Africa.

In the camps paved with many a baby's grave,
"He loves his home; it is a way men have".
But no; the slander-storm went none the slower,
Your courage comes a little late, Pro-Boer.

For you, New Tory of the ink-soiled trade,
Whom foreign foes bid call a spear a spade,
Who on Dutch kicks and Yiddish bribes have thriven,
Whose trembling fingers have torn down and given
The Union Jack up to this first of foes
To wipe his bloody knife and blow his nose—
Lie down; curl up; do anything you can,
You will not be mistaken for a man.
(from *The New Witness*, April 2, 1914)

THE MAY QUEEN
(Adapted and set to music by Lord Reading of Earley)[1]

If they take me, call me Earley, call me Earley, brother dear.[2]
Tomorrow will be the rummiest start of all the glad New Year,
Of all the glad New Year, brother, so much the maddest day.
For I'm to be L.C.J.[3] Chase me! I'm to be L.C.J.

There's many a black, black eye, they say, but none so blacked as mine;
Samuel[4] and George[5] and Murray[6] stood to be thumped in line;
Yet none so thumped as Rufus in all the land they say,
So I'm to be L.C.J. Rummy! I'm to be L.C.J.

[1] Lord Reading of Earley—Rufus Isaacs (1860–1935) Lord Reading of Erleigh, Lord Chief Justice and later Viceroy of India, was alleged to be involved in insider trading in shares of the American Marconi Company in 1912, an accusation which led to the prosecution of G. K. Chesterton's brother Cecil, editor of *The Eye Witness* for libel.

[2] Godfrey Isaacs (?–1925), Chairman and managing director of the Marconi Company, brother of Rufus.

[3] Lord Chief Justice, head of the English legal system and Speaker of the House of Lords.

[4] Herbert Samuel (1870–1963), Post-Master General responsible for awarding contracts for the establishment of a British Empire-wide telegraph service.

[5] David Lloyd George (1859–1940), later prime Minister 1916–1922.

[6] Alexander Murray (1870–1920), chief whip of the British Liberal Party.

I thought they'd hoof me out before, but still alive I am,
And all the Tories[7] round me are bleating like the lamb,
And now I think it can't be long before I find release,
And that good man, the Party Man, has told me words of peace.

To live and live in Parliament,[8] where rich men feel at home,
And there to wait a little while till you and Harry[9] come;
To live like old Boccacio's boys[10] that camped beyond the Pest;
Where the honest cease from troubling, and the wicked are at rest.

(April 16, 1914)

ALLITERATIVISM
(the Latest School)
"French airmen have been flying over Baden
and Bavaria, violating Belgian neutrality."
Stated on German authority in the *Westminster Gazette*

See the flying French depart
Like the bees of Bonaparte,
Swarming up with a most venomous vitality.
Over Baden and Bavaria,
And Brighton and Bulgaria,
Thus violating Belgian neutrality.

And the injured Prussian may
Not unreasonably say
"Why, it cannot be so small a nationality!
Since Brixton and Batavia,
Bolivia and Belgravia,
Are bursting with the Belgian neutrality.

---

[7] Members of the British Conservative Party.

[8] The Lord Chief Justice is entitled to live in a suite of rooms in the Victoria Tower of the Palace of Westminster.

[9] Godfrey and Harry Isaacs, Rufus Isaac's brothers.

[10] In Boccacio's *Decameron* tales are told by a group camping outside Florence to escape the effect of the plague which is rampant in the city.

By pure Alliteration
You may trace this curious nation,
And respect this somewhat scattered principality;
When you see a B in Both
You may take your Bible oath
You are violating Belgian neutrality.
          (from *The New Witness*, August 13, 1914)

BALLADE OF THE SECRET OF OUR HAPPINESS

Why do the English sing and dance all day?
Why does their rapture never seem to pall?
It is a mystery. We can but say
No French conscription keeps us all in thrall,
No German bread our people can appall,
No Russian censor blackens our free press
Our breakfast rolls are round and rather small;
It is the secret of our happiness.

Our uniforms are red, the German's grey.
The French footguards are short and ours are tall,
The Paris traffic turns the other way
To what we all are used to by Whitehall.
Our middle class hold tea-cups when they call,
Our upper classes dine in evening dress,
Our lower classes never dine at all;
It is the secret of our happiness.

Envoi

Prince, take this packet folded very small
    Of such minute and precious littleness
That some declare it isn't there at all;
    It is the secret of our happiness.
          (ca. 1914)

Scribbled on the end papers of GKC's undated, small-format edition of William
Makepeace Thackeray's *Book of Snobs* issued by Collins.

THE GREAT MINIMUM

It is something to have wept as we have wept,
It is something to have done as we have done,
It is something to have watched when all men slept,
And seen the stars which never see the sun.

It is something to have smelt the mystic rose,
Although it break and leave the thorny rods,
It is something to have hungered once as those
Must hunger who have ate the bread of gods.

To have seen you and your unforgotten face,
Brave as a blast of trumpets for the fray,
Pure as white lilies in a watery space,
It were something, though you went from me to-day.

To have known the things that from the weak are furled,
Perilous ancient passions, strange and high;
It is something to be wiser than the world,
It is something to be older than the sky.

In a time of sceptic moths and cynic rusts,
And fatted lives that of their sweetness tire,
In a world of flying loves and fading lusts,
It is something to be sure of a desire.

Lo, blessed are our ears for they have heard;
Yea, blessed are our eyes for they have seen:
Let thunder break on man and beast and bird
And the lightning. It is something to have been.

(pre-1915)

VII

POEMS WRITTEN FOR
FREDERICA ELIZABETH
SPENCER
1914–1919

The Beaconsfield Fancy Dress Fair.

Miss Freda Spencer accused of being the Queen of Beauty at a Tournament. —

From 1914 until 1919 Frederica "Freda" Elizabeth Spencer (1892–1973) was G. K. Chesterton's secretary. Walter Opsomer, a refugee Flemish boy whose family was billetted next door during the Great War of 1914–1918, noted that she was extremely pretty.

[THE WOOING OF JULIAN ALVAREZ]

A CIGAR-MAKER'S ROMANCE

Smoke for me only with thine eyes
And I'll inhale with mine
And save the Belgian matches while
Thy brighter eyes shall shine.
The ritual incense still doth rise
In Wheatfield's jewelled shrine.
But had I thuribles three score
The incense should be thine.

I gave thee once a good Cigar
Not so much meant for thee,
As that I thought that, if begun,
It would not finished be,
But thou thereon didst only glance
And chucked it back to me
Since when it glows and smells, I swear,
Not of itself but thee.

Julian Alvarez
From the Companion Volume to
"A Cigarette-Maker's Romance"
by F[rancis] Marion Crawford
(ca. 1915)

HABAÑA

Julian the Unapostate—undismayed
By Frederica's coldness, shows his face,
Worn by long waiting, by fierce longing frayed,
To such wan charms and thin ethereal grace.

Chesterton seems to have delighted in teasing his secretary Frederica Spencer about possible suitors by imagining that Julian Alvarez, the cigar manufacturer whose portrait appeared on his cigarboxes and cigarbands was one of them. Billets-doux in the form of poems would be left near the cigar-box or alongside the stubs in the ashtray. For another jest about suitors see "To Freda Spencer", *Collected Poetry*, Part I, p. 329.

Look, girl, upon the pallid wreck you made;
Demon, behold your work, let conscience hiss
You have reduced a substance to a shade,
A fairly solid gentleman to this.

Yet still his portraits shall pursue your ways
And every portrait frailer than the last,
Yet leaner than the form on which you gaze,
Ghastlier than this which leaves you now aghast,

Till even these last faint lines of loveliness
Shall fail and vanish in the void coerulean;
And a black doom shall smite and stun you. Yes!
To look no more upon the face of Julian.

                                        (ca. 1915)

FRAGMENT BY F.E.S.

Who stood to catch me when I fell
From work, and gave me tales to tell
To read as fast as I could spell?
                My Mother

Who saved me from the wrath of Pam
As lightsome as a London tram,
Which made me—rhyme with Mary's lamb?
                My Mother

Who saved me from the blasted bore
Of typing rubbish more and more
By that ...
                    (*Hiatus Valde defendus*)[1]
                    (ca. 1916)

See "Lines by the Late Lord Tennyson", *Collected Poetry*, Part I, p. 299 and "Bal-
lade of Apologies to a Secretary", Part II, p. 458.
    [1] "The omission vigorously defended"

TO ELFREDA
That she should write a Romance

Elfreda, take your pen and write,
Or take your typewriter and rattle.
Trust me, it is not lies so white
That wrong the royal truth of battle.

Now hearts have first, in parting, met,
And men grow simple in strong pain,
A novel may be novel yet
And old Romance ride home again.

Dare what our boldest spinsters banned,
Who left the crimes of *Cranford*[1] dark,
Or tell us why no human hand
Murdered Miss Price in *Mansfield Park*.[2]

In passion's scarlet hieroglyphs
Tell us Miss Yonge[3] is young again,
Give us an heir of Redder Cliffs,
A yet more crimson *Daisy Chain*.

Give us a Hero marked from men,
Put in the house with haunted wings,
Shove in the dear old Dreary fen—
—Believe me there are drearier things.

Ah, lady, there are duller dreams,
And lies that are not white—or pink,
Where Harmsworth's[4] hireling scrawling reams,
Splashes in English blood for ink.

See "Lines to a Young Lady Born Before April Fool's Day", *Collected Poetry*, Part I, p. 301–2.

[1] The novel (1853) by Mrs. Elizabeth Gaskell (1810–1865).

[2] The novel (1814) by Jane Austen (1775–1817).

[3] Charlotte Mary Yonge (1823–1901), author of *Heir of Redclyffe* (1853) and over a hundred other books.

[4] Alfred Harmsworth (1865–1922), 1st Viscount Northcliffe, newspaper proprietor of the *Daily Mail* (1896), *Daily Mirror* (1903) and *The Times* (1908).

Things spies have pilfered, hacks have penned,
And false as only facts can be—
Here falsehood sells her slaves, my friend,
Walk into fiction and be free.

Family Heralds shift the tale,
Yvonne to Viola, Joan to Jill,
Leave the pale clerk his *Daily Mail*,
Stick to the *Weekly Female* still.

He reads the Leaders that mislead,
The News that is not even new,
What Cowards, as they run, may read,
—Walk into fiction and be true.

Write, that the England of our sires
With you returning, may return,
With books to read beside our fires
And newspapers to make them burn.

That we, in this deserted house,
Far down the Oxford road may see
Blaze in a more emblazoned blouse
The Herald of the Family.

                              (ca. 1916)

The Habit of — Changing Hats —

Miss Freda Spencer and the Bolshevik Ambassador
A Study on Hampstead Heath

See "Ballade of a Hat Forgone", *Collected Poetry*, Part II, p. 458.

LINES TO A FRIEND
APPREHENSIVE OF A SHORTAGE
OF FOOD IN BEACONSFIELD

Lady, you will not, when you come,
Devour us out of house and home,
Nor do I think you come, indeed,
Impelled by undiluted greed,
Or merely seek our poor abodes
To over-eat at Overroads,
Or merely come to make the Rectory
Alter its name to the Refectory,
Out of mere vanity to win
A double or a treble chin,
Or hope to shake this wood and weald,
A larger Mrs. Inglefield.

Dear Freda, no. Food has been seen
Between Hall Barn and Knotty Green.
Men walk our ways, whose pasts reveal
The far-off memory of a meal.
Your fatter friends, through all the dearth,
Fill their appointed space on earth.
Lord Burnham (if by force of will)
Is stouter than Lord Stopford still;
And Becky Child, on closer view,
Is still a shade more thick than you.
And I, a frailer lily, last
—Bent but not broken by the blast.

Shelley, the ethereal bard, who had
A tidy income from his dad,
Sang (as his month's allowance came)
That poets live on love and fame:

Food shortages were common during the First World War (1914–1918). See "Songs to an Old Tune", *Collected Poetry*, Part I, p. 316.

The Poet who has penned these lines
On more material matter dines;
And with his fame and love, will take
A casual Ham, a trifling Steak;
And sends, in this disgraceful verse you view,
His fame to blazes and his love to you.

(ca. 1917)

WARSASH, 1917

The clotted woods are dim, the day
Ever expires and still expands:
The River finds its wandering way
From what unfathomable lands,
And God who made our hearts so great,
Our little hearts that hold the world,
Hangs this high moment with a weight
Of banners drooping, but not furled.

For we too broaden though we fade,
And we too deepen though we die,
Waste in what fashion we were made
And die of immortality—
And something rooted like the tree
Can hear unquelled, although it quiver,
Ancestral voices of the sea
That call the unreturning river.

Wide windows of the soul enlightened
Of these wide waters and the light—
Seeing whatever stars have brightened
Since eyes of men were sad and bright.
Fear not the dust or dusk hereafter
That darkens this dear land and leaves
The loves that found us and the laughter
Upon so many summer eves.

For not in rains of weeping rotten
Nor choked in thorns of thwarting, ends
The greatness of the unforgotten,
The silence of the pride of friends.
And sad with songs yet good and gay
And weak with no ignoble things
We look on this white waste of day
Where silence is alone and sings.

The clustered trees are all a cloud,
A vision and a voiceless wraith;
Fading in fulness, like a cloud
Of final thoughts that fade to faith:
But richer than the jewelled nights
That build beyond Southampton Bar
A ladder of the harbour-lights
From England to the evening star.

(1917)

Chesterton accompanied Winston Churchill on a trip to Warsash on the Solent. Freda Spencer, Churchill's cousin and Chesterton's secretary, fell into the water and was rescued by her cousin, who was inspecting sea-plane production.

TO FREDERICA

When pigs can fly and seas are dry
In the impossible bye-and-bye,
When you are shaved and I am saved
And little Mac is well behaved,
When Mrs. Wace improves her face
And God redeems the Hebrew race,
When the flashing Gerald saves hosts imperilled
In a brilliant tale for the *Family Herald*,
When poor Miss Watts comes out in spots
From drinking beer in pots and pots,
When kind Miss Woods gives all her goods
To Roman Catholic sisterhoods,
When old Le Pla drinks at the bar
And says "You know what barmaids are!"
When Mrs. Timms composes hymns
Suited to choirs of cherubims,
When Mr. Bord, grown legs absurd,
Obeys his partner's lightest word,
When Mrs. Commeline[1] ceases pummelin'
(I really can't drag Cayley Drummle in),
When the inspector arrests the Rector
As a bogus company director,
When we see Miss Homan a travelling showman
In the uniform of an Ancient Roman,
When poor old Wink takes pen and ink
To prove he is the Missing Link,
When Auntie Frances has psychic trances
(Whereby the Astral Self advances),
When Cecil Palmer, at last grown calmer,
Shall seek at last some other charmer,

---

[1] The wife of the Vicar of Beaconsfield. The others are all neighbors in Beaconsfield, some of whom are mentioned in "Ballade of an Ethical Lady", also written for Freda Spencer in *Collected Poetry*, Part II, p. 461.

In short when we at last shall see
The ineffable things that cannot be,
Then shall a weaker, more breathless speaker,
Finish your poem, Frederica.

(ca. 1917)

LINES BY THE WEDDING MARCH HARE
ST. GEORGE'S DAY 1919

Lady, I think that long ago
A man so mixed we fail to pen him,
The splendid schemer of your house,
Laid out a bolder plan than Blenheim:
Great Churchill to Godolphin spoke,
Peruques together, to provide
A plan that, by such wandering ways
Should lead the bridegroom and the bride.

So should Godolphin's gold preserve
In school and scholar yet to come
The iron tongue our fathers loved,
The laurel and the lyre of Rome:
And Churchill's tree should spread and speak
To each chance heir and far succeeder
"For Woe and Winston weep no more,
Rejoice in Freedom and in Freda."

Thus could new Sarum[1] wax and bloom
And bear for England's eye the apple
(For the large building you observe
Is not the Seventh Day Baptist chapel)

Freda Spencer married Thomas Henry Bayley on St. George's Day, April 23, 1919,
after which she took a position at Godolphin House School in Salisbury. See "Lines to
the Air of 'Godolphin Horne'", *Collected Poetry*, Part I, p. 303, and "To a Poetess", p. 319.
  [1] Salisbury.

While the old sank in sloth and slime
And venal shame, and heard the alarum
Of Cobbett[2] on the Accursed Hill,
The abuse and not the use of Sarum.[3]

Had you been there of old, my friends,
With lies and bribery unbesotted,
Old Sarum never had grown old
Nor any rotten borough rotted,
Who keep in this waste-paper world
The touch that tells that rot is rot,
When ninety new religions rise
Where all the rubbish has been shot.

You unreturning have attained,
As I some rude mode have meant,
To serve even in this pool of ink
The things that are more excellent.
Love may be made a test for apes
And Latin changed for Cherokee,
And God be gas, and Gas be God,
But not for you, and not for me.

Here let me leave this final rag
Upon our rubbish-heap of rhymes
With wishes for the good new years
In memory of the good old times
When once we passed, in paradox
And topsy-turvydom of fun,
For Patience to The Bat and Ball
And Westward to The Rising Sun.[4]

[2] William Cobbett (1763–1835)
[3] The Use of Sarum, or Sarum Rite, is a Latin rite of the Mass which preceded the Tridentine Rite. Old Sarum had few voters but returned a member of Parliament.
[4] Pubs.

FRAGMENT
(From Tennyson's "Idylls of the Queen":
"The Passing of Freda")

Then spake the journalist, as one that dreams
And dreaming, breaks the bed up with his weight,—
And shakes cubicular walls and wakens not:
"The sequel of today unsolders all
The goodliest fellowship of old and young
Of which the old keep record; and the young
Sometimes remember, kindly, being fled:
For when shall we at any future time
Delight our souls with utter misery
With poker and with patience: what remains
Is patience; and the poker pokes no more.

Patience of souls not sullen, nor as one
That casts his cards into the Rubbish Row
And kicks down tables, cursing; but as he
That plays a lonely game under the lamp
When the bleak panes are shuttered on the frost
And *The White Hart* is whiter, and young ice
Calls to young Gerald and his troop of dames
Wild for their skates; and winter comes amain,
So is our table; seeing we yet can match—
Two of a kind, but never Four and Five
And the Full House is empty till I die."

Then answered Freda of her courtesy:
"The old Sec. skidaddles, yielding place to new,
But if indeed the winter come, quaint saws
Declare "Christmas is Coming": and it comes,
Showing strange truth in stored-up prophecies,
And all we sware that I should come again,
With Christmas in its coming: therefore rest
And trust the Sequence still; for in no time

Christmas shall fail or vows of Christian men."
So spake the Lady: and the Journalist
Dreaming no more, slept only; and his snores
Rolled from the Chilterns to the changing sea.

(1919)

POEMS 1915–1919

THE BATTLE OF THE STORIES

In the Caucasus

They came uncounted like the stars that circle or are set,
They circled and they caught us as in a sparkling casting-net
We burst it in the mountain gate where all the guns began,
When the snow stood up at Christmas on the hills of Ardahan.
The guns—and not a bell to tell that God was made a man—
But we did all remember, though all the world forget.

Before Paris

The kings came over the olden Rhine to break an ancient debt,
We took their rush at the river of death in the fields where first we
    met,
But we marked their millions swaying; then we marked a standard fall;
And far beyond them, like a bird, Maunoury's[1] bugle call:
And there were not kings or debts or doubts or anything at all
But the People that remembers and the peoples that forget.

In Flanders

Empty above your bleating hordes his throne abides the threat,
Who drew the sword of his despair to front your butcher's bet:
You shall scan the empty scabbard; you shall search the empty seat.
While he along the ruined skies rides royal with retreat,
In the judgment and the silence and the grass upon the street.
And the oath the heavens remember and you would fain forget.

In Poland

A cloud was on the face of God when three kings met,
What hour the worst of men were made the sun hath suffered yet.
We knew them in their nibbling peace or ever they went to war.
In petty school and pilfered field we know them what they are.
And we drank the cup of anguish to the pardon of the Czar,
To the nations that remember and the empires that forget.

---

[1] General Michel Maunoury (1847–1923), an artillery officer recalled to the colours in August 1914 at the age of 67 to command the "Army of Lorraine". Redeployed to defend Paris against the invading Germans, he was the victor in the 1st Battle of the Marne (see *The Ballad of St. Barbara*). Posthumously made Maréchal de France.

In the Dardanelles

To the horned mount of the high Mahound of moon and of
  minaret
Labouring go the sieging trains whose tracks are blood and sweat.
The ships break in a sanguine sea; and far to the front a boy
Fallen, and his face flung back to shout with the Son of God for joy.
And the long land under the lifted smoke; and a great light on Troy,
And all that men remember and madmen can forget.

In the Balkans

They thrice on crags of death were dry and thrice in Danube wet
To prove an old man's empty heart was empty of regret,
For the Turks have taken his city's soul: his spurs of gold are dross,
And the Crescent hangs upon him while we hang upon the Cross.
But we heave our tower of pride upon Kossovo[2] of the loss,
For a proof that we remember and the infidels forget.

In the Alps

Master of Arts and mastery of arms, master of all things yet,
For the musket as for the mandolin the master fingers fret;
The news to the noise of the mandolin that all the world comes
  home,
And the young are young and the years return and the days of the
  kingdom come.
When the wars wearied, and the tribes turned: and the sun rose on
  Rome,
And all that Rome remembers when all her realms forget.

In the North Sea

Though the seas were sown with the new dragons that knew not
  what they ate,
We broke St. George's banner out to the black wind and the wet,
He hath broken all the bridges we could fling, the world and we,
But the bridge of death in heaven that His people might be free,
That we straddled for the saddle of the riders of the sea.
For St. George that shall remember if the Dragon shall forget.

[2] Kossovo, a battle (1389) in which the Serbs lost to the Turks.

All the Voices

Behold, we are men of many lands, in motley seasons set,
From Riga to the rock of Spain, from Orkney to Olivet,
Who stand up in the council in the turning of the year,
And, standing, give the judgement on the evil house of fear;
Knowing the End shall write again what we have written here,
On the day when God remembers and no man can forget.

(from *The New Witness*, August 12, 1915)

THE BALLAD OF ST. BARBARA

When the long grey lines came flooding upon Paris in the plain,[1]
We stood and drank of the last free air we never could taste again:
They had led us back from the lost battle, to halt we knew not where
And stilled us; and our gaping guns were dumb with our despair.
The grey tribes flowed for ever from the infinite lifeless lands
And a Norman to a Breton spoke, his chin upon his hands.

"There was an end of Ilium; and an end came to Rome;
And a man plays on a painted stage in the land that he calls home;
Arch after arch of triumph, but floor beyond falling floor,
That lead to a low door at last; and beyond there is no door."

And the Breton to the Norman spoke, like a small child spoke he,
And his sea-blue eyes were empty as his home beside the sea:
"There are more windows in one house than there are eyes to see,
There are more doors in a man's house, but God has hid the key:

Barbara was a maiden of great beauty shut up in a tower by her father in order to discourage suitors. When she became a Christian her father killed her not only for her faith, but also for having a third window to honor the Trinity built in his bathhouse. After slaying his daughter, he was struck dead by a bolt of lightning and burnt to ashes. It is her association with the explosive lightning bolt that has made her patron saint of artillery and those in danger of sudden death.

[1] On September 9, 1914 the German forces broke through the French defensive lines during the Battle of Mondemont. By the next morning the Germans had been pushed back by Moroccan, Norman and Breton artillery men.

Ruin is a builder of windows; her legend witnesseth
Barbara, the saint of gunners, and a stay in sudden death."

It seemed the wheel of the world stood still an instant in its turning,
More than the kings of the earth that turned with the turning of
    Valmy mill:
While trickled the idle tale and the sea-blue eyes were burning,
Still as the heart of a whirlwind the heart of the world stood still.

"Barbara the beautiful
Had praise of lute and pen:
Her hair was like a summer night
Dark and desired of men.

Her feet like birds from far away
That linger and light in doubt;
And her face was like a window
Where a man's first love looked out.

Her sire was master of many slaves
A hard man of his hands;
They built a tower about her
In the desolate golden lands,

Sealed as the tyrants sealed their tombs,
Planned with an ancient plan,
And set two windows in the tower,
Like the two eyes of a man."

Our guns were set toward the foe; we had no word, for firing.
Grey in the gateway of St. Gond the Guard of the tyrant shone;
Dark with the fate of a falling star, retiring and retiring,
The Breton line went backward and the Breton tale went on.

"Her father had sailed across the sea
From the harbour of Africa
When all the slaves took up their tools
For the bidding of Barbara.

She smote the bare wall with her hand
And bade them smite again;

She poured them wealth of wine and meat
To stay them in their pain.

And cried through the lifted thunder
Of thronging hammer and hod
'Throw open the third window
In the third name of God.'

Then the hearts failed and the tools fell,
And far towards the foam,
Men saw a shadow on the sands
And her father coming home."

Speak low and low, along the line the whispered word is flying
Before the touch, before the time, we may not loose a breath:
Their guns must mash us to the mire and there be no replying,
Till the hand is raised to fling us for the final dice to death.

"'There were two windows in your tower,
Barbara, Barbara,
For all between the sun and moon
In the lands of Africa.

Hath a man three eyes, Barbara,
A bird three wings,
That you have riven roof and wall
To look upon vain things?'

Her voice was like a wandering thing
That falters yet is free,
Whose soul has drunk in a distant land
Of the rivers of liberty.

'There are more wings than the wind knows
Or eyes than see the sun
In the light of the lost window
And the wind of the doors undone.

For out of the first lattice
Are the red lands that break
And out of the second lattice
Sea like a green snake,

But out of the third lattice
Under low eaves like wings
Is a new corner of the sky
And the other side of things.' "

It opened in the inmost place an instant beyond uttering,
A casement and a chasm and a thunder of doors undone,
A seraph's strong wing shaken out the shock of its unshuttering,
That split the shattered sunlight from a light beyond the sun.

"Then he drew sword and drave her
Where the judges sat and said
'Caesar sits above the gods,
Barbara the maid.

Caesar hath made a treaty
With the moon and with the sun,
All the gods that men can praise
Praise him every one.

There is peace with the anointed
Of the scarlet oils of Bel,[2]
With the Fish God, where the whirlpool
Is a winding stair to hell,

With the pathless pyramids of slime,
Where the mitred negro lifts
To his black cherub in the cloud
Abominable gifts,

With the leprous silver cities
Where the dumb priests dance and nod,
But not with the three windows
And the last name of God.' "

They are firing, we are falling, and the red skies rend and shiver us,
Barbara, Barbara, we may not loose a breath—
Be at the bursting doors of doom, and in the dark deliver us,
Who loosen the last window on the sun of sudden death.

[2] God of the Babylonians. The half-man, half-fish god is Dagon.

"Barbara the beautiful
Stood up as queen set free,
Whose mouth is set to a terrible cup
And the trumpet of liberty.

'I have looked forth from a window
That no man now shall bar,
Caesar's toppling battle-towers
Shall never stretch so far.

The slaves are dancing in their chains,
The child laughs at the rod,
Because of the bird of the three wings,
And the third face of God.'

The sword upon his shoulder
Shifted and shone and fell,
And Barbara lay very small
And crumpled like a shell."

What wall upon what hinges turned stands open like a door?
Too simple for the sight of faith, too huge for human eyes,
What light upon what ancient way shines to a far-off floor,
The line of the lost land of France or the plains of Paradise?

"Caesar smiled above the gods
His lip of stone was curled,
His iron armies wound like chains
Round and round the world,

And the strong slayer of his own
That cut down flesh for grass,
Smiled too, and went to his own tower
Like a walking tower of brass,

And the songs ceased and the slaves were dumb
And far towards the foam
Men saw a shadow on the sands;
And her father coming home....

Blood of his blood upon the sword
Stood red but never dry.

He wiped it slowly, till the blade
Was blue as the blue sky.

But the blue sky split with a thunder-crack,
Spat down a blinding brand,
And all of him lay back and flat
As his shadow on the sand."

The touch and the tornado; all our guns give tongue together
St. Barbara for the gunnery and God defend the right,
They are stopped and gapped and battered as we blast away the
    weather.
Building window upon window to our lady of the light.
For the light is come on Liberty, her foes are falling, falling,
They are reeling, they are running, as the shameful years have run,
She is risen for all the humble, she has heard the conquered calling,
St. Barbara of the Gunners, with her hand upon the gun.
They are burst asunder in the midst that eat of their own flatteries,
Whose lip is curled to order as its barbered hair is curled....
Blast of the beauty of sudden death, St. Barbara of the batteries!
That blow the new white window in the wall of all the world.

For the hand is raised behind us, and the bolt smites hard
Through the rending of the doorways, through the death-gap of the
    Guard,
For the cry of the Three Colours[3] is in Condé and beyond
And the Guard is flung for carrion in the graveyard of St. Gond,
Through Mondemont and out of it, through Morin marsh and on
With earthquake of salutation the impossible thing is gone,
Gaul, charioted and charging, great Gaul upon a gun,
Tiptoe on all her thousand years and trumpeting to the sun:

As day returns, as death returns, swung backwards and swung home,
Back on the barbarous reign returns the battering-ram of Rome;
While that that the east held hard and hot like pincers in a forge,
Came like the west wind roaring up the cannon of St. George,[4]

---

[3] The French tricolor.
[4] British cannon to the West.

Where the hunt is up and racing over stream and swamp and tarn
And their batteries, black with battle, hold the bridgeheads of the
   Marne,
And across the carnage of the Guard, by Paris in the plain,
The Normans to the Bretons cried and the Bretons cheered again....
But he that told the tale went home to his house beside the sea
And burned before St. Barbara, the light of the windows three,
Three candles for an unknown thing, never to come again,
That opened like the eye of God on Paris in the plain.[5]

(from *The New Witness*, September 7, 1916)

TO F.C.[1]

In Memoriam Palestine, 1919

Do you remember one immortal
Lost moment out of time and space,
What time we thought, who passed the portal
Of that divine disastrous place
Where Life was slain and Truth was slandered
On that one holier hill than Rome,
How far abroad our bodies wandered
That evening when our souls came home?

The mystic city many-gated,
With monstrous columns, was your own:
Herodian stones fell down and waited
Two thousand years to be your throne.
In the grey rocks the burning blossom
Glowed terrible as the sacred blood:

[5] The poem was written as a celebration in the wake of the victory. However, within a few weeks Chesterton was stricken by the severe illness which caused him to be kept under sedation for several months; when he recovered the war had lapsed into the long attrition of the trenches which was to continue until its end in 1918. When the poem was eventually published in September 1916, two years had passed since Mondemont had fired hopes of a swift and successful end to hostilities.

[1] Frances Chesterton.

It was no stranger to your bosom
Than bluebells of an English wood.

Do you remember a road that follows
The way of unforgotten feet,
Where from the waste of rocks and hollows
Climb up the crawling crooked street
The stages of one towering drama
Always ahead and out of sight....
Do you remember Aceldama[2]
And the jackal barking in the night?

Life is not void or stuff for scorners:
We have laughed loud and kept our love,
We have heard singers in tavern corners
And not forgotten the birds above:
We have known smiters and sons of thunder
And not unworthily walked with them,
We have grown wiser and lost not wonder;
And we have seen Jerusalem.

(1919)

SONGS OF EDUCATION

I. GEOGRAPHY

The earth is a place on which England is found,
And you find it however you twirl the globe round;
For the spots are all red and the rest is all grey,
And that is the meaning of Empire Day.

Gibraltar's a rock that you see very plain,
And attached to its base is the district of Spain.
And the island of Malta is marked further on,
Where some natives were known as the Knights of St. John.

---

[2] The Potter's Field purchased with the thirty pieces of silver returned by Judas Iscariot.

Then Cyprus, and east to the Suez Canal,
That was conquered by Dizzy and Rothschild[1] his pal
With the Sword of the Lord in the old English way;
And that is the meaning of Empire Day.

Our principal imports come far as Cape Horn;
For necessities, cocoa; for luxuries, corn;
Thus Brahmins are born for the rice-field, and thus,
The Gods made the Greeks to grow currants for us;
Of earth's other tributes are plenty to choose,
Tobacco and petrol and Jazzing and Jews:
The Jazzing will pass but the Jews they will stay;
And that is the meaning of Empire Day.

Our principal exports, all labelled and packed,
At the ends of the earth are delivered intact:
Our soap or our salmon can travel in tins
Between the two poles and as like as two pins;
So that Lancashire merchants whenever they like
Can water the beer of a man in Klondike
Or poison the meat of a man in Bombay;
And that is the meaning of Empire Day.

The day of St. George is a musty affair
Which Russians and Greeks are permitted to share;
The day of Trafalgar is Spanish in name
And the Spaniards refuse to pronounce it the same;
But the day of the Empire[2] from Canada came
With Morden and Borden and Beaverbrook's fame[3]
And saintly seraphical souls such as they:
And that is the meaning of Empire Day.

                    (from *The New Witness*, July 11, 1919)

---

[1] Dizzy, Benjamin Disraeli (1804–81), British Prime Minister. Meyer Rothschild, 1st Baron Rothschild (1840–1915).

[2] May 24, Empire Day, was instituted in 1902.

[3] Newspaper proprietors.

II. ENGLISH HISTORY
Form 9734.A. Education Department, Whitehall

The Roman threw us a road, a road,
And sighed and strolled away:
The Saxon gave us a raid, a raid,
A raid that came to stay;
The Dane went west, but the Dane confessed
That he went a bit too far;
And we all became, by another name,
The Imperial race we are.

Chorus
The Imperial race, the inscrutable race,
The invincible race we are.

Though Sussex hills are bare, are bare,
And Sussex weald is wide,
From Chichester to Chester
Men saw the Norman ride;
He threw his sword in the air and sang
To a sort of a light guitar;
It was all the same, for we all became
The identical nobs we are.

Chorus
The identical nobs, individual nobs
Unmistakable nobs we are.

The people lived on the land, the land,
They pottered about and prayed;
They built a cathedral here and there
Or went on a small crusade:
Till the bones of Becket[1] were bundled out
For the fun of a fat White Czar,[2]

---

[1] Thomas à Becket (1118–1170), Archbishop and martyr (St. Thomas of Canterbury).
[2] Henry VIII (1491–1547).

And we all became, in spoil and flame,
The intelligent lot we are.

Chorus

The intelligent lot, the intuitive lot,
The infallible lot we are.

O Warwick woods are green, are green,
But Warwick trees can fall:
And Birmingham grew so big, so big,
And Stratford stayed so small.
Till the hooter howled to the morning lark
That sang to the morning star;
And we all became, in freedom's name,
The fortunate chaps we are.

Chorus

The fortunate chaps, felicitous chaps,
The fairy-like chaps we are.

The people they left the land, the land,
But they went on working hard;
And the village green that had got mislaid
Turned up in the squire's back-yard:
But twenty men of us all got work
On a bit of his motor car;
And we all became, with the world's acclaim,
The marvellous mugs we are:

Chorus

The marvellous mugs, miraculous mugs,
The mystical mugs we are.

(from *The New Witness*, July 18, 1919)

III. SONG FOR THE CRÈCHE
Form 9736.B. Education Department, Whitehall

I remember my mother, the day that we met,
A thing I shall never entirely forget;
And I toy with the fancy that, young as I am,
I should know her again if we met in a tram.
 But mother is happy in turning a crank
 That increases the balance at somebody's bank;
 And I feel satisfaction that mother is free
 From the sinister task of attending to me.

They have brightened our room, that is spacious and cool,
With diagrams used in the Idiot School,
And Books for the Blind that will teach us to see;
But mother is happy, for mother is free.
 For mother is dancing up forty-eight floors.
 For love of the Leeds International Stores,
 And the flame of that faith might perhaps have grown cold,
 With the care of a baby of seven weeks old.

For mother is happy in greasing a wheel
For somebody else, who is cornering Steel:
And though our one meeting was not very long,
She took the occasion to sing me this song:
 "O, hush thee, my baby, the time will soon come
 When thy sleep will be broken with hooting and hum;
 There are handles want turning and turning all day,
 And knobs to be pressed in the usual way;

O, hush thee, my baby, take rest while I croon,
For Progress comes early, and Freedom too soon."

(from The New Witness, July 25, 1919)

IV. ARITHMETIC
Form 9736.B. Education Department, Whitehall

Twice one is two,
Twice two is four,
But twice two is ninety-six if you know the way to score.
Half of two is one,
Half of four is two,
But half of four is forty per cent, if your name is Montagu:
For everything else is on the square
If done by the best quadratics;
And nothing is low in High Finance
Or the Higher Mathematics.

A straight line is straight
And a square mile is flat:
But you learn in trigonometrics a trick worth two of that.
Two straight lines
Can't enclose a Space.
But they can enclose a Corner to support the Chosen Race:
For you never know what Dynamics do
With the lower truths of Statics:
And half of two is a touring car
In the Higher Mathematics.

There is a place apart
Beyond the solar ray,
Where parallel straight lines can meet in an unofficial way.
There is a room that holds
The examiner or his clerks,
Where you can square the circle or the man that gives the marks.
Where you hide in the cellar and then look down
On the poets that live in the attics;
For the whole of the house is upside down
In the Higher Mathematics.

(from The New Witness, August 1, 1919)

V. CITIZENSHIP

Form 9736.B. Education Department, Whitehall

How slowly learns the child at school
The names of all the nobs that rule
From Ponsonby to Pennant;
Ere his bewildered mind find rest,
Knowing his host can be a Guest,
His landlord is a Tennant.[1]

He knew not, at the age of three,
What Lord St. Leger next will be
Or what he was before;
A Primrose in the social swim
A Mr. Primrose is to him,
And he is nothing more.

But soon, about the age of ten,
He finds he is a Citizen,
And knows his way about;
Can pause within, or just beyond,
The line 'twixt Mond[2] and Demi Mond[e],
'Twixt Getting On—or Out.

The Citizen will take his share
(In every sense) as bull and bear;
Nor need this oral ditty
Invoke the philologic pen
To show you that a Citizen
Means Something in the City.

Thus gains he, with the virile gown,
The fasces and the civic crown,
The forum of the free;
Not more to Rome's high law allied

---

[1] All are names of influential families.
[2] Alfred Moritz Mond (1868–1930), 1st Baron Melchett, chairman of the Mond Nickel Co.

Is Devonport[3] in all his pride
Or Lipton's[4] self than he.

For he will learn, if he will try,
The deep interior truths whereby
We rule the Commonwealth;
What is the Food-Controller's fee
And whether the Health Ministry
Are in it for their health.
(from *The New Witness*, August 8, 1919)

VI. HYGIENE [I]

When Science taught mankind to breathe
    A little while ago,
Only a proud and panting few
    Were really in the know:
Nor could the Youth his features wreathe,
    Puffing from all the lungs beneath:
When Duty whispered softly "Breathe!"
    The Youth would answer "Blow!"

When Science found by fearless research
    The need for exercise,
Our careless Youth was climbing trees
    Or idly blacking eyes:
To thoughtless schoolboys breaking bounds
    For leapfrog or for hare-and-hounds,
Or fighting hard for fourteen rounds,
    It came as a surprise.

She tells us how to wash and walk
    And when to woo and wed,

---

[3] Hudson Ewbanke Kearley (1856–1934), 1st Viscount Devonport (1917), Liberal politician and grocer.

[4] Sir Thomas Lipton (1850–1931), grocer best known for his tea and for racing yachts in The Americas Cup.

And how to live when we're alive
  And not when we are dead:
Unless we know the Latin terms
  For each invertebrate that squirms,
Our corpses might not turn to worms
  But water-snakes instead.

(1919)

HYGIENE [II]

"All practical eugenists are agreed on the importance
of sleep."—*The Eugenic Congress*

When Science taught mankind to breathe
A little while ago,
Only a wise and thoughtful few
Were really in the know:
Nor could the Youth his features wreathe,
Puffing from all the lungs beneath:
When Duty whispered softly "Breathe!"
The Youth would answer "Blow!"

When Science proved with lucid care
The need of Exercise,
Our thoughtless Youth was climbing trees
Or lightly blacking eyes:
To reckless idlers breaking bounds
For football or for hare-and-hounds,
Or fighting hard for fourteen rounds,
It came as a surprise.

But when she boldly counsels Sleep
To persons when in bed,
Then, then indeed men blush to see
The daybreak blushing red:
The early risers whom we term
Healthy, grow sickly and infirm;

The Early Bird who caught the Worm
Will catch the Germ instead.

For this at least be Science praised
If all the rest be rot,
That now she snubs the priggish child
That quits too soon his cot:
The pharisaic pachyderm
Of spiritual pride shall squirm:
The Early Bird catches the worm,
The Worm that dieth not.

                    (between 1919–1922)

POEMS OF THE
EARLY 1920s

En Voyage to North America, 1921

VARIATIONS ON AN AIR

Composed on having to appear in a pageant as Old King Cole

Old King Cole was a merry old soul,
And a merry old soul was he;
He called for his pipe,
He called for his bowl,
And he called for his fiddlers three.

AFTER LORD TENNYSON

Cole, that unwearied prince of Colchester,
Growing more gay with age and with long days
Deeper in laughter and desire of life,
As that Virginian climber on our walls
Flames scarlet with the fading of the year;
Called for his wassail and that other weed
Virginian also, from the western woods
Where English Raleigh checked the boast of Spain,
And lighting joy with joy, and piling up
Pleasure as crown for pleasure, bade men bring
Those three, the minstrels whose emblazoned coats
Shone with the oyster-shells of Colchester;
And these three played, and playing grew more fain
Of mirth and music; till the heathen came,
And the King slept beside the northern sea.

AFTER W. B. YEATS

Of an old King in a story
　　From the grey sea-folk I have heard,
Whose heart was no more broken
　　Than the wings of a bird.

As soon as the moon was silver
　　And the thin stars began,
He took his pipe and his tankard,
　　Like an old peasant man.

And three tall shadows were with him
　　And came at his command;
And played before him for ever
　　The fiddles of fairyland.

And he died in the young summer
　　Of the world's desire;
Before our hearts were broken
　　Like sticks in a fire.

AFTER ROBERT BROWNING

Who smoke-snorts toasts o' My Lady Nicotine,
Kicks stuffing out of Pussyfoot, bids his trio
Stick up their Stradivarii (that's the plural)
Or near enough, my fatheads; *nimium*
Vicina Cremonæ; that's a bit too near).
Is there some stockfish fails to understand?
Catch hold o' the notion, bellow and blurt back
　　"Cole"?
Must I bawl lessons from a horn-book, howl,
Cat-call the cat-gut "fiddles"? Fiddlesticks!

AFTER WALT WHITMAN

Me clairvoyant,
Me conscious of you, old camarado,
Needing no telescope, lorgnette, field-glass, opera-glass, myopic
    pince-nez,
Me piercing two thousand years with eye naked and not ashamed;
The crown cannot hide you from me;
Musty old feudal-heraldic trappings cannot hide you from me,
I perceive that you drink.
(I am drinking with you. I am as drunk as you are.)
I see you are inhaling tobacco, puffing, smoking, spitting
(I do not object to your spitting),
You prophetic of American largeness,
You anticipating the broad masculine manners of these States;
I see in you also there are movements, tremors, tears, desire for the
    melodious,
I salute your three violinists, endlessly making vibrations,
Rigid, relentless, capable of going on for ever;
They play my accompaniment; but I shall take no notice of any
    accompaniment;
I myself am a complete orchestra.
So long.

AFTER SWINBURNE

In the time of old sin without sadness
    And golden with wastage of gold
Like the gods that grow old in their gladness
    Was the king that was glad, growing old;
And with sound of loud lyres from his palace
    The voice of his oracles spoke,
And the lips that were red from his chalice
    Were splendid with smoke.

When the weed was as flame for a token
    And the wine was as blood for a sign;
And upheld in his hands and unbroken
    The fountains of fire and of wine.

And a song without speech, without singer,
  Stung the soul of a thousand in three
As the flesh of the earth has to sting her,
  The soul of the sea.

                              (pre-1932)
(from *The New Witness*, December 10, 1920)

FANTASIA

The happy men that lose their heads
They find their heads in heaven
As cherub heads with cherub wings,
And cherub haloes even:
Out of the infinite evening lands
Along the sunset sea,
Leaving the purple fields behind,
The cherub wings beat down the wind
Back to the groping body and blind
As the bird back to the tree.

Whether the plumes be passion-red
For him that truly dies
By headsman's blade or battle-axe,
Or blue like butterflies,
For him that lost it in a lane
In April's fits and starts,
His folly is forgiven then:
But higher, and far beyond our ken,
Is the healing of the unhappy men,
The men that lost their hearts.

Is there not pardon for the brave
And broad release above,
Who lost their heads for liberty
Or lost their hearts for love?
Or is the wise man wise indeed

Whom larger thoughts keep whole?
Who sees life equal like a chart,
Made strong to play the saner part,
And keep his head and keep his heart,
And only lose his soul.

(from "Christmas Spirit",
Toc H[1] *Annual*, Christmas 1920)

[FIVE TRAVELLERS]

Five travellers in a fairy tale
Whose feet went forth as one,
They went towards the sunset
   To find the rising sun.

They ate the crabs they did not catch
In place of fowl or meat.
They got into a boat and caught
The crabs they did not eat.

(incomplete, ca. 1920)

GOD AND GREEN GINGER

For God and Green Ginger[1] I take the high way
With cutlass and compass and Hullabelay,
With rum and religion and all that is right,
For God and Green Ginger I go for to fight.

(ca. 1920)

[1] Toc H—Morse pronunciation of the letters T.H. standing for Talbot House, recreational centres run by Rev. P.B. "Tubby" Clayton on an interdenominational basis.

[1] The land of Green Ginger is a fabulous place. It is also the name of a street in Hull in East Yorkshire.

TARGAR-ATOLL

When lions lie down on the terrace of Targar-Atoll,
When the plant that is wide as a carpet curls up like a scroll,
And the weeds that are tall as the Temple bow down to the floor,
In the heart of the town of the tombs there is opened a door.

In the streets of the dead, it is moved on the hinges of doom,
And one stands in the gateway whose name is erased from the tomb,
But the death rooms are sealed and none stirs in the terrible place,
For even the dead would have died at the smile on his face.

The grasses stand up in the streets, in the dust of the street,
For an instant a blossom's unfolded, fire-red and rose-sweet
And its fume is like wine and its heart is like Heaven or Hell,
And the name of that flower is the news that no travellers tell.

Then the door and the bloom are shut, and a shudder runs through
The air that is cold as with earthquake and blood-wrinkled blue,
And the lions rise up in a great roaring, and thunder clouds roll
In sulphur and sable and purple on Targar-Atoll.

(ca. 1920)

FOR FIVE GUILDS

I. THE GLASS-STAINERS

To every Man his Mystery,
A trade and only one:
The masons make the hives of men,
The domes of grey or dun,
But we have wrought in rose and gold
The houses of the sun.

The shipwrights build the houses high.
Whose green foundations sway

Alive with fish like little flames,
When the wind goes out to slay.
But we abide with painted sails
The cyclone of the day.

The weavers make the clothes of men
And coats for everyone;
They walk the streets like sunset clouds;
But we have woven and spun
In scarlet or in golden-green
The gay coats of the sun.

You whom the usurers and the lords
With insolent liveries trod,
Deep in dark church behold, above
Their lance-lengths by a rod,
Where we have blazed the tabard
Of the trumpeter of God.

II. THE BRIDGE-BUILDERS

In the world's whitest morning
As hoary with hope,
The Builder of Bridges
Was priest and was pope;
And the mitre of mystery
And the canopy his,
Who darkened the chasms
And domed the abyss.

To eastward and westward
Spread wings at his word
The arch with the key-stone
That stoops like a bird;
That rides the wild air
And the daylight cast under;

The highway of danger,
The gateway of wonder.

Of his throne were the thunders
That rivet and fix
Wild weddings of strangers,
That meet and not mix;
The town and the cornland;
The bride and the groom;
In the breaking of bridges
Is treason and doom.

But he bade us, who fashion
The road that can fly,
That we build not too heavy
And build not too high:
Seeing always that under
The dark arch's bend
Shine death and white daylight
Unchanged to the end.

Who walk on his mercy
Walk light, as he saith,
Seeing that our life
Is a bridge above death;
And the world and its gardens
And hills, as ye heard,
Are borne above space
On the wings of a bird.

Not high and not heavy
Is building of his:
When ye seal up the flood
And forget the abyss,
When your towers are uplifted,
Your banners unfurled,
In the breaking of bridges
Is the end of the world.

III. THE STONE-MASONS

We have graven the mountain of God with hands,
As our hands were graven of God, they say,
Where the seraphs burn in the sun like brands
And the devils carry the rains away;
Making a thrift of the throats of hell,
Our gargoyles gather the roaring rain,
Whose yawn is more than a frozen yell
And their very vomiting not in vain.

Wilder than all that a tongue can utter,
Wiser than all that is told in words,
The wings of stone of the soaring gutter
Fly out and follow the flight of the birds;
The rush and rout of the angel wars
Stand out above the astounded street,
Where we flung our gutters against the stars
For a sign that the first and the last shall meet.

We have graven the forest of heaven with hands,
Being great with a mirth too gross for pride,
In the stone that battered him Stephen stands
And Peter himself is petrified:
Such hands as have grubbed in the glebe for bread
Have bidden the blank rock blossom and thrive,
Such hands as have stricken a live man dead
Have struck, and stricken the dead alive.

Fold your hands before heaven in praying,
Lift up your hands into heaven and cry;
But look where our dizziest spires are saying
What the hands of a man did up in the sky:
Drenched before you have heard the thunder,
White before you have felt the snow;
For the giants lift up their hands to wonder
How high the hands of a man could go.

IV. THE BELL-RINGERS

The angels are singing like birds in a tree
In the organ of good St. Cecily:
And the parson reads with his hand upon
The graven eagle of great St. John:
But never the fluted pipes shall go
Like the fifes of an army all a-row,
Merrily marching down the street
To the marts where the busy and idle meet:
And never the brazen bird shall fly
Out of the window and into the sky,
Till men in cities and shires and ships
Look up at the living Apocalypse.

But all can hark at the dark of even
The bells that bay like the hounds of heaven,
Tolling and telling that over and under,
In the ways of the air like a wandering thunder,
The hunt is up over hills untrod:
For the wind is the way of the dogs of God:
From the tyrant's tower to the outlaw's den
Hunting the souls of the sons of men.
Ruler and robber and pedlar and peer,
Who will not hearken and yet will hear;
Filling men's heads with the hurry and hum
Making them welcome before they come.

And we poor men stand under the steeple
Drawing the cords that can draw the people,
And in our leash like the leaping dogs
Are God's most deafening demagogues:
And we are but little, like dwarfs underground,
While hang up in heaven the houses of sound,
Moving like mountains that faith sets free,
Yawning like caverns that roar with the sea,

As awfully loaded, as airily buoyed,
Armoured archangels that trample the void:
Wild as with dancing and weighty with dooms,
Heavy as their panoply, light as their plumes.

Neither preacher nor priest are we:
Each man mount to his own degree:
Only remember that just such a cord
Tosses in heaven the trumpet and sword;
Souls on their terraces, saints on their towers,
Rise up in arms at alarum like ours:
Glow like great watchfires that redden the skies
Titans whose wings are a glory of eyes,
Crowned constellations by twelves and by sevens,
Domed dominations more old than the heavens,
Virtues that thunder and thrones that endure
Sway like a bell to the prayers of the poor.

V. THE SHIPWRIGHTS

The sea that is above the sky
Low on it like a load did lie,
The skies grew green and black and nigh
And broke: and the Flood came.
But through the inky violet sea
A candle-lighted ship went she
Whose master made our Mystery
With Noah for his name.

The high impossible horns and hair
The beards of bestial kings were there.
Birds of the East, red-gold and rare,
Crowded the mast for crown.
Grey giant birds stood gaunt and strong
But over them sang all day long
The little lark that makes a song
A mile from London town.

Hard as the world God nailed with stars
That ship that on its decks and spars
Carried the world and all its wars
Troy and eternal Rome.
Hard were old Noah's timbers found,
And those we smite as hard and sound
That shall have girt the green world round
When all our ships come home.

Redeem we from that world undone
Huge stones that shall outshine the sun
And crowns and bones of gods, o'errun
With leprosies of foam.
For God regathers his ancient rights
And heaven itself has newer sights,
Happier in all its harbour-lights
When all our ships come home.

                                        (ca. 1920)

To the Charioteers of St Louis.

(with regrets & apologies)

What time you launch the cars of Art
  Toward the Olympian fale
Numbers the lecturer's donkey-cart
  From Omaha to Yale

That I must miss your wheels of fire
  Is not my fault at all.
The race around Patroclus' pyre
  Is not my funeral

Keep silence on my painful part
  I pass as I arrive:
Alas, it is a donkey-cart
  I draw and do not drive.

———————

G.K. Chesterton

March. 19. 1921.

TO THE CHARIOTEERS OF ST. LOUIS[1]

(with regrets and apologies)

What time you launch the cars of Art
    Toward the Olympian pale
Lumbers the lecturer's donkey-cart
    from Omaha to Yale.

That I must miss your wheels of fire
    Is not my fault at all.
The race around Patroclus' pyre
    Is not my funeral.

Keep silence on my painful part
    I pass as I arrive:
Alas, it is a donkey-cart
    I draw and do not drive.
                    (March 19, 1921)

[A PROPHECY]

This curious rhymed prophecy, anonymous and of uncertain date, was discovered by the president of the Buckinghamshire Archeological Society in his recent excavations in the district.

When folk shall find, as it is fated,
    That Overroads is overrated,[1]
And Topmeadow, whereto they hop
    Still wants a little bit on top—
When Winter comes to instruct the mind
    That Spring is rather far behind,

[1] A poem given to George S. Johns, President of the St. Louis Artists' Guild who drove Chesterton about when he was lecturing in St. Louis.

[1] Over-roads was the Chestertons' house in Beaconsfield from 1909 until they moved across the road to their new house, Top Meadow, in 1922.

All folk shall gather to review them
  Poems that have no Poets to them,
And in a noise of nails and bricks
  Shall read them hard from five to six.
            (November, 1921)

[ON THE WEDDING OF THE PRINCESS ROYAL]

If only Princess Mary[1]
Had worn the garb of a Guide,
I needn't be quite so chary
Of describing the dress of the bride.
The writer, for proper payment,
Will describe what he couldn't see;
But the facts about ladies' raiment
Are a little too much for me.
I'll imagine a Duke or Duchess
Or even invent a priest
With a hundred accurate touches
From the greatest thing to the least:
From the great bells rocked and ringing
With a nation's vast accord
To a gilded tassel swinging
On the soldier's hilted sword:
But the trouble with Viscount Lascelles,
Otherwise Lord Lascelles,
Is whether he rhymes to tassels
Or whether he rhymes to bells.
                (1922)

[1] Princess Mary (1897–1965), the Princess Royal and daughter of King George V, actively promoted the Girl Guide movement. On February 28, 1922, she married Henry, Viscount Lascelles (1882–1947), later 6th Earl of Harewood.

THE JAZZ [II]

A Study of Modern Dancing, in the manner of Modern Poetry

TLANNGERSHSHSH!
Thrills of vibrant discord,
  Like the shivering of glass;
Some people dislike it; but I do not dislike it.
  I think it is fun,
Approximating to the fun
Of merely smashing a window;
But I am told that it proceeds
  From a musical instrument,
Or at any rate
  From an instrument.

  Black flashes ...
... Flashes of intermittent darkness;
Somebody seems to be playing with the electric light;
  Some may possibly believe that modern dancing
  Looks best in the dark.

  I do not agree with them.
I have heard that modern dancing is barbaric,
  Pagan, shameless, shocking, abominable.
No such luck—I mean no such thing.
  The dancers are singularly respectable
  To the point of rigidity,
With something of the rotatory perseverance
  Of a monkey on a stick,
But there is more stick than monkey
  And not, as slanderers assert,
More monkey than stick.

If I were writing an essay
—And you can put chunks of any number of essays

Cf. shorter version in *Collected Poetry*, Part I, pp. 442–44.

Into this sort of poem—
I should say there was a slight disproportion
   Between the music and the dancing;
For only the musician dances
   With excitement,
While the dancers remain cold
   And relatively motionless
(Orpheus of the Lyre of Life
   Leading the forests in fantastic capers;
Here is your Art eclipsed and reversed,
   For I see men as trees walking.)

If Mr. King stood on his head,
Or Mr. Simon butted Mr. Gray[1]
   In the waistcoat,
Or the two Burnett-Browns
Strangled each other in their coat-tails,
   There would then be a serene harmony,
     A calm unity and oneness
   In the two arts.
   But Mr. King remains on his feet,
And the coat-tails of Mr. Burnett-Brown
   Continue in their customary position.

And something else was running in my head—
—Songs I had heard earlier in the evening;
   Songs of true lovers and tavern friends,
     Decent drunkenness with a chorus,

   And the laughter of men who could riot.
And something stirred in me;
   A tradition
Strayed from an older time,
   And from the freedom of my fathers:
That when there is banging, yelling and smashing to be done,

---

[1] Neighbors of the Chestertons.

I like to do it myself,
     And not delegate it to a slave,
          However accomplished.
And that I should sympathise,
     As with a revolt of human dignity,
If the musician had suddenly stopped playing,
And had merely quoted the last line
Of a song sung by Mrs. Harcourt Williams:[2]
"If you want any more, you must sing it yourselves."
               (from *Beaconsfield Parish Magazine*, March 1922)

THE JAZZ [III]
[Fragment or Earlier Variation]

Let us be moderate.
There are a lot of jolly people doing it
     (Whatever it is).
Patches of joyful colour shift sharply
Like a kaleidoscope,
Green and gold and red and splashes of splendid black,
     Familiar faces and unfamiliar clothes;
I see a nice-looking girl, a neighbour of mine, dancing
     After all,
She looks nearly as well as when she is not dancing
     (Bound, O Terpsichore, upon the mountains,
          With all your nymphs upon the mountains,
     And Salome who held the heart of a King
          And the head of a Prophet,
     For the height of this tribute
     Your Art has come.)

I see certain others, less known to me, also dancing.
     They do not look very much uglier
     Than when they are sitting still.

[2] Jean Sterling Mackinley, actress, singer and diseuse, in 1908 married Ernest Harcourt Williams, a fellow member of Frank Benson's Bensonian Players.

If I were writing an essay
—And you can put chunks of any number of essays
   Into this sort of poem—
I should say there was a slight disproportion
   Between the music and the dancing,
   For only the musician dances
      With excitement,
   While the dancers remain cold
      And relatively motionless.
   (Orpheus Immortal
      Leading the forests in fantastic dance
         Calling up the capering rocks,
         Such things can your Art achieve.)

                                        (1922)

THE CONVERT

After one moment when I bowed my head
And the whole world turned over and came upright,
And I came out where the old road shone white,
I walked the ways and heard what all men said,
Forests of tongues, like autumn leaves unshed,
Being not unlovable but strange and light;
Old riddles and new creeds, not in despite
But softly, as men smile about the dead.

The sages have a hundred maps to give
That trace their crawling cosmos like a tree,
They rattle reason out through many a sieve
That stores the sand and lets the gold go free:
And all these things are less than dust to me
Because my name is Lazarus and I live.

                                        (1922)

Chesterton, who had been an Anglican, converted to Roman Catholicism in 1922.

[YOU WILL HEAR MANY TALES]

Some say the earth's first king and conqueror, Cain,[1]
Traced in his brother's blood that burned like fire
The plan of all this place as on a slate
On great plains grey with night and so gave up
His sin in that red hieroglyph to heaven.
While others tell how Nimrod the great hunter[2]
Drove his huge herds of mammoth and elephant
To labour here and lift up a new town
With towers as wild as their own tusks and horns
Made on the scale of monsters and not men
To be a witness to the ends of the Earth
That strength and the strong riders rule the world.
And some that Alexander like Apollo[3]
Came like the sun an Emperor from the East
Trailing all Asia here made sacrifice
To Nike and Anagke above all gods,[4]
Set a winged Victory without a head
For the blind spirit of speed.

      While others say
That Jack climbed up the Beanstalk and fell down
Bringing a giant tumbling from the sky
With other trifles. Friend, I have studied not
In desert fables but the ways of men,
And men are always men even in the desert.
I know what moves such folk into such freaks
Not inexcusably. These tribes have seen
Truths as tremendous as your fictions are,
Earthquakes on Earth and not in fairyland,

[1] Eldest son of Adam and Eve, murderer of his brother, Abel.

[2] The Mesopotamian monarch described in Genesis, founder of Babel or Babylon.

[3] Alexander III of Macedon (356–323 B.C.), aka Alexander the Great. Apollo, the Greek god of the sun.

[4] Nike, Greek goddess of victory, daughter of Styx and Pallas. Anagke, Greek god of necessity.

Seesaw of life and death and in broad day,
Grown dizzy because the real world goes round.
They saw our fathers storm Jerusalem
On swaying towers that charged like chariots,
And Godfrey[5] in a glory of Greek fire
Perch on the high roofs of the holy town.
Then came the Christian curse; quarrel of princes,
Hattin[6]; and streamed along the striped dark sand
Like a green flame the flag of Saladin,
And the cross flat before it; then new dawns
Saw the Red Ship of Richard burn the sea.[7]
The trumpets of the Lion tell a tale
They publish yet in the streets of Ascalon[8]
Then a new ruin; more quarrels; and far away
They saw the light around St. Louis' head[9]
In the lost battle like a sunken sun
And the same foe retreating as we charged,
And the same foe returning as we turned,
And all things turning and returning still
Till these men cried "All change is chance and doom,
And an indifferent juggler tosses up
Alternately the Crescent and the Cross,
But we will wait upon the wheel of the world
And blazon on our flag the Wheel of Fortune."

(ca. 1922)

---

[5] Godfrey de Bouillon (1058–1100), Margrave of Antwerp, Duke of Lower Lorraine, Crusader knight.

[6] Hattin, definitive defeat of Crusader forces on July 4, 1187 by Saladin (1138–1193), Sultan of Egypt and Syria.

[7] Richard I (1157–1199), King of England known as the Lionheart.

[8] A strategic city on the coast of Palestine.

[9] Louis IX (1214–1270), King of France (1226–1270), leader of the 7th and 8th Crusades.

THE BALLAD OF THREE HORNS

An experiment in narrative verse in the metre of the old ballads

When Robin Hood in Sherwood shot
(Though prigs pretend to know
That not the bowman but the bard
Was drawing the long bow),

In Lincoln Green he gaily trod,
With sword and arrows keen
(Some say only the bard was sharp,
Only the hearers green).

Where the green wood grew thin and showed
A shimmer of pale gold,
He came out from the forest fringe,
Out on the great grey wold.

And as he went by the Franklin's farm
He idly wound his horn;
And the Franklin cried from his banquet-hall
With a sleepy roar of scorn,

"What boots your barren horn, Robin,
Methought you blew it when
You laid the hounds to the hurtling deer
Or called up your merry men.

"There is naught in your hollow horn, Robin,
But air and empty sound,
But my horn is full of the Gascon wine
That makes the world go round.

"I ride this bench, my wooden horse,
Happy as huntsman can,
Nor need I call to my merry men,
I am the merriest man."

This poem was written for a miniature book in the library of Queen Mary's doll's house at Windsor Castle.

"I drink of the brook," said Robin,
"Or the brown Nottingham ale;
But if you had come from Nottingham Fair,
When the reeling stars were pale,

"Dizzy among the dancing trees,
Treading the heaving ground,
You would know there's brew in Merry England
To make the world go round."

He went by the graven Abbey, grey
And wrinkled with ancient tales,
And blew his horn by the vaulted cell
Of the wise Monk from Wales.

The Monk looked out of the lattice,
Saying "Why blow ye so?"
And Robin laughed, saying "Father,
Why, horns were made to blow."

"Nay, horns were made for a hundred things,
Money or mead or beer,
And I have better than wealth or wine
Out of my ink-horn here.

"With naught but an old reed-pen to use,
A parchment-page to stain,
I dwell with Michael and Mary the Queen
And Arthur and Charlemagne.

"And he that knows not wind or wine
But only an ancient tale
Can blow the horn that Roland blew
And drink of the Holy Grail."

Till he saw by a gate in a long grey wall,
Like the wall at the world's end,
A lone old man with a crooked smile
That was neither of foe or friend.

He opened the gate, saying "Enter ye
Who have come to the world's desire."

And the chambers of that great grey keep
Were lined with gold like fire.

The first room had a dizzy dome
Where moons and planets swim,
And the second room had a solemn dome
Stooping with seraphim.

The door of the third was strong and high,
And when it did open stand
There was naught beyond but the empty sky
And the endless falling land.

Only grey groves of Druid oak
Looked down on a rushy fen,
But through the mist came a monstrous shape
Shaking the bones of men—

An Ox; but in the fields of earth
Are no such oxen found:
And the horns of its head were a black crescent
Like the crescent of Mahound.

"Here is your boon," the old man said,
"Your vision come to pass,
For this is the Black Bull of the North
That has trampled spears like grass.

"Stones that were towns are in his track,
Bones that were hosts of war;
This is the door of the treasure-house;
Go where your treasures are.

"You have hounded the timid stag, Robin,
And the running deer in play,
Here is a deer that will not run
And a stag that turns to bay.

"The room is roofed with a shining dome
And strewn with rushes free,

There are oaken pillars on either hand
And the horns are plain to see."

In Robin's eyes yet wondering
A slow strange welcome woke,
Till his lungs were filled with laughter,
And he lifted his head and spoke:

"In the green heart of England,
Under the greenwood tree,
I ought to have learnt the lesson
I have come so far to see.

"Bows are not born with bow-strings,
Though men be born with hands,
But the yew-tree of the unyielding dead
Like a dark green dragon stands.

"The feathered arrows do not spring
Like feathered twigs on a tree,
But the wild-goose cries from the scudding sky
That the wild-goose chase is free.

"And though this brute tread down the world
Behind me shall not fail
The good green trees and the merry men
And the old songs and the ale.

"After all sport and idleness
This soul shall still go forth
When a man from the heart of Merry England
Meets hell out of the North."

Like a toppling hill with hair for grass
The Thing grew vast and nigh
Till the horns of its head were far aloft
Like the young moon in the sky.

And high on that hairy mountain
By that star-staggering horn

The eye of the Black Bull of the North
Red-rimmed, was white with scorn.

And Robin remembered a Southland down
As high in heaven and wide
With a tiny target red and white,
A speck on the far hill-side,

When he shot with the Sussex archers
For the prize of a Sussex ram,
And over the vast vale hit the white
For the honour of Nottingham.

But naught was here but the towering beast
And the ruinous falling land
When Robin lifted his soul to God
And took his bow in his hand.

There was naught alive but a living death
To freeze the stars with fear
When Robin went upon one knee
And drew the cord to his ear.

And the whole earth shook with the monster
And the whole world swayed and swam
When Robin shot, and hit the white
For the honour of Nottingham.

The Bull came down like a Babel-Tower
With the feathered bolt in his brain:
And Robin sprang on the hairy hill
And blew his horn again.

He blew his horn and drew his sword
And hacked at either horn
And carried them back to merry Barnsdale
And the place where he was born.

Robin went back to merry Barnsdale
And saw the grey goose fly

And the greenwood rise and the red deer run
And his soul sang in the sky.

He gave one horn to Friar Tuck
And the other to Little John
And since that day in merry England
The tales and songs go on.

The ballads and books of Merry England
Of Man's most holy mirth
That are as the laughter of giants,
An earthquake on the earth:

Their ink shall madden the world like wine,
Their wine like water flow,
The men that go on the wild-goose chase
And find where the wild horns grow.

And this is a dull and common tale
To the dizzy tales divine
The bards of a better time shall tell
Whose ink is mixed with wine.

They shall pluck their pens in the wild-goose chase
Wherever the wild geese go,
For this is the latest not the last
Of the tales of the Long Bow.

EXPLICIT LAVS DEO

*Mr. Chesterton has collected a number of opinions of the press,
of which some are appended:*

"There is perhaps in some parts of the narrative something almost verging on the improbable."— *The Spectator*

"It has neither the psychology of Balzac nor the quiet observation of Jane Austen."— *Times Literary Supplement*

"Had not the Bull been a decent self-respecting Vegetarian, he could have made a mouthful of Robin Hood."—Mr. G. Bernard Shaw

"Tiens!"—M. Anatole France

"If each one of us saw himself as a black ox, experiencing the ox psychology, we should outgrow this custom of poking bulls in the eye."—Mr. J. Galsworthy

"He by the brain-congesting Black Bull Complex controlled is."
—Professor Freud

"Robin Hood was clearly a Sun Myth like Lord Leverhulme of Port Sunlight, or the legendary 'Kaiser' with his Place in the Sun."
—Mr. Edward Clodd

"It is the ambition of my life to act the hind legs of the Bull."
—Mr. Charles Chaplin

THE OUTSIDER

The lattice of my window
Is a cage that holds the world.
The shrubs are brown against the glow,
The blanching leaves are curled
Like tongues of captive beasts that lick
The glass cage of the world.

Earth and sky live in glass houses
Of our windows, like glass frames
Holding green grotesques of nature,
Palms and cactus with queer names:
Moon: a bulb of spotted silver,
Sun: a golden gourd that flames.

Or when noon's tall blue palm and houses
Darken to night instead
The nights are tanks where children
Bend down a curious head,
Seeing the moon like a phosphorous shell,
The sun like a sunfish red.

God made the world a peepshow,
And men outside the show.
Broad unconscious backs of things
Not of our looking know,
We are the world's outsiders
—We only see it so.

(early 1920s)

THE EXPERIMENTALIST

"Personality does not survive death."—Mr. Edison

Truth's test is in experiment:
And with empiric care
He went into the other world
And found he wasn't there.

We must believe, if this by rule
Of science may be read,
That he has died while still alive
And lives to say he's dead.

But till that last discovery
His dogma stands disputed:
Nor need we be electrified
Till he's been electrocuted.
(*G.K.'s Weekly*, April 4, 1925)

BALLADE OF THE PRIMROSE SPHINX

"Tories of the *Morning Post* school are now frankly Anti-Semite."
—A Correspondent

How we were mild in the days gone by
When England swallowed the Semite pill,
All that the Orient leech could try
Could not make us feel really ill;

Samuels gave us a passing chill,
Mond affects us with mild fatigue,
Here is the fever; here is the thrill,
What has become of the Primrose League?[1]

None of the Jewish need apply:
Great Spinoza reduced to nil,
Heine's songs are a hollow cry,
Elman's music and Steinmetz' skill,
David Ricardo gives place to Mill,
Brahms and Mendelssohn yield to Grieg,
Never a post for a Yid to fill.
What has become of the Primrose League?

Where is he that was wont to lie
A primrose meek by the brim of the rill,
Nearly as yellow if not as shy,
Flaunting the boast that the years fulfill;
All his Tories are out to kill
With *Judenhatze* and *Krieg ist Krieg*
Where there is Israel's blood to spill.
What has become of the Primrose League?

Envoy

Prince of Judah, a statue still,
After that wonder of wild intrigue,
Lying and fighting and wit and will,
What has become of the Primrose League?
(*G.K.'s Weekly*, April 25, 1925)

---

[1] Primrose League, an organization founded in 1883 within the British Conservative party to support the ideals of Benjamin Disraeli (1804–1881). The name was chosen because of the mistaken belief that primroses were his favorite flower after Queen Victoria sent a wreath of primroses to his funeral.

UTOPIA

"No one suggests that any judge in England does not wish to act quite fairly or try every case properly."— *The Spectator*

> The judges in Sweden delight in the sport
> Of trying improperly cases in court;
> The judges in Spain would exult to a man
> In acting unfairly whenever they can:
> But the judges in England by climate and kin,
> Have been always exempt from original sin,
> One startling exception to earth and her tribes,
> Since Jeffreys took brandy and Bacon took bribes.[1]
>
> (*G.K.'s Weekly*, June 27, 1925)

THE TRAGIC WOMEN

CAST

Princess of the Shadowy Waters, Sheila
Mrs. Tanqueray
Princess Melisande

FADING THOUGHTS
[A Prelude]

> Forgive us you, whose pageant flames
> With youth and beauty and the morning.
> If blows like dust across your stage

[1] Judge George Jeffreys (1648–1689), Lord Chancellor (1685–1688), best known for the so-called Bloody Assizes following the Monmouth rebellion. Francis Bacon (1561–1626), Lord Chancellor (1618), was imprisoned for accepting bribes and banished from government; also a philosopher and author.

"The Tragic Women" was written for the actress Barbara Morley Horder (b. 1908). She married the engineer Roger Rollerton West and adopted Barbara West as her stage name. She was understudy to Sybil Thorndyke in the London production of Bernard Shaw's *St. Joan* and then acted for the BBC.

The breath of things too stale for scorning;
How should you flout these mummied queens
Or mock them when you never met them—
In lost Victorian scenes, so far
That men forget that they forget them?

How should you guess, of these grey jests.
If mocked or mocker be more silly—
With Maeterlinck[1] a Missing Link
And Willie Yeats[2] a Weary Willie,
Or if Conviction or Convention
Marshalled those fashions long ago
Or if Pinero[3] rhymes to Hero
Or only rhymes to "in a row"?

Cras vobis.[4] Even the fervent youth
Who faintly murmurs, "Rather rotten"
Shall rot with Shelley[5] and St. Paul
These that forget shall he forgotten,

Even in Arlen[6] time shall quench
St. Michael's faith, the ecstatic flame
And Mr. Coward[7] toes no more
The crest of his crusading name

Forgive these Phantasmal things,
The ghosts of *Ghosts*, in Ibsen's[8] day
For he that writes them is a ghost
And as you gaze, he fades away.

---

[1] Maurice Maeterlinck (1862–1949), Belgian symbolist dramatist.
[2] William Butler Yeats (1865–1939), Irish poet.
[3] Arthur Wing Pinero (1855–1934), dramatist.
[4] "Tomorrow [is] for you."
[5] Percy Bysshe Shelley (1792–1822), Romantic poet.
[6] Richard Arlen (1898–1976), American actor.
[7] Noël Coward (1899–1973), English actor and playwright.
[8] Henrik Ibsen (1828–1906), Norwegian dramatist.

A subdued background, curtains with a quiet decoration of skulls or what not. Three ornamental cups of green poison on a table. In the centre the Princess of the Shadowy Waters, named, I fancy, Dectora, but here called for convenience Sheila. To her enter on the right Mrs. Tanqueray, by kind permission of Sir Arthur Pinero; on the left the Princess Melisande, by kind permission of M. Maeterlinck.

Mrs. T.	I am the Second Mrs. Tanqueray The saddest of all wives, except the First, Who stood it longer. This is Melisande From Belgium, which suffered from depression Until it tried oppression for a change. A welcome change; and we, a mournful pair, Have come to seek the most oppressed of all The lady of the Irish poet's vision Pitying her sorrows.
Sheila (politely).	You are very good.
Mrs. T.	You must not say that I am very good It must be grasped that I am very bad. And very bad before the play begins, And only sad, or mad, before it ends; But surely you are saddest of us all.
Sheila.	I am the Princess of the Shadowy Waters.
Mrs. T.	But you are only shadowy, I am shady.
Sheila.	I am the Princess of the Shadowy Waters, And, as you may have possibly observed, I am more beautiful than sun or moon Or than the shivering casting-net of the stars.
Mrs. T.	You are taken in a net of evil stars I can believe the English have undone you. For Mr. Tanqueray was English too.
Sheila.	It may be I am saddest of you all. I have borne much, and mockeries worse than wounds

> And for the Irish, being the Tragic Woman
> Is some relief from being the Comic Man:
> We have a right to gloom; since graceless masters
> Forbidding us the Wearing of the Green
> Condemned us to the Wearing of the Grin.

Mrs. T.

> I also am not feeling very well,
> I am so old.

Sheila.

>   Why, yes, I understand
> That it was long ago when you appeared
> And even some considerable time
> Since anyone produced you on the stage.

Mrs. T (crossly).

> No; that is not my meaning in the least.
> I mean that I am like the Mona Lisa
> In Mr. Pater's prose; and changing time
> Found many men pledged to put up with me
> And me unable to put up with them;
> For I was Eve; and wronged my lord because
> He would not dress for dinner. I was Balkis
> Going to seek great Solomon, of whose glory
> The half had not been told me. For I never
> Allowed a man to finish more than half
> Of any sentence: for the subject palled
> And so did Solomon. I was Cleopatra ...

Sheila (in a society tone).

> Surely you must be Mrs. Patrick Campbell.

Mrs. T.

> Yes. I was she. She is no longer I.

Sheila.

> That is so very mystical and that ...
> And quite like Mr. Yeats and Mr. Russell.
> The cycles of the travelling soul. Eh, what?

Mrs. T.

> I am Salome: I am Melisande ...

Melis.

> Oh, pardon me. *So* sorry. Some mistake.
> For *I* am Melisande; and I have waited

For some considerable time to say
That a Pale Mouse is nibbling at the door....
And then he will come in.... He will come in.

Mrs. T.   The modern woman does not fear a mouse.

Shelia.   The fear is often absent in the cat.

Melis.   There are so many things that must be feared.
A lonely lamppost when it does not move....
Until we fear that it will never move.
A cloud that looks like something in the sky,
A stone we shut our eyes and try to pass,
And cannot pass, and scream, and try again:
And all the railings down our quiet street
Looking like things that we have seen before.

Mrs. T.   You seem upset.

Melis.   I would say something more
But a Pale Mouse is nibbling at my skirt.

Mrs. T.   The modern woman wants but little skirt
Nor wants that little long.

Melis.   But does it strike you
That we are not extremely modern women?
Maeterlinck made of mediaeval cut
My garments; Sheila of the Shadowy Waters
Is in herself a rather shadowy person
Of prehistoric date and dress to match
But you, you are the hoarier monument
Of ages infinitely more remote.
Aeons of night primordial called the 'nineties,
Whose books were yellow and whose devils blue,
Since when the world has seen all hell let loose
And brightened up a bit. We are not modern.
We are old huddled women, grey as winter,
Like the three witches with their cauldron cold.

Mrs. T.   Yes; it is true that our dark day is done,
The better reason we should end it darkly
With all the pomp of the last Pessimists;
For people will no longer kill themselves
Finding it jollier to kill each other,
And so indeed it may be; but we three
The Tragic Fates, can make our tragedies.
There is green poison in that triple cup
Or if you like a dagger—here it is. (Produces a dagger.)

Sheila.   Must we all three then with a single dagger (Takes dagger.)
Be stabbed? Oh, very well then. You begin.

(She stabs Mrs. Tanqueray.)

Mrs. T.   It is apparent to my failing reason
That it is you, in this case, who begin
And I have nothing left to do but end.

(She sinks to the floor.)

Melis.   Is it a dagger that I see before me?
I do not know a dagger when I see it. (Takes dagger.)
And a Pale Mouse ... well, well, ... I am not glad.

Sheila.   As you appear to be infirm of purpose
Plus some infirmity of intellect,
Give me the dagger.

(She stabs Melisande.)

Melis.   Oh ... (Sinks to the ground.) I am not glad
And a Pale Mouse is nibbling at my heart.

Mrs. T.   Now you! The compact! Everything is settled (to Sheila).

Sheila.   I am not glad when everything is settled,
Especially without consulting me.
For me, it may be that my Celtic Twilight
Was darkened by the 'nineties into night
But even then, my friends, I never gathered
Out of my barren bogs and huts of clay

Anything quite so dismal and depressing
As you the British and the Belgians,
Made from your wealth of banks and factories
And now it seems that you are getting left:
For many cataracts of shadowy waters
Have flowed under the bridge of time since then
And I, even I, that have some right to tears,
Because the waters have gone over me,
Because I was overwhelmed in the water floods,
Have found and known by title in the torrent
The thing that many waters cannot quench;
And being come from the waters and the shadows,
It seems to me that I am on the Land
And an ancestral trick of driving pigs
Has taught me how to deal with politicians.

Melis. (faintly).   There is a red bird fluttering round the tower.
A small red bird upon the ivory tower
From which alarming detail it will be
Apparent to the dullest intellect
That I am dying. I would hear a song
The sort of song that one can hardly hear
Telling of old blind men beside the sea
A fruit-tree flowering on a lonely islet—
An empty chair beside an open window,
A crowned King lost at a desolate cross-roads
A silver wine-cup and a golden well;
A dead man sitting smiling in the sun.
Sing, in low tones, some soft and simple lay
Dealing if possible with all these things.

Mrs. T.   Yes; a soft music. When we decadents
Decayed in heaps about the drawing-room
It was quite usual for a piano
To be played softly in the other room.
Croon to me, Sheila of the Shadowy Waters,
Very piano; soft as Celtic Twilight,
And with your sleepy runes sing me to sleep.

Sheila (at the top of her voice, like a blare of trumpets).

And shall Oirland then be free?

Says the Shan Van Voght[1]

Shall Oirland then be free?

Says the Shan Van Voght.

Yes, Oirland shall be free

From the centre to the sea.

And Hurrah for Libertee!

Says the Shan Van Voght.

(She begins the steps of an Irish Jig. The two others sit up suddenly and watch.)

(1925)

ANSWERS TO THE POETS

THE SKYLARK REPLIES TO WORDSWORTH
(As it might have appeared to Byron)

Ephemeral minstrel, staring at the sky,
   Dost thou despise the earth where wrongs abound,
Or, eyeing me, hast thou the other eye
   Still on the Court, with pay-day coming round,
That pension that could bring thee down at will
Those rebel wings composed, that protest still?

Past the last trace of meaning and beyond
   Mount, daring babbler, that pay-prompted strain
'Twixt thee and Kings a never-failing bond
   Swells not the less their carnage o'er the plain.
Type of the wise, who drill but never fight,
True to the kindred points of Might and Right.

(from G.K.'s Weekly, March 21, 1925)

---

[1] The poor old woman.

THE SEA REPLIES TO BYRON
(As it might have appeared to Wordsworth)

Stroll on, thou dark not deep "blue" dandy, stroll,
  Ten thousand duns call after thee in vain.
Thy tailor's marked with ruin; his control
  Stops with my shore; beyond he doth retain
No shadow of a chance of what's his own,
But sinks above his bills with bubbling groan,
  "Absconded; gone abroad; address unknown."

Thy songs are speeches, void of all save Thee,
  Childe Harold, Lara, Manfred, what care I?
My water washed them down—you got it free,
  And many a wine-cup since when you were dry,
Till nature blows the man-hater sky-high,
Howling against his gods in stark D.T.,
And dashes him against the Truth. There let
  him *lie.*
          (from *G.K.'s Weekly*, March 21, 1925)

DOLORES REPLIES TO SWINBURNE

Cold passions, and perfectly cruel,
  Long odes that go on for an hour,
With a most economical jewel
  And a quite metaphorical flower.
I implore you to stop it and stow it,
  I adjure you, relent and refrain,
Oh, pagan Priapean poet,
              You give me a pain.

I am sorry, old dear, if I hurt you,
  No doubt it is all very nice
With the lilies and languors of virtue
  And the raptures and roses of vice.

But the notion impels me to anger,
   That vice is all rapture for me,
And if you think virtue is languor
                    Just try it and see.

We shall know when the critics discover
   If your poems were shallow or deep;
Who read you from cover to cover,
   Will know if they sleep not or sleep.
But you say I've endured through the ages
   (Which is rude) as Our Lady of Pain,
You have said it for several pages,
                So say it again.
       (from *G.K.'s Weekly*, March 28, 1925)

FROM THE SPANISH CLOISTER

Grrrr—what's that? A dog? A poet?
   Uttering his damnations thus—
If hate killed things, Brother Browning,
   God's Word, would not hate kill us?

If we ever meet together,
   Salve tibi! I might hear
How you know poor monks are really
   So much worse than they appear.

There's a great text in Corinthians
   Hinting that our faith entails
Something else, that never faileth,
   Yet in you, perhaps, it fails.

But if *plena gratia* chokes you,
   You at least can teach us how
To converse in wordless noises,
   Hy, zi; hullo!—Grrrr—Bow-wow!
   (from *G.K.'s Weekly*, April 4, 1925)

LADY CLARA VERE DE VERE REPLIES
TO MR. ALFRED TENNYSON

Alfred, Alfred Tennyson,
  So you've come up to town as well!
We saw you in the Park to-day,
  And scarcely knew you, such a swell.
You don't desire the *Daily Wire*
  Should print your name with father's guests;
We'd ask you here to meet the Prince,
  But you have loftier interests.

Listen, Alfred Tennyson,
  It's not the best of taste, you know,
To blame me for what I myself
  Was forced to suffer, years ago.
Your Muse forgets the racing debts
  I paid three times before the day
When Laurence in the lime-walk flung
  His panic-stricken life away.

Alfred, Alfred Tennyson,
  Till she can see me clapped in gaol
His mother's pledged my name; and you
  Still sit and let the creature rail.
The jury found his mind unsound,
  And hers is balanced none too well;
But in what dark unstable realms
  Your generous soul prefers to dwell!

Really, Alfred Tennyson.
  You move a bit behind the times.
There's not an orphan, girl or boy,
  That can't by heart repeat your rhymes.
For girls indeed are taught to read
  While beggars at the castle gate
Don't find much use for simple faith.
  Oh, Alfred, do get up to date!
                (from *G.K.'s Weekly*, May 2, 1925)

BY A CAPTAIN, OR PERHAPS A COLONEL,
OR POSSIBLY A KNIGHT-AT-ARMS
[TO MILTON]

Poet or pamphleteer, or what you please,
Who chance behind this space of wall to dwell,
Upon my soul I cannot very well
Correct my fire for arguments like these,
The great Emathian conqueror be blowed!

I have not got a spear or you a bower.
London is packed with poets; temple and tower
Swarm with them; where the devil should we be
Storming a town, if the repeated plea
Of Puritanic poets had the power
To stop a piece of ordnance with an ode?
                    (from *G.K.'s Weekly*, May 9, 1925)

THE FAT WHITE WOMAN SPEAKS

Why do you rush through the field in trains,
Guessing so much and so much.
Why do you flash through the flowery meads,
Fat-head poet that nobody reads;
And why do you know such a frightful lot
About people in gloves as such?

And how the devil can you be sure,
Guessing so much and so much,
How do you know but what someone who loves
Always to see me in nice white gloves
At the end of the field you are rushing by,
Is waiting for his Old Dutch?
                    (from *G.K.'s Weekly*, May 9, 1925)

Cf. Frances Cornford's "To a Fat Lady Seen from the Train".

TO A MODERN POET

Well,
What
about it?

I am sorry
if you have
a green pain
gnawing your brain away.
I suppose
quite a lot of it is
gnawed away
by this time.

I did not give you
a green pain
or even
a grey powder.
It is rather you, so winged, so vortical,
Who give me a pain.
When I have a pain
I never notice
the colour.

But I am very unobservant.
I cannot say
I ever noticed that the pillar-box
was like a baby
skinned alive and screaming.
I have not
a Poet's
Eye
which can see Beauty
everywhere.

Now you mention it,
Of course, the sky
is like a large mouth

                    shown to a dentist,
          and I never noticed
          a little thing
                    like that.

     But I can't help wishing
          You got more fun out of it;
          you seem to have taken
               quite a dislike
                    to things
     They seem to make you jump
     And double up unexpectedly—

     And when you write
          like other poets,
               on subjects
     not entirely
               novel,
          such as, for instance,
               the Sea,
     It is mostly about
          Sea-sickness.
     As you say—
     It is the New Movement,
          The Emetic Ecstasy.
     (from *G.K.'s Weekly*, May 30, 1925)

               POST-RECESSIONAL
               [TO KIPLING]

God of your fathers, known of old,
   For patience with man's swaggering line,
He did not answer you when told
   About you and your palm and pine,
Though you deployed your far-flung host
And boasted that you did not boast.

Though drunk with sight of power and blind,
   Even as you bowed your head in awe,

You kicked up both your heels behind
  At lesser breeds without the law;
Lest they forget, lest they forget,
That yours was the exclusive set.

We fancied heaven preferring much,
  Your rowdiest song, your slangiest sentence,
Your honest banjo banged, to such
  Very recessional repentance;
Now if your native land be dear,
Whisper (or shout) and we shall hear.

Cut down, our navies melt away.
  From ode and war-song fades the fire,
We are a jolly sight to-day
  Too near to Sidon and to Tyre
To make it sound so very nice
To offer ancient sacrifice.

Rise up and bid the trumpets blow
  When it is gallant to be gay,
Tell the wide world it shall not know
  Our face until we turn to bay.
Bless you, you shall be blameless yet,
For God forgives and men forget.
          (from *G.K.'s Weekly*, July 4, 1925)

LUCASTA REPLIES TO LOVELACE

Tell me not, friend, you are unkind,
  If ink and books laid by,
You turn up in a uniform
  Looking all smart and spry.

I thought your ink one horrid smudge,
  Your books one pile of trash,
And with less fear of smear embrace
  A sword, a belt, a sash.

Yet this inconstancy forgive,
　　Though gold lace I adore,
I could not love the lace so much
　　Loved I not Lovelace more.
(from *G.K.'s Weekly*, August 8, 1925)

AMERICANISATION

Britannia needs no Boulevards,
　　No spaces wide and gay:
Her march was through the crooked streets
　　Along the narrow way.
Nor looks she where, New York's seduction,
The Broadway leadeth to destruction.

Britannia needs no Cafés:
　　If Coffee needs must be,
Its place should be the Coffee-house
　　Where Johnson growled for Tea;
But who can hear that human mountain
Growl for an ice-cream soda-fountain?

She needs no Russian Theatre,
　　Where Father strangles Mother,
In scenes where all the characters
　　And colours kill each other:
Her boast is freedom had by halves,
And Britons never shall be Slavs.

But if not hers the Dance of Death,
　　Great Dostoievsky's dance,
And if the things most finely French
　　Are better done in France—
Might not Americanisation
Be best applied to its own nation?

Ere every shop shall be a store
　　And every Trade a Trust ...

Lo, many men in many lands
  Know when their cause is just.
There will be quite a large attendance
When *we* Declare our Independence.
    (from *G.K.'s Weekly*, May 2, 1925)

GEORGE LANSBURY[1]

He does not want Oil Magnates boiled in oil
Even in Olive Oil, the Chrism of Peace.
He does not wish to arm the sons of toil
Quite otherwise; he wants all arms to cease,
Arms and the Man I sing who, forced by Fate,
Leads us by Love and makes us long for Hate.
    (from *G.K.'s Weekly*, December 5, 1925)

THE PREMIER

What does little Baldwin[1] say
In his bed at break of day?
(Let us hope he smokes in bed),
Will it be like what he said
Long ago, of Birkenhead,[2]
Just suggest, in wish or doubt
Things that we could do without;
Then, regretting that he spoke it,
Put it in his pipe and smoke it,
Take such people as a joke,
Laugh, and let it end in smoke?
    (from *G.K.'s Weekly*, December 5, 1925)

---

[1] George Lansbury (1859–1940), British Labour Party politician, Christian pacifist and newspaper editor who opposed rearmament in the 1930s. The actress Angela Lansbury is his granddaughter.

[1] Stanley Baldwin (1867–1947), British Conservative Party leader and Prime Minister, was well known as a pipe-smoker.

[2] A seaport on the River Mersey opposite Liverpool. F. E. Smith, 1st Earl of Birkenhead, is also a possibility.

RIMA

What wish has Epstein's art portrayed,
Toward what does Rima rise?[1]
Those little hands were never made
To tear out eagles' eyes:
She for *Green Mansions* yearns; but not
So green a mansion as she got.
(from *G.K.'s Weekly*, December 5, 1925)

THE TURKEY AND THE TURK
The Mummer's Play

CAST

Father Christmas
St. George
A doctor from Berlin
A Turkish Knight
The Princess of the Mountains

Father C.   Here am I, Father Christmas; well you know it,
            Though critics say it fades, my Christmas Tree.
            Yet was it Dickens who became my poet,
            And who the Dickens may the critics be?

St. G.   I am St. George, whose cross in scutcheon scored,
               Red as the Rose of England on me glows,
            The Dragon who would pluck it, found this sword
               (*Draws sword.*)
            Which is the thorn upon the English Rose.

Doctor.   I am the doctor from Berlin. I kill
            Germs and diseases upon handsome terms

---

[1] Rima was the heroine of W. H. Hudson's *Green Mansions: A Romance of the Tropical Forest* (1904). A female equivalent of Tarzan and Mowgli, Rima the Bird Girl was a petite, dark-haired seventeen-year old brought up in the forests of South America. In 1925 a statue of Rima sculpted by Jacob Epstein was erected in Kensington Gardens in London.

—There are so many ways of being ill—
Some trust the Germans. Some prefer the Germs.

Turk.   I am the Turkish Knight: to sink and rise
In every Mummer's Play has been my work,
I am that Wrath that falls but never flies,
A Turkish Knight, but a most knightly Turk.

Princess.   I am the Princess come from mountains shady
That are the world's last wall against the Turk,
I had to come; or there would be no lady
In this remarkable dramatic work.

(*Enter Father Christmas with Christmas pudding, turkey, flagons, etc.*)

Father C.   I will not drink; let the great flagon here
Till the great toasts are drunk, stand where it is.
But Christmas pudding comes but once a year
But many times a day. And none amiss (*Cuts off a piece*).
The Christmas pudding, round as the round sky.
Speckled with better things than stars.

Doctor. (*rushing in and arresting his hand*)
                         Forgive
My haste. But men who eat that pudding die.

Father C.   And men who do not eat it do not live (*Eats*).

Doctor.   Our last proofs show, for perils that appal,
A Christmas pudding is a cannon ball.
But you grow old—

Father C.   And you grow always new
And every year you take a different view.
My every Christmas brings, with change and chills,
New doctors' doctrines with new doctors' bills.
Next year this pudding where I plant my knife
Will be the only food sustaining life.
The proverb holds: who shall decide or choose
When doctors disagree—with their own views?
Your drugs turn poisons and your poisons food.

And still this round and solid fact holds good—
While with themselves the doctors disagree
No Christmas pudding disagrees with me.

Doctor.   Progress is change; so is the whole world's youth
Afoot betimes to catch the newest truth,
While you in night-long wassail waste your breath
The early bird catches the worm of death,
Conquers the grave; and doth the secret know
Of life immortal.

Father C.   For a month or so.
That, too, will change. Soon you will tell us all
That early rising is a daily fall,
That fever waits in fiery morning skies,
And Bed is the most bracing exercise.
You'll find for sluggards some more pleasing term
And cry "The Early Bird catches the Germ."

(*Enter the Princess of the Mountains.*)

Princess.   Save me and harbour me, all Christian folk,
For I am fleeing from the heathen might.
My mountain city is a trail of smoke,
My track is trampled by the Turkish Knight,
Already where I sink they shake the ground,
The flying towers, the horsemen of Mahound.

Doctor.   Mahound. More properly Muhammad. Quaint!
The wars of creeds—or demons—smoke and smother,
Each of the demons calls himself a saint
Until two men can tolerate each other.

Princess.   So were we taught by many Turkish kings
To tolerate intolerable things.

Father C.   I have a creed, Its name is charity
And at my table all men may agree.

Princess.   Folk of the West, bethink you, far from strife,
Through what more weary ages than you think,
Our broken swords covered your carving knife

And with our blood you bought the wine you drink,
That you might ply your kindlier Christmas work
And kill the Turkey while we killed the Turk.

Father C.   I see one from the mountains ride amain
           Who rather comes to slay than to be slain.

        (*Enter Turkish Knight.*)

Turk.   I am the master of the sons of battle.
      The cohorts of the Crescent of the night,
      I for whom queens are slaves and slaves are cattle,
      I claim this queen and slave out of my right.
      I have burned her town and slain her sire in strife,
      Is there a better way to earn a wife?

Princess.   A wife! This Turkish dog, like sheep in pen,
          May herd a hundred wives—or bondwomen.

Doctor.   Consider. Set above the smoke of passion
       Where high philosophy and reason reign.
       I can give counsel in a cooler fashion
       Who am the friend of peace, the foe of pain.
       Consider—should this gentleman insist—
       He might be worse than a polygamist.

Princess.　What could be worse, and what unworthier?

Doctor.　He might, like Bluebeard, be a widower.
The habit which enjoys a hundred wives
Suggests at least, that every wife—survives.

Princess.　Such are not things that such as I survive,
Nor shall such bridal see us both alive,
Nor I consent.

Turk.　　　　　　Nor did I ask consent.
I did not ask your banner to be rent,
Your sire to fall, your battle-line to break,
I do not ask for anything I take.

Doctor.　She will find comfort in Philosophy.

Father C.　You were right, Doctor; I am old. Woe's me,
My knife is a clown's sword for cutting grease.
(*Flings down his carving-knife.*)

Doctor. (*looking piously upward*)
Peace! Is not this the certain road to Peace?

(*Enter St. George.*)

St. G.　Stop! For the doors are shut upon your treason,
I, George of Merry England, bar the way.
Not all so easily, not for a season,
You brave the anger of the saints at bay.
Red shall your cohorts be, your Crescent faint,
The hour you find—what will provoke a Saint.

Doctor.　Who is this mad Crusader?

Father C. (*lifting his flagon*)
He is come!
Let burst the trumpets, dance upon the drum!
Shout till you deafen the dead! I drain the flagon.
England in arms! St. George that beat the Dragon!

Doctor.　You dream, old dotard, and your drunken tales
Are fumes of Yuletide vintages and ales.

The wine is in your head. Water and wine.
A Dragon! Snapdragon is more your line.

Father C.   It may be. Who shall choose between us twain
Wine in the head or water on the brain!
But what of you, most prudent paragon,
You are as frightened of the snapdragon
As of the dragon, that St. George has beaten,
More scared to eat than he was to be eaten.

St. G.   At least I come in time to do redress
On a new Dragon for a new Princess.

Turk.   Sir, if my hundred wives indeed be sheep
I am the shepherd, who can count and keep,
And I keep this; had you a hundred lives
This sword should teach you to respect my wives.

St. G.   I will respect your widows.

Turk.   They that keep
          The oracles of the Prophet see you sleep
          Dead on your shield.

St. G.   I bear upon my shield
          Death, and a certain lesson how to die.
          Your Prophet lived too late to prophesy.

          (*Turkish Knight rushes forward.*)

Princess.   See how the face of your strange Doctor sneers!

Doctor.   How should Peace stay when Piety appears
          And men do murder for a change of words?
          Yet might the Peace be held. Ere you cross swords
          Knights of the Cross and Crescent, count the loss.

St. G.   Two swords in crossing make the sign of the cross
          That frightens fiends.

          (*Doctor leaps back from the clash of swords.*)
                         He's wounded in the hand;
          Doctor, a Doctor—let the battle stand.

Doctor.   I am a doctor, sir, and I can cure
          Complaints and maladies such Turks endure;
          In Turkish camps where air and water taints....

Turk.   You will find maladies, but not complaints.

Doctor.   But who will pay me if I cure the Turk?

St. G.   This hand will give you pay, which gives you work.

(*He hangs up his Red Cross shield behind the Turkish Knight and doctor.*)

St. G.   For proof that Christian men war not as cattle
          Above my foeman's head I hang my shield,
          That shows far off o'er hideous wastes of battle
          My sword has shattered but my shield has healed.

Father C.   They say to every shield there are two sides.
          So shall our champion show them as he rides,

And milder servants follow him in fight,
The Red Cross nurses to the Red Cross Knight.

Doctor.   Nurses and knights and all your chivalry
Would still be barren mercies but for me.
While you with liberal words would mend the Turk,
The healing hand of Science does your work,
While you show generous gestures, vague or grand
The healing hand of Science finds a hand.

(*Produces a mailed fist or any sort of big pantomime glove of armour.*)

Father C.   Here is the sort of trick the doctors love
To take a hand and give us back a glove.

Turk.   What would you do? I do not understand.

Doctor.   The Gauntlet shall be mightier than the hand,
Science has found the hand of your desire
An iron hand, a hand for flinging fire,
A mailed fist, the ensign of your legions,
And from the fingers of it flames shall go,
Smoke and thick flames that poison vasty regions,
And blight the fields as well as blight the foe.
Fool and fantastic in your red-cross coat,
A more than human hand is at your throat,
A hand that chokes.

St. G.   I know that this is sure
Whatever man can do, man can endure,
Though you shall loose all laws of fight, and fashion
A torture-chamber from a tilting-yard,
Though iron hard as doom grow hot as passion,
Man shall be hotter, man shall be more hard,
And when an army in your hell-fire faints,
You shall find martyrs who were never saints.

Doctor.   I am weary of your sainthood. If you knew
You would, as even I do, quake. But you
Who in a painted halo put reliance
Fear naught.

St. G.   Not even the healing hand of science.

Doctor. (*furiously*)
                Then at him, wound him, waste him utterly. (*They fight.*)

Turk.   Ere I could wound him he has wounded me.

Princess.   The Turk is wounded in the leg.

Father C.   Well fought!

Turk.   A Doctor, quick, a doctor! It is naught,
                To heal such scathe should be a petty task.
                I answer for my answering of it. Ask
                The Princess of the Mountains, for she knows.
                How long wars wage in Eastern sands or snows.
                No splitting of a slender tilting lance
                For a crowd's gaping or a lady's glance.
                War to the knife!

Doctor.   The surgeon's knife, my lord
                The surgeon's knife is mightier than the sword.
                Answer me now, old driveller, as you can,
                When your great carving-knife has cured a man,
                Or if these bones the war-dogs crush and crunch
                Can be patched up with pudding or with punch.
                Lady, I tell you all your mountain dead
                Who on Kossovo of the Blackbirds bled,
                There where the hero dies as a dog dies,
                Might have re-risen as this man shall rise.
                Answer me now, proud lady, as you can.
                Does Science help? Can Science save a man?
                What do you see, for all your savage pride?

Princess.   I see it always helping the wrong side.

Father C. (*to St. George*)
                This is not just. You fight not one but three,
                I think that you grew wearier than he.

Princess.   Why should we patch this pirate up again?

Why should you always win, and win in vain?
Bid him not cut the leg, but cut the loss.

St. G.   I will not fire upon my own Red Cross.

Princess.   If you lay there, would he let *you* escape?

St. G.   I am his Conqueror and not his ape.

Doctor.   Be not so sure of conquering. He shall rise
On lighter feet, on feet that vault the skies.
Science shall make a mighty foot and new,

(*Produces a sort of pantomime leg in armour and with wings.*)
Light as the feather feet of Perseus flew,
Long as the seven-leagued boots in tales gone by,
This shall bestride the sea and ride the sky.
Thus shall he fly, and beat above your nation
The clashing pinions of Apocalypse,
Ye shall be deep-sea fish in pale prostration
Under the sky-foam of his flying ships.

(*The Turkish Knight advances with the new leg, to fight again.*)
When terror above your cities, dropping doom,
Shall shut all England in a lampless tomb,
Your widows and your orphans now forlorn
Shall be no safer than the dead they mourn.
When all their lights grow dark, their lives grow grey,
What will those widows and those orphans say?

St. G.   St. George for Merry England!

(*They fight again, with more doubtful effect, but St. George at last smites
the Turkish Knight on the head and he falls.*)

Princess.   Down is the Crescent and its crest abased!

Doctor.   A Head is very easily replaced.

Father C.   More of this ironmongery that he hires.

Doctor.   Here is a Head no headache ever tires
Which never wants its hair cut, singed or curled,
The Business Head of all the Working World.

(*Produces pantomime head of a German with a spiked helmet and spectacles, perhaps rather like the Doctor's own.*)

Father C.   Shall we again grant respite to our foe?

St. G.   I tell you Yes, man!

(*The Turkish Knight suddenly lifts himself on his elbow.*)

Turk.   And I tell you No.
             I'll have no more of your pale wizardry,
             Leave me my wounded head and let me be.

Doctor.   What do you mean? A wound is only pain,
             And why should I who twice, and now again,
             Lead you to conquer, leave you now to die?

Turk.   Something may conquer. It will not be I.
             If always thus you mend me when I fall,
             There will be nothing of myself at all.
             You arm me and you tame me and you trim,
             Each time I gain a tool and lose a limb.
             In wings and wheels all that I was will fade
             And I shall be a monster you have made.

Doctor.   You hoped to have his head when you began.

Turk.   Base leech, I hoped to be the better man
             And not the better mantrap. Leave alone!
             I hoped to have his head—and keep my own (*rousing
                 himself*).
             When I came riding from the tents of morning
             Clean as an arrow from my bended bow,
             I had not need of such dead things' adorning,
             No, by the panoply of the Prophet, no! (*Rises.*)
             Lady, if we be less than you in love,
             At least our hate as high as yours shall stand.
             And I have lost. The Devil take my glove (*Flings away the
                 mailed hand.*)
             And George of Merry England take my hand.

Princess.   Now is the Turkish Knight a knight at least.

Doctor.   A Knight! They will be snivelling for a priest
To wed you to your Red Cross cut-throat here,
With all the mummeries of Faith—and Fear—
To suit this medieval mummery,
These fighting-cocks are caught in—Chivalry!
That in a tangle of fantastic rules
Makes them first foes, then friends, and always fools;
I would have rapt your souls to clearer rages,
On the top wave of Time, alive, alert,
I had done all that could outdare the ages.

Father C. (*poking him with the carving knife*).
Friend, did you ever laugh? And did it hurt?
No matter—if you cannot laugh, my friend,
You can be laughed at; let us laugh—and end.
Dragon and snapdragon alike take flight
With cockcrow. Take a slash at Turkish Knight,
Or take a slice of turkey, as you choose,
And have the German Doctor for the goose—
And if the goose must cackle—if he tease
With talk of medieval mummeries,
Ask him what else but Mummery, I pray,
He asks from Mummers upon Christmas Day?
(from *G.K.'s Weekly*, December 5, 1925)

X

POEMS ADDRESSED TO MARGARET HALFORD
1921–1923

ON ACTOR-MANAGERS

I have known doubt, and even damn, in fact
Actors who manage, managers who act,
But never you, in whose magnanimous sway
To manage is indeed to *ménager*.
Your *ménage* knows you: take these thanks from me,
The heaviest beast in your menagerie.

(early 1920s)

THE APOLOGY OF THE CLOWNS

I. BOTTOM THE WEAVER

Once when an honest weaver slept
And Puck passed by, a kindly traitor,
And on his shoulders set the head
Of a Shakespearean commentator.

The man had walked proverbial ways
Fair science frowned not on his birth
Nor lost in long and tangled dreams
The mother-wit of mother-earth,

Elaborate surgeons had not found
The cobweb made the cure too brief
Nor vegetarians taught the rule
Of eating mustard without beef,

Mrs. Margaret Halford was a professional actress who after her marriage moved to Beaconsfield, where she started the neighborhood theater group the Players Club. She became a friend of the Chestertons, who performed in some of her productions. Although ostensibly an amateur group, the club included some young members, such as John Gielgud, who went on to make professional acting careers. See "The Players Club", *Collected Poetry*, Part I, p. 312 and "The Club" on p. 364 in this volume.

In July 1921, under the direction of Mrs. Margaret Halford, GKC played Theseus in the Players Club short version of Shakespeare's *A Midsummer Night's Dream*. See "A Midsummer Night's Dream", *Collected Poetry*, Part I, p. 307.

Only in that green night of growth
Came to him, splendid, without scorn,
The lady of the dreams of men
The rival of all women born.

And he, for all his after weaving
Drew up from that abysmal dream
Immortal Art, that proves by seeming
All things more real than they seem.

The dancing moth was in his shuttle
The pea's pink blossom in his woof
—Your driving schools, your dying hamlets,
Go through them all and find the proof.

That you where'er the old crafts linger
Draw in their webs like nets of gold
Hang up their banners for a pattern
The leavings of the looms of old.

And even as this home-made rhyme
Drags but the speech of Shakespeare down
These home-made patterns but repeat
The traceries of an ancient clown.

And while the modern fashions fade
And while the ancient standards stream
No psycho-analyst has knocked
The bottom out of Bottom's dream.

II. STARVELING THE TAILOR

When the dancing is done and the laughter
And the Carnival garments must go
Not to Starveling who tailored in Athens
But Simmons who lives in Soho,

When the Journalists' tales and their pictures
Have gone like their trousers to press
Is there place for these dubious echoes
That linger and wonder and guess
From the sermons in stone and the symbols
From the songs that are older than books
That the fool of Shakespearean fancy
Is not such a fool as he looks?

That his heart was not hungry in leisure
That his task and his time were in tune
That the man on the earth did not labour
Alone like the man in the moon,
When the School of the Guild was unbroken
That taught men to colour and carve
When the gold of the Guild was unrifled
That suffered not Starveling to starve,
That the changes hang heavy with question
In the land where our fathers were free
That took from us flagons and fairies
And gave us tobacco and tea?

When the songs die away and the jesting
And our pleasures that vanish too soon
Like the dog of dramatic departure
That bayed but obeyed not the moon,
Suffice it that here for a season
Unbroken of clatter and clang
Merry England, our mother, returning
Stood up in her gardens and sang.
And the clothes that we wore were a challenge
For all elfland to rise from the dead
And to ask how the hat of the tailor
Had ever come into his head

III. SNUG THE JOINER

Stranger manners are in fashion.
Bolder words are coined
Since the day when Snug the joiner
Saw the lovers joined.
We should feel the fun was faded
Feel the jests were forced
Seeing Dukes of Athens married—
Dukes are all divorced.
Come to the Divorce Feast, each
In solitude sublime,
Mendelssohn's Divorce March sounding
(Syncopated time).
Hushed the high ancestral house
Where the pairs were mated
Crash the cymbals ... we shall soon
All be syncopated.
Pictures flung about in patches
Music torn to rags
(Even such a star as Thisbe
Guilty of some gags)
The triumphal arch of ages
Cloven to the abyss.
Architecture rent and rhyming
Turned to rant like this.

Newer morals are the measure
Stranger fates fulfilled
Since the day when Snug the Joiner
Joined the Joiners' Guild.
Only you shall find forgotten
Fencing house and hall
Doors that do not warp or wither
Beams that do not fall,
Strengthened of the storm of ages
Spared of frost and thunder

Things that man has joined and God
Has not put asunder.

IV. FRANCIS FLUTE THE BELLOWS-MENDER

It's very well for Mr. S.
And all those literary fellows
To laugh when we are acting plays—
Supposing they were mending bellows.

If Shakespeare had been Snug the Joiner
The joining might be far from snug
And he might mend himself a pot
And only make himself a mug.

There would be smiles more delicate
Among discriminating drapers
Raised by an actor cutting [lines]
Than by a tailor cutting capers.

And if he plied my trade at Court
I fancy that Queen Bess would send
And bellow at the bellows-mender
And break more things than he could mend.

In many a shop of broken bits
Men seek the art they tore to shreds,
The warming pan is on their walls
They counted vulgar in their beds,

Thus what we know as dish or flagon
Is called a Wedgwood now, and thus
That we poor clowns would call a fiddle
Is called a Stradivarius.

A picture's called a Botticelli
(At which the man in Punch was mute)
So, to make music for the ages
My Bellows shall be called a Flute.

V. QUINCE THE CARPENTER

This is Quince the Prompter, he
As Stage Carpenter may be
Suited to the Carpentry
More than to the Stage,
Yet the workman must be far
Prompter than the prompters are
Welding out of beam and bar
Props for youth and age.

Theseus friend of man and dog
Did not like the expiring frog,
Really sit upon a log
But upon a throne,
If the chair on which he sat
Let him down and laid him flat
Even he might curse at that
In an undertone.

Did we feel where'er we tread
Rafters thump us on the head
Seams like blossoms lightly shed
Down from roof and gables,
Grand pianos strewn in scraps
The mahogany collapse
We might own that Quince perhaps
Might have turned the tables.

When this incident occurs
People, if with some demurs
Will be just to carpenters
And the Duke when wedded
May his scornful bride remind
That the men who have designed
Wooden legs for all mankind
Are not wooden-headed.

VI. SNOUT THE TINKER

"Hard-handed men are they who never
Have laboured in their minds till now".
The master of the Thesean revels
He knew it. But I wonder how.

The mind of Snout had surely pondered
On other points than walls and chinks
Surely the tinker is a thinker
Surely he thinks of what he tinks.

Those fingers stretched to frame the cranny
Could mend with many a hook and crook
Well nigh as taxing to the talents
As carrying wands before a Duke.

In modern streets, in mighty cities
Have we not wished that things were so
That other bricks were as obliging,
That other walls away would go?

There are that do disfigure walls
With the trade-marks of meaner trades
And Wall Street knows unworthier whispers
Than is the way of men and maids.

No more; the cities of Destruction
Shall be destroyed as they were made
Before the earth of days unending
Has seen the end of Bunyan's trade.

Under the hedge the tinker tinkers
At my own garden's weedy edge;
Shall I not choose the cheaper fancy
And use the tinker for the hedge?

(1921)

THE CLUB

The Players Club is turned to the Club of a Giant
      To crush or wreck
Before whose feet I stand up small but defiant
      A spot or speck.
But YOU shall rule and remain in our thanks and praises
      And face without loss
Colossal cities, the vast Babylonian mazes
      Of Gerrard's Cross.
You won us the Crown: and led us where Victory beckoned
      Established our soul
If after we nobly abjured it and deigned to come second
      To Hogs-In-The-Hole.
If Craig-and-a-Bittock outran us ahead,
      Or Tooting, in rage:
Without You we had always been almost as dead
      As the Regular Stage.
Forgive, if this Modern and rugged original metre
      By accident Rhymes
And for lack of Young Poets to round it and make it completer,
      Means something at times:
For these things began when Reason and Rhyme were in season,
      And trite and tame
Is the Rhyme: but for writing to you, dear Lady, the Reason
      Is always the same.

                    (ca. 1922)

For note on the Players Club, see p. 357. See also "The Players Club", *Collected Poetry*, Part I, p. 312.

[TO ONE RETURNING FROM AMERICA]

When you were in the land of your late mission,
The land of cocktails and prohibition
(Vaster not greater in its art or song:
For spires are high, sky-scrapers only long:
Music we had, but they discovered Sound.
If we have poets, they have Ezra Pound.)[1]
A dreadful fear possessed us, for we knew
Their joy in picking up a thing or two:

We knew how they secure our precious things,
Towers of our earls or jewels of our kings,
Bid for the shrine that pointed to the stars,
Or match cathedrals as they match their cars—
A charming compliment! So very kind!
But had you stayed with them we still should find
The International Exchange too dear,
With you out there and Lady Astor[2] here.

Had you returned not for the pantomime
We had made war upon that western clime,
Avenging Saratoga and Yorktown:
We would set back those stars in England's crown,
If anybody wanted such a gem—
(Just now we see a bit too much of them).

See "Ad Amicos", *Collected Poetry*, Part I, p. 266.

[1] Ezra Pound (1885–1972), American Poet and Critic, then best known in England
as a proponent of a style of poetry based on Anglo-Saxon alliteration.

[2] Lady Astor, Nancy Witcher Langhorne (1879–1964), daughter and heiress of an
American tobacco manufacturer, who in 1919 married Waldorf Astor (1879–1952)
who in 1919 succeeded to the hereditary title of 2nd Viscount Astor, thus debarring
himself from the British House of Commons. Nancy Astor was then elected to replace
him as Member of Parliament for Plymouth, becoming the first woman to enter the
British Parliament.

NO.... We would ransom you and not be shabby,
Let them have Lady Oxford[3] and an abbey.

(ca. 1922)

APOLOGY OF AN ABSENTEE PRESIDENT

Alas! I was not there when, led by you,
Our stage all earthly stages overthrew:
Athens and Stratford and Beyreuth went down
Forgotten in the fame of this our town:
When—but I fear I mix the details ... well
Some rollicking gay Russian farce was played
Till shouts of laughter shook the house; and made
Howard de Walden shed the woes of birth
And lose his monocle in tears of mirth:
With tears of woe I say it in despair.
Alas! I may be wrong. I was not there.

(ca. 1922)

IN ACKNOWLEDGEMENT OF A SNAKE

The Spotted Snake has lost his tongue
In emulation of that young
And wondering wife of that romance
Of ancient France—by modern France
Who in fantastic garb antique
Could charm us when she could not speak:
And should that leech the bond dissever,
Would please us though she talked for ever.

[3] Lady Oxford—Margot Tennant (1864–1945), a society figure and brilliant hostess who led the "Souls", a group advocating greater freedom for women. In 1894 she married the politician Herbert Asquith who went on to become Prime Minister in April 1908 and then Earl of Oxford and Asquith. After her husband's resignation in 1916 she wrote two autobiographies considered indiscreet at that time.

The Serpent took the tip but bossed it.
He tried to hold his tongue and lost it.

                                        (ca. 1922)

[TO MRS. MARGARET HALFORD]

Had we in London, not in London End,[1]
    First seen you flame in footlight of renown,
We had not dreamed what neighbour or what friend
    Could tread the tiny stages of our town.

They talk of Arts impersonal illusion,
    And men must in the mask forget the face:
Puck is but Puck and yields without confusion
    The Duchess or Dick Whittington his place.

Yet tho' our souls be cowed with Critic thunder
    And private warmth be frighted with stage fire,
Yet pardon us who know whereat we wonder,
    Suffer us still to love what we admire.

Whatever Optional Fancy-dress you are Opting,
    When revels call us back, you shall be still[2]
Fairy and Lady and leader of our adopting,
    Queen, Empress of Twelfth Night—Or What You will.

                                        (ca. 1922)

[1] The Halfords lived in London End, Beaconsfield, until 1927.
[2] The Players Club New Year Revels or party.

XI

THE QUEEN OF SEVEN SWORDS
1926

IN MEMORIAM
J.S.P.

You go before me on all roads
  On bridges broad enough to spread
Between the learned and the dunce
Between the living and the dead
            (December 1926)

THE QUEEN OF SEVEN SWORDS*

I had dreamed of a desolate land, deformed to its crooked skyline,
As if the round earth itself could be bent out of shape in its shame,
Its plants stamped flat like a pattern, by marching of more than
    mammoths,
Huge things, more naked and nameless; too old or new for a name.

And I knew what Spirit had passed, who is vast beyond meaning or
    measure,
The blank in the brain of the whirlwind, the hollow, the hungry
    thing,
The Nothing that swells and desires, the void that devours and
    dismembers,
In the heart of barbarian armies or the idle hours of a king

Low light on the flat-topped hills, like headless creatures of chaos,
Long shadows striping the slime, like ghosts laid flat in the grave,

GKC dedicated *The Queen of Seven Swords* to John Swinnerton Phillimore (1873–
1926), a professor of classics at the University of Glasgow. The volume included the fol-
lowing from *Collected Poetry*, Part I: "The Ballad of King Arthur, p. 531, "The Black
Virgin", p. 122, "In October", p. 545, "Laughter", p. 226, "A Little Litany", p. 356,
"The Paradox", p. 154, "A Party Question", p. 510, "Regina Angelorum", p. 156, "The
Return of Eve", p. 160, "The Trinkets", p. 180, "The Towers of Time", p. 177, "The
Two Maidens", p. 183, and "The White Witch", p. 185.

* It will be obvious that the Seven Champions of Christendom who are here used
as types of the different nations are only the imaginary paladins of the old boyish romance;
and have no connection with the historical saints who bore their names [GKC].

371

Low clouds lying flattened and spread, as if heaven itself lay prostrate;
And I looked on the world-wide waste; and I said, "There is none
    to save."

I knew not if time out of mind, last night or now or to-morrow,
Had broken that obscene dawn; on the strange, scarred hills I trod,
I saw on their breaking terraces, cracking and sinking for ever,
One shrine rise blackened and broken; like a last cry to God.

Old gold on the roof hung ragged as scales of a dragon dropping,
The gross green weeds of the desert had spawned on the painted
    wood:
But erect in the earth's despair and arisen against heaven interceding,
Whose name is Cause of Our Joy, in the doorway of death, she stood.

The Seven Swords of her Sorrow held out their hilts like a challenge,
The blast of that stunning silence as a sevenfold trumpet blew
Majestic in more than gold, girt round with a glory of iron,
The hub of her wheel of weapons; with a truth beyond torture, true.

And it seemed as I gazed, from afar, from the cracks of the withering
    mountains,
That seven sad knights came riding from seven points of the sky,
Yet I knew their crests from of old, who had ridden in the faerie
    tourney,
When all the days were daydreams, in the truant days gone by.

The green rust and the red had rotted their bronze and iron,
The green slime and the grey had stained them with many lands
The sheath of the sword hung hollow; but before the shrine in the
    twilight
They ranked their empty scabbards; they raised their empty hands.

And each man spoke, but in each was more than of one man speaking;
A sound as of many waters, a tumult of many men.
And I heard through my heaving dream the noise of the breaking of
    nations,
And tribes that the terror scatters and the trumpet gathers again.

ST. JAMES OF SPAIN

Mine eyes were strong with sorrows; none other blood shall say
What lay on my heart for a hundred years ere the stone was rolled
    away,
When crushing the vines and statuary, the rock of Mahound was hurled,
Featureless, faceless, enormous; the rolling stone of the world.

The haters of wine, the horsemen, came on us like night at noon.
The veiled knights with the crooked swords that sware by the crooked
    moon
We endured to go down under darkness, beholding, as men that die,
The name of their God of Battles scrawled backwards across the sky.

Queen, if our own gold rotted what no man's iron could rend,
Bronzed gold, dark wine of the dust; if we stiffened and stood at the
    end
A gilded skeleton army brittle and brown in the sun,
Forget not what all have forgotten; this field was won.

ST. DENYS OF FRANCE

Mine eyes were fierce with fever; I was lord of the sleepless land
Where the foot sticks to the stirrup and the sword-hilt to the hand,
A torment of banners tossing when no wind blows
Of the men that have made all marvels, except repose.

On the East and the West gate graven our name was Victory;
We took all nations captive that we might set them free;
We could not endure the endurance of all slaves under the sun;
We spat at them rights and riches, out of a gun.

Mother, if hell came after and the world laid waste for a word,
If some of our blows fell upon thee, if some blows erred,
It fell of a fury of justice that fell from thee—
Lo, we have freed all peoples. Oh, set us free!

ST. ANTHONY OF ITALY

Mine eyes were blind with splendours; I have stood too long in the
sun.
The heat and the light and the laurels, in the days when the world was
one,
And merry where all was ancient and careless where all was known,
We dwelt in the gay glass houses that beckon the booby's stone.

The force of the foolish peoples, that herd, that follow a king,
On the light-winged thought came crashing with the weight of a
thoughtless thing
And the Virgins, the high Republics, that were wed to the Vision and
free,
Imperial clowns took captive, holding in harlotry.

Lady of lilies in heaven, thy lilies on earth burn red,
We built and the wide world ruined; we wove and they rent the
thread;
We carved and the whole world shattered; we bound and the world
disbands.
In the day I arise for requital—hold thou mine hands.

ST. PATRICK OF IRELAND

Mine eyes were alive with anger; for the gag was in my mouth.
They bound me to a broken tree, with my face towards the South,
And hucksters watched and betted, when would the great heart break,
And pygmy pedants whipped me, for Thy name's sake.

Thee, though the myrrh be bitter with the crushing of all sweet things,
Though we fed upon hope and hatred, and the pride of the ragged
kings,
And the two-edged sword of the spirit that wounds the hand,
Torture could not take from us; this is thy land.

O smitten, O dolorous Mother, if the cross fall thwart of the crown,
If thy rose grew dark in our garden, thy moon on our wrath went
down,

If too close be the cloud on Kiltartan,[1] too deep the debt,
Forgive us when we forgive not; let us forget.

ST. ANDREW OF SCOTLAND

Mine eyes were hard with horror; I walked on the heights alone
And the winds were winged bulls walking, clashing their wings of stone,
And the Lord was rolled in the thunder, like the Bible in the plaid,
And for fear of the Feet above them, the stars went mad.

On the seventh day from the seventh halted the earthquake feet,
And they made an evil silence, a silence in the street.
And men walked damned or chosen, as it was with the world begun,
For the Day, that awaited all men, for us was done.

Mother of mirth and pardon, of laughter and tears and truce,
Queen of the kind and careless knights that rode with the heart of
     Bruce,
Does there not wait upon wisdom a last surprise?
Are we not weary of wisdom? Oh, make us wise!

ST. DAVID OF WALES

Mine eyes were shy with secrets; I was hunted to the hills,
The shadow-hunt of the rider that, riding, never kills
But is lost in the heights and hears, over horrible chasms hung,
The voice of his vanished foeman sing in a strange tongue.

But ours was the Hound of Arthur, whose leap was long as the day,
And the buried name of Britain that none but the Druids say,
And a song is hid in my speech; that sways like a tolling bell
For the men that went forth to battle; but they always fell.

Thine is no pride, Princess, in the proud, the palpable things,
In the vast flat plans of the plains, that are traced in the charts of kings:
He is thine that was born in the cavern, that died on the hill;
A hymn is hid in my speech; it may cry to thee still.

[1] An area in Co. Galway associated with Lady Augusta Gregory (1852–1932) and
W. B. Yeats.

ST. GEORGE OF ENGLAND

Mine eyes were sealed with slumber; I sat too long at the ale.
The green dew blights the banner; the red rust eats the mail.
And a spider spanned the chasm from the hand to the fallen sword,
And the sea sang me to sleep; for it called me lord.

This was the hand of the hero; it strangled the dragon's scream,
But I dreamed so long of the dragon that the dragon was a dream:
And the knight that defied the dragon deserted the princess.
Her knight has stolen her dowry; she has no redress.

Mirror of Justice, shine on us; blaze though the broad sky break,
Show us our face though it shatter us; shatter and shake us awake!
We were not tortured of demons, with Berber and Scot,
We that have loved have failed thee. Oh, fail us not!

ALL THE SEVEN

"We have lost our swords in the battle; we have broken our hearts in
  the world
Since first we went forth from thy face with the gonfalon's gold unfurled,
Disarmed and distraught and dissundered thy paladins come
From the lands where the gods sit silent. Art thou too dumb?"

They waited; and minute by minute the hush grew hollow with
  horror
From doubt; till a far voice spoke, as faint with pain and apart,
"Knew ye not, ye that seek, wherein I have hidden all things?
Strewn far as the last lost battle; your swords have met in my heart."

And it seemed that the swords fell down with a shock as of
  thunderbolts falling,
And the strange knights bent to gather and gird them again for the fight:
All blackened; a bugle blew; but all in that flash of blackness,
With the clang of the fallen swords, I awoke; and the sun was bright.

IMAGES

I saw a mirror like the moon
   Made splendid by a sunken sun
Framing the wrinkled face of kings
   And haloed harlots one by one
And many a judge with livid lips,
   And many a thief with thankful eyes,
Like his who climbed the torturing tree
   And drank that night in Paradise;
     And something like a floating word
     Behind a curtain, overheard
     By chance, from a strange chamber, found me
     "The mirror is a woman's eyes."
     (*Speculum Justitiae, ora pro nobis.*)[1]

Rose up through one clear rent of sky
   The midmost of a monstrous tower
Far up, far down, all earthly scale
   Escaping in its pathless power
Such strength as only burst from sight
   In some lost epic vast and wild
Where giants piling up their tower
   Were pygmies by the thing they piled.
     And the heart knew without a word
     A strength below all strength had stirred
     Lifting the load of all the world
     A woman's arm under a child.
     (*Turris Davidica, ora pro nobis.*)[2]

Broad was the house of burning gold
   Like sunrise standing on the mountains
A million mirrored flames that glowed
   On golden peacocks, golden fountains,

---

[1] Mirror of Justice, pray for us.
[2] Tower of David, pray for us.

As tree by tree stood rayed with flame
   Like seven-branched candlestick or fan
All glories in the Age of Gold
   Glowed equal when the world began
      But a voice speaking dreamily
      Said in my ear, but not to me,
         "One gold thread of a woman's hair
         Has blown across the eyes of man."
         (*Domus Aurea, ora pro nobis.*)[3]

Deep in a silver wintry wood
   In secret skies where sleepers rove
An ivory turret from the trees
   Rose clearer than the sky it clove
Too wan for flame, too warm for snow,
   Which gold most delicate would defile
And near but never nearer growing
   Though one should labour mile on mile.
      And with it—in the flash that brings
      Sight of the world of little things,
      A woman's finger lifted up,
      A finger lifted with a smile.
      (*Turris Eburnea, ora pro nobis.*)[4]

Down through the purple desolation
   Of deserts under stars they strode
Who bore the dark and winged pavilion
   Of their ungraven god for load;
Strange if the secret of the skies
   Behind low crimson curtains hid,
Or if that vagrant booth defied
   The huge hypnotic Pyramid.

---

[3] House of Gold, pray for us.
[4] Tower of Ivory, pray for us.

Then, in an instant come and gone,
Green fields and one that stood thereon
Flashed like green lightning; and the thunder
"A woman was his walking home"
(*Foederis Arca, ora pro nobis*)[5]

O breakers! great Iconoclasts!
  When will your raking hammers find
What statues spring up with a word,
  What icons have built up the mind,
Or learn by hacking if the Form
  Be all a part or part a whole,
Or grind out of your gods made dust
  What is the sign and what the soul
    Or chase what images have hung
    In the air where any song was sung,
    Seeing if the sword can put asunder
    All that was wedded with the tongue?
    (*Sedes Sapientiae, ora pro nobis.*)[6]

AN AGREEMENT

Mr. William Clissold[1] *regards birth-control as the test of liberality: those against it are reactionary: those in favour are for the progressive revolution.*

Where you have laid it, let the sword divide;
And your unmotherly Medea be
Here sundered from our human trinity,
The Mother and the Virgin and the Bride.

Why should we falter? Ours shall be the mirth
And yours the amaze when you have thinned away

[5] Ark of the Covenant, pray for us.
[6] Seat of Wisdom, pray for us.

[1] *The World of William Clissold* (1926) was a novel by H. G. Wells (1866–1946).

Your starving serfs to fit the starveling pay
And seen the meek inheriting the earth.

That Christ from this creative purity
Came forth your sterile appetites to scorn.
Lo: in her house Life without Lust was born,
So in your house Lust without Life shall die.

XII

POEMS 1926–1929

PROPAGANDA

"And why does Mr. Chesterton drag Catholic propaganda even into detective stories?"—From a very indulgent reviewer

> Under that blue Italian dome,
> Men throned the Thunderer in the sky
> And still his priests creep forth from Rome
> And walk *Sub Divo*[1] on the sly:
> And painters, under priestly strictures,
> Must drag the sky into their pictures.
>
> Priests in the School; each astral chart
> Must show the sun on pain of sin:
> Priests in the Home; in rooms apart
> Some window drags the daylight in
> And private portraits still are made
> Of cunning blends of light and shade.
>
> Since Jupiter Capitoline
> Was set above the storms on high,
> No landscape-painter yet has dared
> To paint the land above the sky.
> Since dead religions will not die,
> What of abolishing the sky?
> (from *G.K.'s Weekly*, July 17, 1926)

ARISTOCRACY

Dr. Marie Stopes,[1] in answering Dr. Fairfield, claims that her principles have been in many cases approved by the House of Lords, that august assembly.

> Lord Hump, whose heritage is all entail,
> Smiles when the spawn of poor relations fail:

[1] *Sub Divo*, in the open; openly.

[1] Dr. Marie Stopes (1880–1958), the birth control pioneer.

Lord Slump, whose family has run to seed,
Can see no reason why the poor should breed:
Lord Grump, who thinks of suicide this spring,
Lord Lump, who does not think of anything,
Lord Zump, long fled from the Levantine shore,
Lord Dump, of Deeds That Won the Empire or
The Contract for the Rubbish-Carts at Wembley
(Who would alone adorn the august assembly—),
Lord Pump, of the *Live Wire*, who makes a mint
From all the things he prints—and does not print—
All these accept the high salute of Stopes,
The tribute proudly held from priests and popes

"Let God and Nature, Birth and Babies die
But spare, O spare our Old Nobility."
                    (from *G.K.'s Weekly*, April 9, 1927)

ALL THROUGH THE NIGHT

(*The effect of these lines depends entirely on their being sung very slowly
indeed to the beautiful Welsh air.*)

Jazz is jerking, jazzers reeling,
          All through the night!
Raucous saxophones are pealing
          All through the night.
Din like all damnation dealing—
Yelling, banging, howling, squeaking,
Suit this air when played with feeling
          All through the night.

Noise that keeps the night-clubs going
          All through the night.
Fizz and cocktails always flowing
          All through the night.
Showy women not worth showing;
Men well-known and not worth knowing—

Loudly their own trumpets blowing
   All through the night.

Naught can stay the mad gyrations
   All through the night.
Or the latest chic sensations
   All through the night,
Save alarming indications
That the local police stations,
Also stretch their operations—
   All through the night.

Woeful poet, sit not weeping
   All through the night.
Peace a wiser world is steeping
   All through the night.
They that have our lives in keeping:
Digging, planting, ploughing, reaping,
Still retain a taste for sleeping—
   All through the night.
   (from *G.K.'s Weekly*, August 20, 1927)

FOLK SONG

Six detectives went fishing
   Down by the sea-side.
They found a Dead Body,
   And enquired how it died.

Father Brown he informed them,
   Quite mild and without scorn:
'Like you and me and the rest of us,
   He died of being born.'

The Detective from the *Daily News*
   Asked 'Where are the Dead?'

Inscribed in the copy of *The Secret of Father Brown* given to Father O'Connor.

And Father Brown coughed gently
  And he answered and said

'If you'll come to St Cuthbert's
  I'll tell you today.'
But the other Five detectives
  Went weeping away.

               (1927)

A SONG OF MODERATION

They have said, the good and wise,
That it pays to advertise,
  And it's only right to speak with moderation
Of a truth that stands so high,
Simply written on the sky,
  Though perhaps with just a touch of ostentation.

The beers that are best known
Are not arsenic alone,
  It is modified by salt and other things.
If you tell a waiter "And please
Will you bring some Gruyère cheese,"
  You can trifle with the substance that he brings.

There's a Port that you can drink,
And distinguish it from ink
  By a something that's not easy to define,
But not only from the poster
Of an after-dinner toaster
  Who has drunk enough to talk of it as wine.

The Yankee car is slick.
Put together very quick.
  When it comes apart with similar rapidity,
It will comfort you to know

It should take an hour or so
   To make it with Victorian solidity.

For it pays to advertise,
And when the engine lies
   On your stomach and the petrol's in a blaze,
And the car lies round you wrecked,
You'll have leisure to reflect
   Upon whom it is exactly that it pays.

                          (1927)

WESLEYAN CHRISTMAS CAROL

How far is it to Bethlehem?
Not very far.
We could visit Him; but them:
Think what they are.

Joseph the working man
Shabby and old;
He's a Roman Catholic
So I've been told.

Mothers I fear are found
Not very far
From any mangers where
Their own babies are.

Ought we to visit her?
Will um or shall um?
How far is it to Bethlehem?
It's nearer to Balham.

              (1927)

Chesterton's response to a request for a revised version of Frances Chesterton's carol for use in Wesleyan Chapels. The revision would have involved the omission of references to Mary.

DEBELLARE SUPERBOS[1]

The golden dust that was the desert lion,
The gilded dust that reared and roared and died,
The Wolf whose wild milk was the Roman pride,
The Eagles that gathered upon the rending of Zion.
These were not all; but vaster, vaguer forms,
Unconscious types—the tortoise of the shields—
Nor was it a Wolf alone that fenced the fields
And saved the sheep from the sea-wolves and the storms.

Wrath of the Lamb? What wrath is in the Lamb?
But when death rent at last the sea-king's keep
Through cracks and chasms not all the dead could dam,
Huge, as a nightmare fills the skies of sleep,
Swelled the enormous visage of a Sheep
Bursting twelve gates, the Roman Battering-Ram.

(*The Radiator*, June 22, 1928.)

[GREEN SUNS]

Green Suns shall glare on worlds eclipsed,
Green hair shall grow on yellow men,
Green blood shall spout in monstrous wars
In the wild journeys of the pen
Only until the soul has seen
That any blade of grass is green.

For by what charter or what claim
When you came naked on the earth
Had you the frenzy to be calm
Before the portents round your birth?
How did you dare expect to see
Not the green man but the green tree?

(ca. 1928)

[1] Virgil, *Aeneid*, book 6, l. 853, "Overthrow the proud."

[THE STORM]

Into steep towers the storm is gathered up,
Tower with the whirlwind for a winding stair,
The fringe brimming, bubbling like a cup,
The deluge huge, unfallen, hung on air—
Then in vast throbs the thunder and light will stare,
Lightning and landscape with white haggard eyes
Stare at each other then shut lids share
A blessed blindness: with the surprise.

Better their weary,   wide, without shade,
The sun itself a brief blazon shone,
Were we but startled once to look thereon
And for one flash be gloriously afraid:
Let there be light: and so a world is made:
Let there be lightning: and the world is gone.

                    (Dudley Chine, Bournemouth, 1929)

FOR THE YOUNG LADIES SUFFERING
EDUCATION AT THE CONVENT
OF THE HOLY CHILD

To be a Real Prophet once
   For you alone did I desire,
Who dragged the Prophet's Mantle down
   And brought the Chariot of Fire.

                    (November 1929)

During his three-month visit to Rome, Chesterton had on several occasions given a talk at the Convent of the Holy Child. Towards the end of their visit, the Chestertons were in St. Peter's to hear Pope Pius XI beatify forty English and Welsh martyrs before a congregation of many thousands. At the conclusion of the ceremony, a group of girls from the Holy Child Convent gathered around the Chestertons only to learn that he was having difficulty making his way up through the seething masses to retrieve his trademark cloak. Some of the young ladies plunged into the milling crowd and returned in triumph; others managed to find a taxi for the Chestertons in St. Peter's Square, no small feat at the best of times, almost miraculous on that day. Later, with his habitual courtesy, Chesterton sent the above poem to their school.

THE ELEVATION[1]

The mighty Monstrance[2] like a silver sun,
And that red lamp, the more than morning star,
That is red dawn at night, sunset at noon,
Red star that led the Magic Kings from far;
Now first the simple know them what they are.
The Sun, moon or stars that rule a secret sky
The happy fallen stars that dwell so nigh
To fallen men and yet no men can mar;
Lover of all men love, whose giant loving
Is so enlarged to love all little things;
Happy is he that to thine altar clings
Though the huge heaven without were shaken and moving
Though he that passed without, leaving this road,
Found the sun darkened and the moon as blood.

(ca. 1929)

[1] The raising of a consecrated host for adoration by the faithful during Mass, or here during Benediction.

[2] An elaborate, often sunray-shaped vessel used to display a consecrated host for veneration.

XIII

POEMS FOR
THE NICHOLL FAMILY
1926–1936

Frances and Gilbert Chesterton with Mrs. Winifrid Nicholl and her
daughters Dorothy and Barbara

[CLUES]

To Whom in Summer long ago
Came the Donor with the Doe,
Comes a Doom more like my own
Red with blood and hard as stone,
Yet will one adorned be,
Whose sister's name is poverty,
Dowering, for those that understand,
A Province of my native land.[1]

One whose name imports in part
Logic and the Reasoner's art,
Yet by contradiction quaint
Blends the Savage with the Saint.
Give one gift of such a sort
As will lead to good report
Pointed to the Beach Hotel:
Blow the ... place to ...
[The inscription is here blurred and indistinct].[2]

WHO, with no mackerel and fishing care,
Yet loosed from all the moorings, dare
To sail strange seas and do not shiver
To make the Port of London River.
Skipper, accept, to whom is due
The raise of such a happy crew,
Little yet Large, the friend of man,
In hope that, hurry as you can,

The meeting of the Chestertons with the widowed Mrs. Winifred Nicholl and her children occurred while the Chestertons were on holiday in Lyme Regis, Dorset, in 1925 or 1926. "To a Tolerant Mother" in *Collected Poetry*, Part I, was written for Mrs. Nicholl.

[1] This stanza contains three clues to Clare Nicholl's name. See "[To Clare Nicholl]" in *Collected Poetry*, Part I, p. 321.

[2] Could be clues for Barbara Nicholl's name, which has the same root word as *barbarian*. St. Barbara is the patron of artillery men.

You won't forget, for such a guest,
To pack his trunk with all the rest.

PIGS may disdain with delicate air,
And bears have more than they can bear:
Only on to one, whose larger grace
Puts up with beasts of every race,
Accepting dogs—and even poodles,
Quoodles, Boodles, Cock-a-doodles.[3]
With whom the timid Shark is safe
Whom Cock-chafers have failed to chafe:
To such a one alone I dare
Bequeath the humbler being here,
Though Poohs may pooh with hasty frown,
And Piglets from their heights look down.[4]

M. mentions him: some, scarce to blame,
Have called relations by his name.

(ca. 1926)

LAMENT FOR DOROTHY WHO HURT HER FOOT[1]

What news alarms us, turning The Three Cups[2]
To cups of trembling, of lament and woe,
That something horrid jumped at Dorothy
And hit her on the light fantastic toe.

[3] Quoodle was the name of the Chestertons' dog.

[4] The Nicholl family nicknames were Cissy or Pig for Cecilia, Pooh for Clare, Mike for Barbara and Diddles for Dorothy. GKC's pet name for Clare was Unicorn. See "An Apology for a Letter Unposted", *Collected Poetry*, Part I, p. 270 and "Lyme Regis Sed Sine Regina", Part I, p. 305.

[1] Retired doctor Wyatt Wingrave spent hours on the shore at Lyme poking among the rocks with a stick. GKC and the Nicholl girls decided that he was looking for prehistoric remains. One day Dorothy Nicholl lost a sweater that was found and handed to the town crier whose voice was heard along the front, "Oyez, oyez, oyez! found a navy blue jersey, belonging to a child," Dorothy's dismay at seeing the distasteful object held out for inspection was compounded when she cut her foot on a piece of glass. See "In the Lyme-Light", *Collected Poetry*, Part I, pp. 283–84.

[2] The hotel where the Chestertons stayed in Lyme.

Did she fall off the Cobb; as was the fashion
With Austen's heroines and the old *elite*,
And, turning somersaults, unlike Louisa,
Retain the power of falling on her feet?

Was it the Shark that came, and did the fishers
Waiting for bites behold the biter bit,
Was it the Shark who opened wide his jaw
And Dorothy who put her foot in it?

Did she, pursuing that elusive Jersey
Fall from the cliffs away by Golden Cap....
And dash herself to bits upon the beach,
Or meet with any other small mishap?

Did Dr. Wingrave's gouty Plesiosaurus
Wake from the sleep of ages, rather riled,
And, being mixed about his dates and doubtful,
Mistake her for a prehistoric child?

Or did the worst and weightiest fate befall her—
Oh load of lamentation, weight of woe!
Did, as we walked the streets of Lyme together,
The present writer tread upon her toe?

(1927)

TO DOROTHY, XMAS

They brought me prunes and big balloons
But still I howled for Macaroons,[1]
And bandsmen playing big bassoons
And palm-trees from the Cameroons
And Roses out of many Junes
And funny Xmas pantaloons
And large supplies of silver spoons
And friendly visits from Baboons,
But still I wail in weary tunes
For Dorothy and Macaroons.

(early 1930s)

[TWO INVITATIONS][1]

*Miss Dorothy Nicholl is warmly invited to come early
and stay late on Thursday March 8th.
—from The Man Who Is Thursday*

I stirred the Biscuits with a spoon
Upon that lonely afternoon
When suddenly I reel and swoon:
I see the sign—the Priceless Boon—
There on my plate ... a Macaroon
　　　from "The Jeremiads of
　　　a Jaundiced Journalist" *in*
Twelve Books and One Rhyme

[1] When Chesterton was ill, Dorothy wrote him a letter, saying she would send macaroons to make him well, but he was not allowed them.

[1] An invitation to tea began the relationship between the Nicholls and the Chestertons. See "A 'Thank-You' for Coming to Tea", Collected Poetry, Part I, p. 317.

Miss Barbara Nicholl is warmly invited to come early
and stay late on Thursday, March 8th.
('Come unto these Yellow Sands and there take hands.')
From an invitation to a jaundiced district
which is nevertheless entirely free from infection.
*   —from The Man Who Is Thursday*

If one shall ask you why Lyme Regis street
Plunges so steeply the steep sea to meet,
Say I walked there in days most dear to me,
And the whole foreshore south into the sea.

If one shall ask why rise the heights above
In dizzy spires as if the hills could move,
Say Barbara on the peaks so lightly tripped,
The rocks danced with her and
The mountains stopped.

(See famous metrical version of the Psalms.)
                                    (1934)

Names.

To Christmas Cottage as Christmas came,
    I dreamed that the Feasts returned:
The name to the place and the feast to the name,
And wherever one old word stood, the flame
    On the fanes of our fathers burned.

And I saw you go like a glistering ghost
    With the candles in your hair
From Christmas Cottage and out beyond
On Candlemas Eve by Candlemas Pond
    As it was in the days that were.

Marts and Lammas and Childermas
    Shall write up their names and stay:
When the light-crowned Lady walks again
The Candlemas Lady in Candlemas Lane
    In the ways you walk today.

Though you walk like an Angel & I like a Goose,
    Our plumes shall unfold alike:
When your Nickname Saint that the toys remember
Takes wing and wakes in the far September
    Where Michaelmas waits for Mike.

NAMES

To Christmas Cottage[1] as Christmas came
    I dreamed that the Feasts returned:
The name to the place and the feast to the name
    And wherever one old word stood, the flame
On the fanes of our fathers burned.

And I saw you go like a glistening ghost
    With the candles in your hair
From Christmas Cottage and out beyond
    On Candlemas Eve[2] by Candlemas Pond,
As it was in the days that were.

Mass and Lammas[3] and Childermas[4]
    Shall write up their names and stay:
When the light-crowned lady walks again,
    The Candlemas Lady in Candlemas Lane,
In the ways you walk today.

Though you walk like an Angel and I like a Goose,
    Our plumes shall unfold alike:
When your nickname saint that the toys remember
    Takes wing and wakes in the far September
Where Michaelmas[5] waits for Mike.[6]

                  (ca. 1934)

---

[1] The Nicholl family moved from Lyme to Christmas Cottage in Beaconsfield, where they became the neighbors of the Chestertons at Top Meadow.

[2] Candlemas Eve on February 1 was the vigil of the Feast of the Purification now renamed as the Presentation of Our Lord.

[3] Lammas on August 1 was the day on which the first fruits of the year were offered in church. Bread for Lammas Day Eucharist is made from the first wheat of the harvest.

[4] Childermas was the old name for the Feast of the Holy Innocents on December 28.

[5] Michaelmas Day on September 29 was the day on which it was traditional to eat goose.

[6] Mike was Barbara Nicholl's family nickname.

GRAND TRIUMPHAL ODE

(on the Occasion of Miss Barbara Nicholl reaching what
are conjectured to be years of discretion)

> The Crier is crying
> In Lyme of the King,
> Lost, Stolen or Strayed
> Is a strange little thing
> The Child that rolled down
> Our steep street to her play,
> The Child that is changed
> And transfigured today.
>
> I will ring to the sea-gulls
>   That dance in their play
> For the girls that go dancing
>   Go dancing away.
> She has gone up to Town
>   In three skips and a hop ...

... But hold! But halt! But stop! But stop! But stop! ...

In English Odes the rule for him who rhymes
Is change the Metre Six or Seven times.

Lo, Bournemouth mourns: that Bourne to which
No traveller (of sense) returns
That in its ten miles of Hotels
All made of gilt and plush and ferns
It is not kept, the feast we keep,
But in this little lesser town

Presented to Barbara Nicholl on her twenty-first birthday. Other poems to Bar-
bara Nicholl include "Ballade of the Mackerel-Catcher", *Collected Poetry*, Part II,
p. 469, "Ballade of Difficult Harmonies", Part II, p. 475, "The Crooner", Part I,
p. 430, and "Barbara", Part I, p. 271.

London: which hid so small and shy
  Till in this feast it finds its crown.

> And Beaconsfield to London
> Like a craven Suburb yields
> (It never had a Beacon
> And it's losing all its Fields)

> And the streets creep outwards ever:
>   Knotty Green is next to Turnham:
> And there's nothing for our Beeches
>   Except perhaps to Burn'em.[1]

> But Little Hampton swells and spreads
>   Grown Larger Hampton for her fame
> The long beach by the southern sea
>   Shakes and reverberates with her name
> Far to that pebbled western wall
>   Of shining shingle where she ran
> A golden arrow and a flame
>   Before the marching years began.
>   But Beaconsfield cries "Out beyond
>   The cottage to the village pond
>   We, only we, have seen her pass
>   From Christmas up to Candlemas."[2]

But hark! High in the northlands dark
  The Swedish Vikings stark
Flashing their axes like the Northern Lights
  Through the long Northern nights
Recall that southern light that on them shone
And shout (after consulting Tennyson):
  "A Sea-King's Daughter from over the sea
  Aryan, Non-Aryan or Yiddish are we

[1] Burnham Beeches is not far from Beaconsfield.
[2] The Nicholls lived in Christmas Cottage near Candlemas Lane.

Brachycephalic, whatever we be—
We are all of us Swede in our welcome of thee
Barbara!"

South, where the blind barbarians drive
On Stephen's City saved alive
There is her Patron's holy name
Acclaimed in cannon-smoke and flame
When up to God through wars and woes
The thunder of the gunners goes
Great with the heart of Austria:
Strong name reversed
Fairest and first
Best of Barbarians—Barbara!

Rejoice all nations under the sun;
Their bishops dance, their aged statesmen run,
Paint the world red and think it frightful fun
That Barbara, Barbara is Twenty-One.

But the Crier is crying
In Lyme of the King
Lost, Stolen or Strayed
Is the Marvellous Thing.
I will ring for the sea-gulls
That dance in the spray
But the girls that go dancing
Go dancing away,
The girls that go dancing,
Go dancing
go dancing,
The girls that go dancing
Go dancing away.
(September 24, 1934)

[A TESTIMONIAL TO BARBARA NICHOLL]

Would it really help you, would it in this cold world truly help
if I broke into song, for instance, and wrote across the form:

> When first I saw dear Barbara
> Rush like a sea-wind to the sea,
> She woke it with a wild ozone
> Not of the sea but all her own:
> That blast of blessing blown and hurled
> Will heal the Wards of all the world,
> The sick will leap from lying flat
> (If you will let her rush like that),
> And wake them as she wakened me.

But would this testimonial be well received? Would the doctors
and nurses think it of close and cogent relevance? ... I doubt it.
I doubt if they would yield even if I tried another metre. As—

> Blow before Barbara, blow the horn for the rider of horses;
>   As for Hector Hippodomio arose the shout:
> For she is the tamer of horses, if sometimes they toss her
> And throw her all over the district and leave her lying about.
> But she that did so in implacable purpose persist
> To break every bone in her body, will surely exist
> To be an expert, experienced, practised Anatomist.

This you will note, is more in the rugged manner: but would this
soothe the modern medical authorities? It is doubtful. There is so
much red tape about. Or even in quieter vein—

> Health follows where she goes: and in her track
> Hospitals rise in Bucks behind her back:

Barbara had decided to train as a nurse and had given GKC's name as a referee.
The request for a testimonial came while the Chestertons were on holiday in France,
and GKC also wrote to Barbara to assure her that the testimonial had been sent off.
It seems likely that these lines may well be the last poetry that he ever wrote; they
certainly post-date other known poems.

Sweden is swept with gusts of youth and sport;
And even Bournemouth is a Health resort.

Forgive me. I send off all this nonsense now because I have a faint fear that my own signature may be needed in some funny official way in your affair....

Yours with love always,
G.K. Chesterton
(May 5, 1936)

Nurse Barbara Nicholl

XIV

POEMS OF THE 1930s

Syracuse, New York, December 4, 1930

ON AN AMERICAN BEST-SELLER

The Decadent's bridges broke down in despair:
It is something that someone could fling
Some sort of a Bridge o'er that dreary abyss
In the name of St Louis the King:
That Art may yet cross to the people, and purged
Of the poisons and slimes that defiled her,
For when I was a child half the world had gone Wilde
But now half the world has gone Wilder.

(*G.K.'s Weekly*, January 10, 1931)

A commentary on the novel *The Bridge of San Luis Rey* by Thornton Wilder.

GKC with his secretary Dorothy Collins and friend Sheila Matier during his visit to California in February 1931.

THE THREE CONQUISTADORS

To Sheila Matier
Who is too old for such picture-books
and her Father
Who is too young for them
and her Mother
to whom I offer these childish thanks for hospitality

THE THREE CONQUISTADORS

To Sheila's home Three Bravoes came
Beyond the Angels' Town,
One Red, one Yellow and one White
Or rather Pinky-Brown.

The Matiers were friends of the Chestertons in Los Angeles. GKC created a pic-
ture book with these verses and illustrations for their daughter Sheila. An abridged
version of this poem is in *Collected Poetry*, Part 1, p. 318.

THE REDSKIN CHIEF

Red Bison of the Hokum Tribe.
His hunting and his fighting
I write of in Red Indian style
—Only in Picture Writing.

JUAN THE DAGO

From Mexico where people drink
  Wild Wine, the brew of Shame,
Came Juan to California, where
  The people do the same.

THE CHINESE PIRATE

Quong, who (unlike your father's friend)
　　Was *not* a Buddhist monk,
A Chinese Pirate spoiled the ships
　　And filled his Junk with junk.

But when they came to Sheila's home
 Those wild marauding three
They felt her softening touch and grew
 Quite as polite as she.

Red Bison climbed to Sheila's house
 As goats that scale an Alp:
But though he much admired her hair,
 He did not take her scalp.

The Dago murdered nobody
 For days and days: and Quong
Found out, with tears, that he belonged
 To Mr. Matier's Tong.

The Dog that up the Ladder goes
 He learned how to descry
With patient pleasure, and without
 One thought of Puppy-Pie.

"For O," they cried, "We come in peace
 Who walk the sunset strand
Far from that bleak but boiling sea
 That breaks on Eastern land,

"That swings and sways with dizzy tides
 Since first the ocean drank
Atlantis to the dregs: and left
 A whirlpool where she sank

"Of storms, Armadas, Vikings, Tars,
 That make its tides terrific:
But Sheila need not shrink from us:
 For we are all Pacific.

     (1931)

GKC planting a tree at Holy Cross College, Worcester, Mass., 1931.

BOB-UP-AND-DOWN

Irresponsible outbreak of one who, having completed a book of enormous length on the Poet Chaucer, feels himself freed from all bonds of intellectual self-respect and proposes to do no work for an indefinite period.

> "Wot ye not wher ther start a litel town,
> Which that icleped is Bob-up-an-down."
> *The Canterbury Tales*

They babble on of Babylon,
They tire me out with Tyre,
And Sidon putting side on,
I do not much admire.
But the little town Bob-up-and-Down,[1]
That lies beyond the Blee,
Along the road our fathers rode,
O that's the road for me.

In dome and spire and cupola
It bubbles up and swells
For the company that canter
To the Canterbury Bells.
But when the Land Surveyors come
With maps and books to write,
The little town Bob-up-and-Down
It bobs down out of sight.

I cannot live in Liverpool,
O lead me not to Leeds,
I'm not a Man in Manchester,
Though men be cheap as weeds:
But the little town Bob-up-and-Down,
That bobs towards the sea,
And knew its name when Chaucer came,
O that's the town for me.

[1] Bob-up-and-Down, the village of Harbledown to the north of Canterbury.

I'll go and eat my Christmas meat
In that resurgent town,
And pledge to fame our Father's name
Till the sky bobs up and down;
And join in sport of every sort
That's played beside the Blee,
Bob-Apple in Bob-up-and-Down,
O that's the game for me.

Now Huddersfield is Shuddersfield,
And Hull is nearly Hell,
Where a Daisy would go crazy
Or a Canterbury Bell,
The little town Bob-up-and-Down
Alone is fair and free,
For it can't be found above the ground,
O that's the place for me.

(from *G.K.'s Weekly*, December 12, 1931)

TO J.L.

Sing a song of Ninepence
    A pocket full of air,
A conscience full of agony,
    A soul full of despair.

For a cause so clear and high
    Misers might fork out;
Only that I quite forgot
    What it was about.

Was it for a fire-engine?
    A church? A cricket club?

When included in *Collected Poetry*, Part I, the identity of J.L. was unknown. Almost certainly it is Joan Lisle-Taylor, fiancée and later wife of Michael Knollys Braybrooke, who was semi-adopted by the Chestertons. The only other Joan in the Chestertons' circle was Joan Nicholl who is adamant that the poem was not addressed to her.

A mission to the Sandwich Isles?
   A model pump—or pub?

Is there in some stately fane
   Earnest Christians build,
Yawning yet the horrid gap
   Ninepence might have filled?

Do the dusky heathen cry
   O'er the southern brine,
"Ninepence more and we are saved,
   All the ninety-nine."

Ah, for all I know, it fed
   Newcastle's need of coal,
A wedding-present for the Pope,
   An ice-box for the Pole.

Only when your face I see
   Visions tower like fate,
Joan as stern as Joan of Arc,
   Love as dread as hate.

Soften that relentless brow
   Pitying this weak pen,
Smile again; and all will be
   As right as ninepence then.

               (ca. 1931)

CROOKED

The little picture of the Mother of God
Hangs crooked upon the wall,
Blue and bright gold like a butterfly pinned askew
Only it does not fall,
As, stooping ever and falling never, an eagle
Hangs winged over all.

And it suddenly seemed that the whole long room was tilted
Like a cabin in stormy seas;
The solid table and strong upstanding lamp and the inkstand
Leaned like stiff shrubs in a breeze
And the windows looked out upon slanted plains and meadows
As on slanted seas.

And I knew in a flash that the whole wide world was sliding;
Ice and not land.
And men were swaying and sliding, and nations staggered
And could not stand:
Going down to the ends of the earth, going down to destruction,
On either hand.

And knowing the whole world stiff with the crack of doom,
I pick up my pen and correct and make notes, and write small:
And go on with the task of the day, seeing unseeing
What hangs over all:
The awful eyes of Our Lady, who hangs so straight
Upon the crooked wall.

(from *G.K.'s Weekly*, September 7, 1933)

THE TWO KINDS

To others and of old I would have said
That dogmas deep as questioning Christendom
Sleep in the sundering of the wine and bread
And that incarnate Christ in every crumb.
For you I find words fewer and more human,
Content to say of him that guards the shrine
To drink this wine he has lost the Love of Woman,
Yea, even such love as yours, to drink this Wine.

(from *G.K.'s Weekly*, September 7, 1933)

Apparently addressed to his wife, Frances, who had questioned the Roman Catholic practice of restricting the chalice to the priest.

A PRESTIGE HOTEL

" The Ballad of the White House "
Too many quires doth fill
" The Ballad of the White Hart "
Would fill more paper still

Hart, for thine Hospitality
Then be thine Horn exalted
Which Cornucopia flowed for me
Since at thy doors I halted

G. K. Chesterton

Sept. /1933

THE BALLAD OF THE WHITE HART[1]

"The Ballad of the White Horse"
Too many quires doth fill;
"The Ballad of the White Hart"
Would fill more pages still.

Hart, for thine Hospitality
Then be thine Horn exalted,
Which Cornucopia flowed for me
Since at thy doors I halted.
                    (September 1933)

[ANOTHER TRIOLET]

My writing is bad,
And my speaking is worse;
They were all that I had,
My writing is bad:
It is frightfully sad,
And I don't care a curse.
My writing is bad,
And my speaking is worse.
(from *The Daily Telegraph*, January 12, 1934)

A BEACONSFIELD BALLAD

Between the load of Ledborough Wood
    To where the thin trees quiver,
Where the road goes by Glory Mill
    That ends beside the river,
Suffer us play the Pastoral fool,
    And rhyme or jest propound,

[1] Printed on the first page of the *à la carte* menu of The White Hart Hotel in Lincoln, where GKC's original used to be displayed in the foyer.

Forgetting while we aid what lives
   In glory's mill are ground.

Still pure in village pales, between
   Wycombe or London End,
The Village Hampden[1] reads these lines
   The Villiage Idiot penned.
Have patience, in our rustic phrase,
   When he, who is no scholar,
Who cannot climb the Greasy Pole,
   Grins through the Horse's Collar.

To us our town remains, to fling
   Wide as its roads and white,
That all men may pronounce it good
   And some pronounce it right;
The flying devils of the foe
   That menace our abodes
Shall flee, beholding faint and far
   The cross of our cross-roads.

Though from the marches of Cockaigne[2]
   The villas creep and cling
Like London Trainbands[3] trailing out
   On Oxford and the King;
Though weaker souls in Gerrard's Cross
   May question and perpend
If grasses still make Knotty Green,
   And where will London End?

               (1934)

---

[1] The Village Hampden—the local patriot John Hampden (1594–1647), Oliver Cromwell's cousin, became the epitome of patriotism.

[2] Cockaigne—an imaginary land of idleness and luxury. Here it means London where the Cockneys live.

[3] Militias (trained bands).

THE UTMOST FOR THE HIGHEST

"... Up, up, up; on, on, on."
Remarkable summary of modern thought and evolutionary
ethics by the Right Hon. Ramsay MacDonald[1]

Since we first were sold a pup,
Till these dead dogs' day is done,
Evolution up, up, up,
Evolutes us on, on, on.

Till we're sacked and left with tup-
-pence a week to live upon.
Mines will blow us up, up, up,
Coppers[2] move us on, on, on.

Till we find the fatal cup
Full, and God's own patience gone,
Till it's plain that all is Up
They will always have us On.

(from *G.K.'s Weekly*, November 8, 1934)

[1] James Ramsay MacDonald—British Labour Party leader, Prime Minister in 1924 and 1929–35. From 1931–35 he led a so-called National government based on support from the Conservative and Liberal parties.
[2] Policemen.

AFTER THE DELUGE
1910–1935

No work is for the worker
No wealth is for the swell:
Even cheats do not get wealthy:
But children still get well.

(1935)

To commemorate the Silver Jubilee of the Children's Convalescent Home, which was celebrated during the Great Depression.

G. K. Chesterton, 1936

BIBLIOGRAPHY

G. K. Chesterton: *Greybeards at Play*, London (Brimley Johnson) 1900 and 1930; reprint, London (Paul Elek) 1974.

G. K. Chesterton: *The Wild Knight*, London (Grant Richards) 1900.

G. K. Chesterton: *Poems*, London (Burns & Oates, Ltd.) 1915.

G. K. Chesterton: *Wine, Water and Song*, London (Methuen) 1915.

G. K. Chesterton: *The Ballad of St. Barbara and Other Verses*, London (Cecil Palmer) 1922.

G. K. Chesterton: *The Queen of Seven Swords*, London and New York (Sheed & Ward) 1926.

G. K. Chesterton: *Collected Poems*, London (Cecil Palmer) 1927; 3rd edition, London, (Methuen) 1933. The 1927 edition has been reprinted as a paperback: *The Works of G. K. Chesterton* in the Wordsworth series.

Kenneth Baker (Ed.): *G. K. Chesterton: Poems*, London (Folio Society) 2007.

R. A. Christophers (Ed.): *The British Library Catalogue of Additions to the Manuscripts* (The G. K. Chesterton Papers), London (The British Library) 2001.

Stephen Medcalf (Ed.): *Poems for All Purposes, Selected Poems of G. K. Chesterton*, London (Random House) 1994.

POEMS DATING FROM 1900–1936
TO BE FOUND IN PART ONE

POEMS DATING FROM 1900–1936
TO BE FOUND IN PART TWO

POEMS WRONGLY ATTRIBUTED
TO G. K. CHESTERTON

The following poems have been wrongly attributed:

Maurice Baring's *Ballade of the Matchless*

Frances Chesterton's *In the Middle West*

[Eheu Fugaces] is from Hilaire Belloc

George C. Heseltine's *Triolet* (I wish I were a jellyfish)

Theodore Maynard's *World's Miser*

W. R. Titterton's *At Eventide*

J.C. Squire's *Friendship's Garland*

POEMS DOUBTFULLY ATTRIBUTED
TO G. K. CHESTERTON

The 32 lines beginning "About the house of Dives" are probably a pastiche by Charles Williams who places them at the end of an essay on Chesterton in *Poetry at Present* [Oxford (At the Clarendon Press)] 1930.

There is no evidence that Chesterton wrote:

> "I searched the parks in all the cities
> But found no statues of committees."

Nor is there evidence that Chesterton wrote the following unsigned poems which appeared in *G. K.'s Weekly*:

Nevercometrue, March 28, 1925

Refutation of the only too prevalent slanders, March 28, 1925

Thank the Goodness and the Grace, April 11, 1925

Birth Control, October 31, 1925

Mind and Matter, November 14, 1925

Whines from the Wood, December 26, 1925

The Song of the Superior Vermin, December 11, 1926

INDEX OF TITLES
Poems 1890–1936

[....] indicates that the title is given by the editor.

445

INDEX OF FIRST LINES